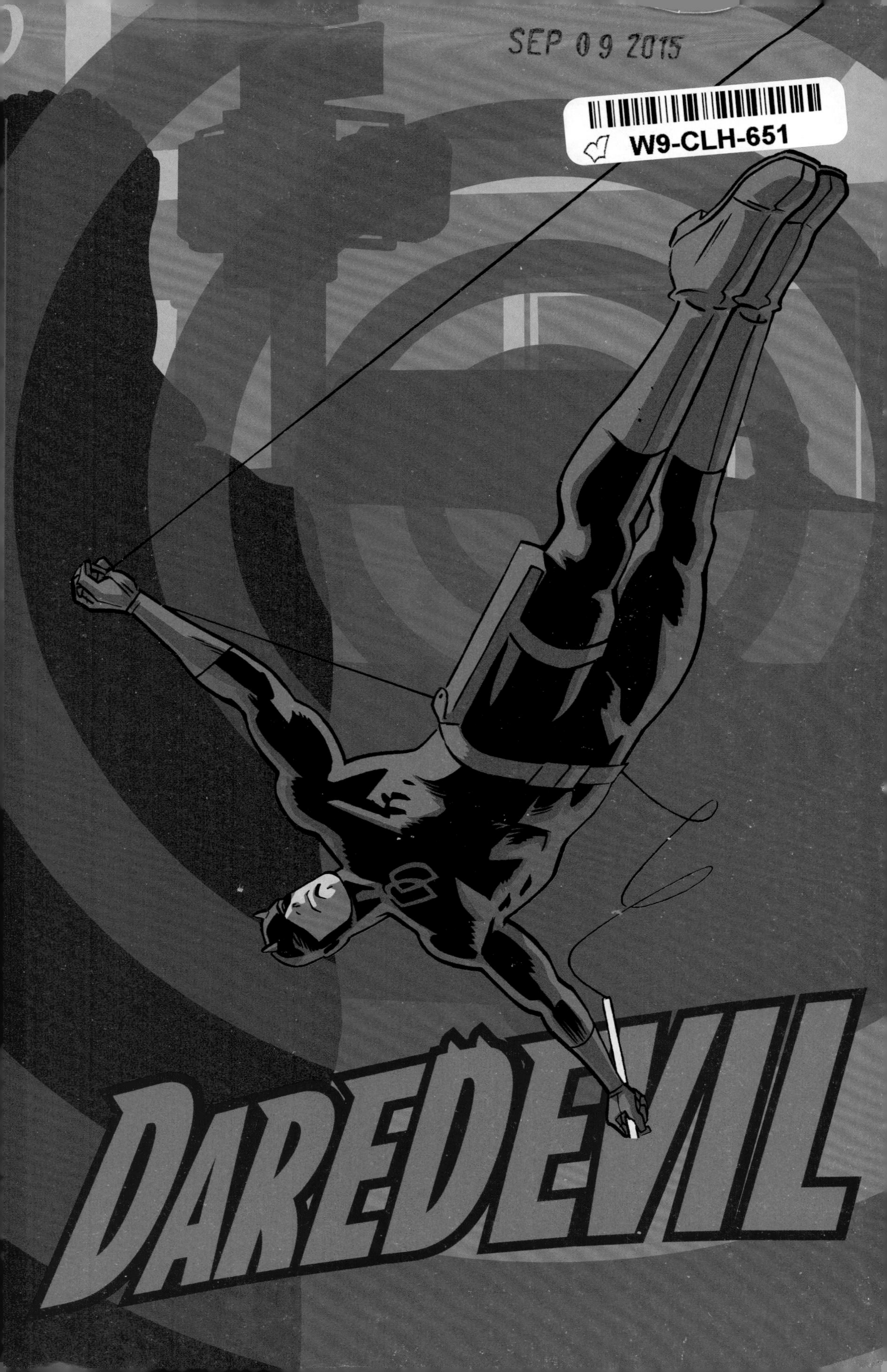
SEP 09 2015
W9-CLH-651
DAREDEVIL

STORYTELLERS
MARK WAID & CHRIS SAMNEE
COLORIST
MATTHEW WILSON
LETTERER
VC'S JOE CARAMAGNA

COVER ART
CHRIS SAMNEE & MATTHEW WILSON

ASSISTANT EDITOR
CHARLES BEACHAM
EDITORS
SANA AMANAT & ELLIE PYLE
SENIOR EDITOR
NICK LOWE

COLLECTION EDITOR
JENNIFER GRÜNWALD
ASSISTANT EDITOR
SARAH BRUNSTAD
ASSOCIATE MANAGING EDITOR
ALEX STARBUCK
EDITOR, SPECIAL PROJECTS
MARK D. BEAZLEY
SENIOR EDITOR, SPECIAL PROJECTS
JEFF YOUNGQUIST
SVP PRINT, SALES & MARKETING
DAVID GABRIEL
BOOK DESIGNER
ADAM DEL RE

EDITOR IN CHIEF
AXEL ALONSO
CHIEF CREATIVE OFFICER
JOE QUESADA
PUBLISHER
DAN BUCKLEY
EXECUTIVE PRODUCER
ALAN FINE

DAREDEVIL VOL. 3: THE DAREDEVIL YOU KNOW. Contains material originally published in magazine form as DAREDEVIL #11-15. First printing 2015. ISBN# 978-0-7851-9228-2. Published by MARVEL WORLDWIDE, INC., a subsidiary of MARVEL ENTERTAINMENT, LLC. OFFICE OF PUBLICATION: 135 West 50th Street, New York, NY 10020. Copyright © 2015 MARVEL. No similarity between any of the names, characters, persons, and/or institutions in this magazine with those of any living or dead person or institution is intended, and any such similarity which may exist is purely coincidental. **Printed in Canada.** ALAN FINE, President, Marvel Entertainment; DAN BUCKLEY, President, TV, Publishing and Brand Management; JOE QUESADA, Chief Creative Officer; TOM BREVOORT, SVP of Publishing; DAVID BOGART, SVP of Operations & Procurement, Publishing; C.B. CEBULSKI, VP of International Development & Brand Management; DAVID GABRIEL, SVP Print, Sales & Marketing; JIM O'KEEFE, VP of Operations & Logistics; DAN CARR, Executive Director of Publishing Technology; SUSAN CRESPI, Editorial Operations Manager; ALEX MORALES, Publishing Operations Manager; STAN LEE, Chairman Emeritus. For information regarding advertising in Marvel Comics or on Marvel. com, please contact Jonathan Rheingold, VP of Custom Solutions & Ad Sales, at jrheingold@marvel.com. For Marvel subscription inquiries, please call 800-217-9158. **Manufactured between 5/29/2015 and 7/6/2015 by SOLISCO PRINTERS, SCOTT, QC, CANADA.**

10 9 8 7 6 5 4 3 2 1

PREVIOUSLY:

The world knows that blind lawyer Matt Murdock is Daredevil. After years of maintaining a secret identity to protect the people he loves, Matt came clean in a court of law. His heightened senses, including his 360-degree radar sense, are now a matter of public record. In order to protect his best friend and former law partner, Foggy Nelson, from Daredevil's enemies, Matt very publicly faked Foggy's death. They then moved to San Francisco, where Matt opened a new law practice with his girlfriend, Kirsten McDuffie.

With his identity out in the open, several of Daredevil's old foes have been popped up in his new city, looking to get revenge. In addition to his super-hero stresses, Matt was recently propositioned by Kirsten's father, a well-to-do publisher, to write an autobiography chronicling his life as the Man Without Fear.

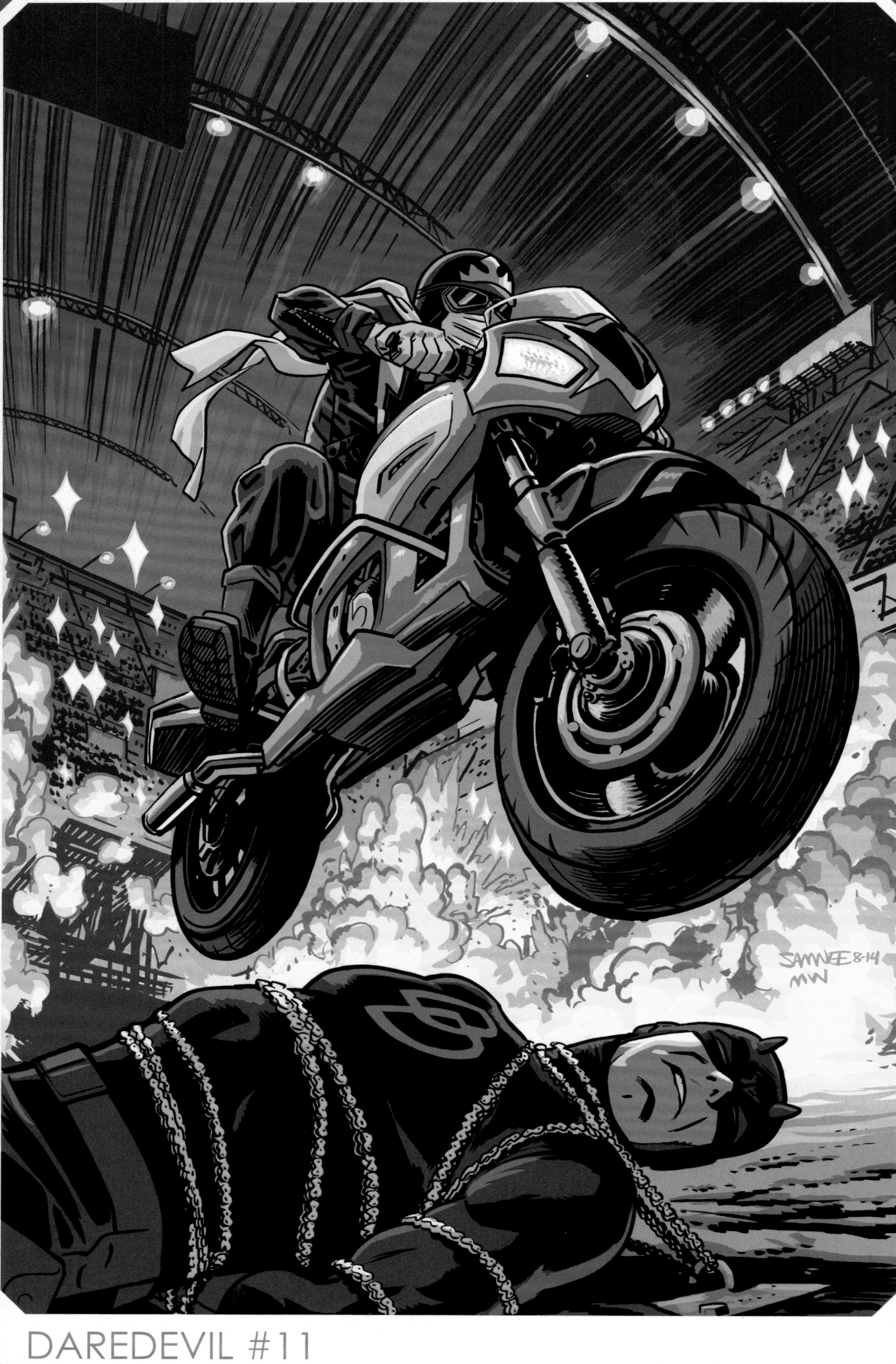
SAMNEE 8-14
MW

DAREDEVIL #11

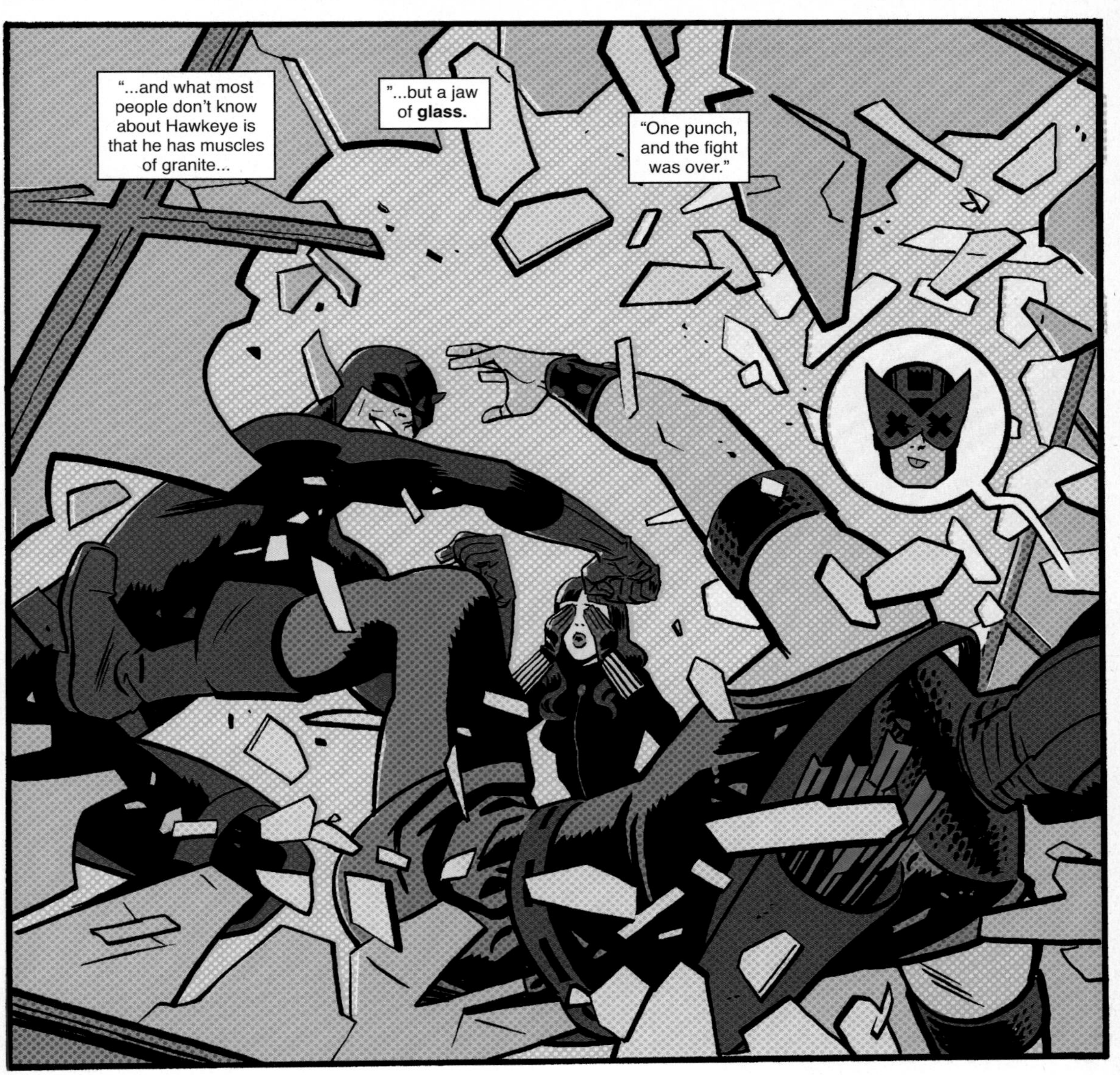
"...and what most people don't know about Hawkeye is that he has muscles of granite...
"...but a jaw of **glass.**
"One punch, and the fight was over."

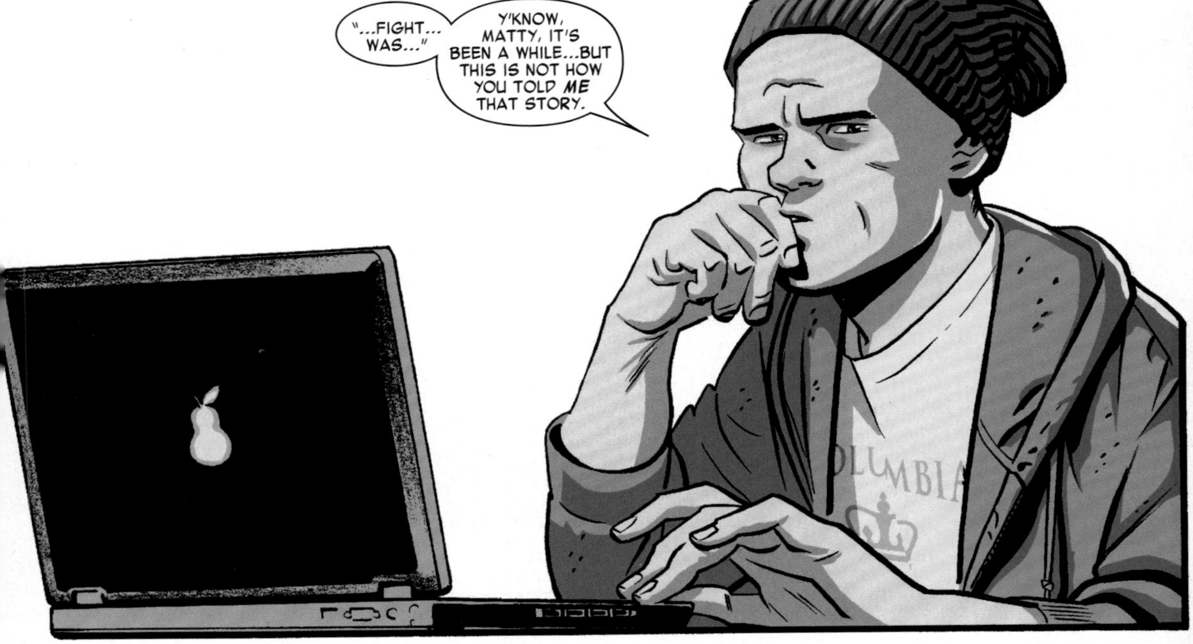
"...FIGHT... WAS..."
Y'KNOW, MATTY, IT'S BEEN A WHILE...BUT THIS IS NOT HOW YOU TOLD *ME* THAT STORY.

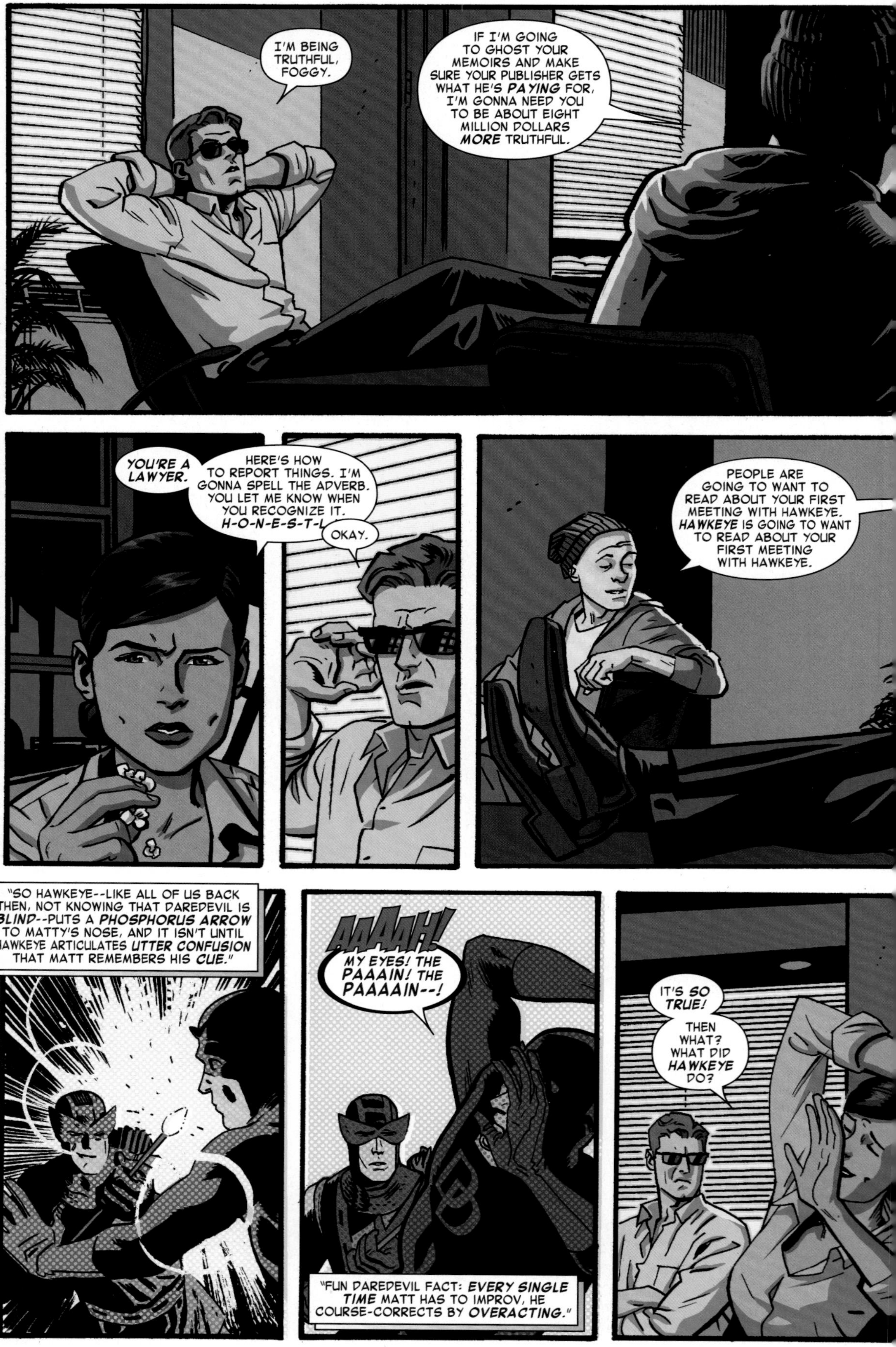

I'M BEING TRUTHFUL, FOGGY.
IF I'M GOING TO GHOST YOUR MEMOIRS AND MAKE SURE YOUR PUBLISHER GETS WHAT HE'S PAYING FOR, I'M GONNA NEED YOU TO BE ABOUT EIGHT MILLION DOLLARS MORE TRUTHFUL.
YOU'RE A LAWYER.
HERE'S HOW TO REPORT THINGS. I'M GONNA SPELL THE ADVERB. YOU LET ME KNOW WHEN YOU RECOGNIZE IT. H-O-N-E-S-T-L
OKAY.
PEOPLE ARE GOING TO WANT TO READ ABOUT YOUR FIRST MEETING WITH HAWKEYE. HAWKEYE IS GOING TO WANT TO READ ABOUT YOUR FIRST MEETING WITH HAWKEYE.
"SO HAWKEYE--LIKE ALL OF US BACK THEN, NOT KNOWING THAT DAREDEVIL IS BLIND--PUTS A PHOSPHORUS ARROW TO MATTY'S NOSE, AND IT ISN'T UNTIL HAWKEYE ARTICULATES UTTER CONFUSION THAT MATT REMEMBERS HIS CUE."
AAAAH!
MY EYES! THE PAAAIN! THE PAAAAIN--!
"FUN DAREDEVIL FACT: EVERY SINGLE TIME MATT HAS TO IMPROV, HE COURSE-CORRECTS BY OVERACTING."
IT'S SO TRUE!
THEN WHAT? WHAT DID HAWKEYE DO?

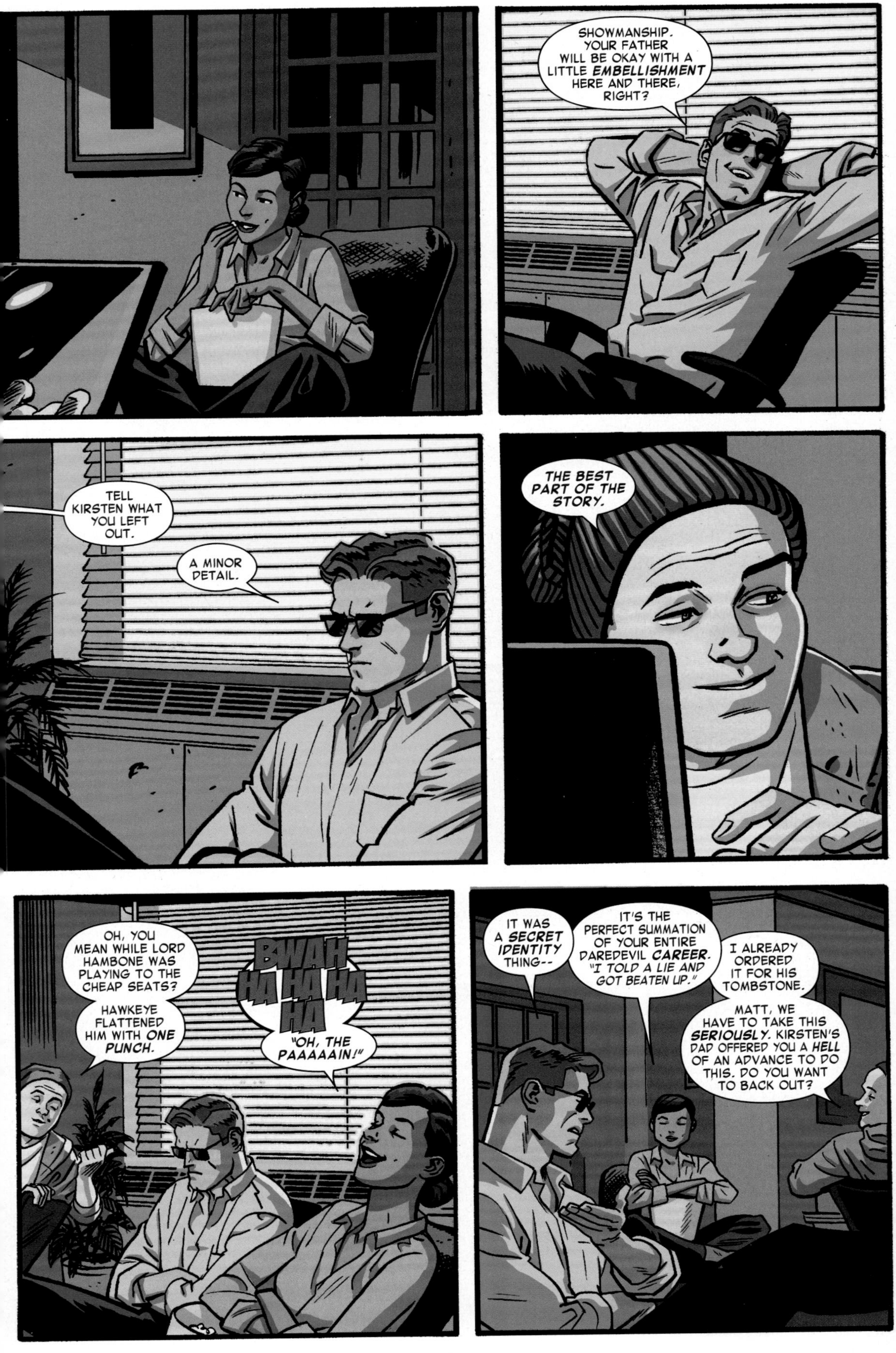
SHOWMANSHIP. YOUR FATHER WILL BE OKAY WITH A LITTLE EMBELLISHMENT HERE AND THERE, RIGHT?
TELL KIRSTEN WHAT YOU LEFT OUT.
A MINOR DETAIL.
THE BEST PART OF THE STORY.
OH, YOU MEAN WHILE LORD HAMBONE WAS PLAYING TO THE CHEAP SEATS?
HAWKEYE FLATTENED HIM WITH ONE PUNCH.
BWAH HA HA HA HA
"OH, THE PAAAAAIN!"
IT WAS A SECRET IDENTITY THING--
IT'S THE PERFECT SUMMATION OF YOUR ENTIRE DAREDEVIL CAREER. "I TOLD A LIE AND GOT BEATEN UP."
I ALREADY ORDERED IT FOR HIS TOMBSTONE.
MATT, WE HAVE TO TAKE THIS SERIOUSLY. KIRSTEN'S DAD OFFERED YOU A HELL OF AN ADVANCE TO DO THIS. DO YOU WANT TO BACK OUT?

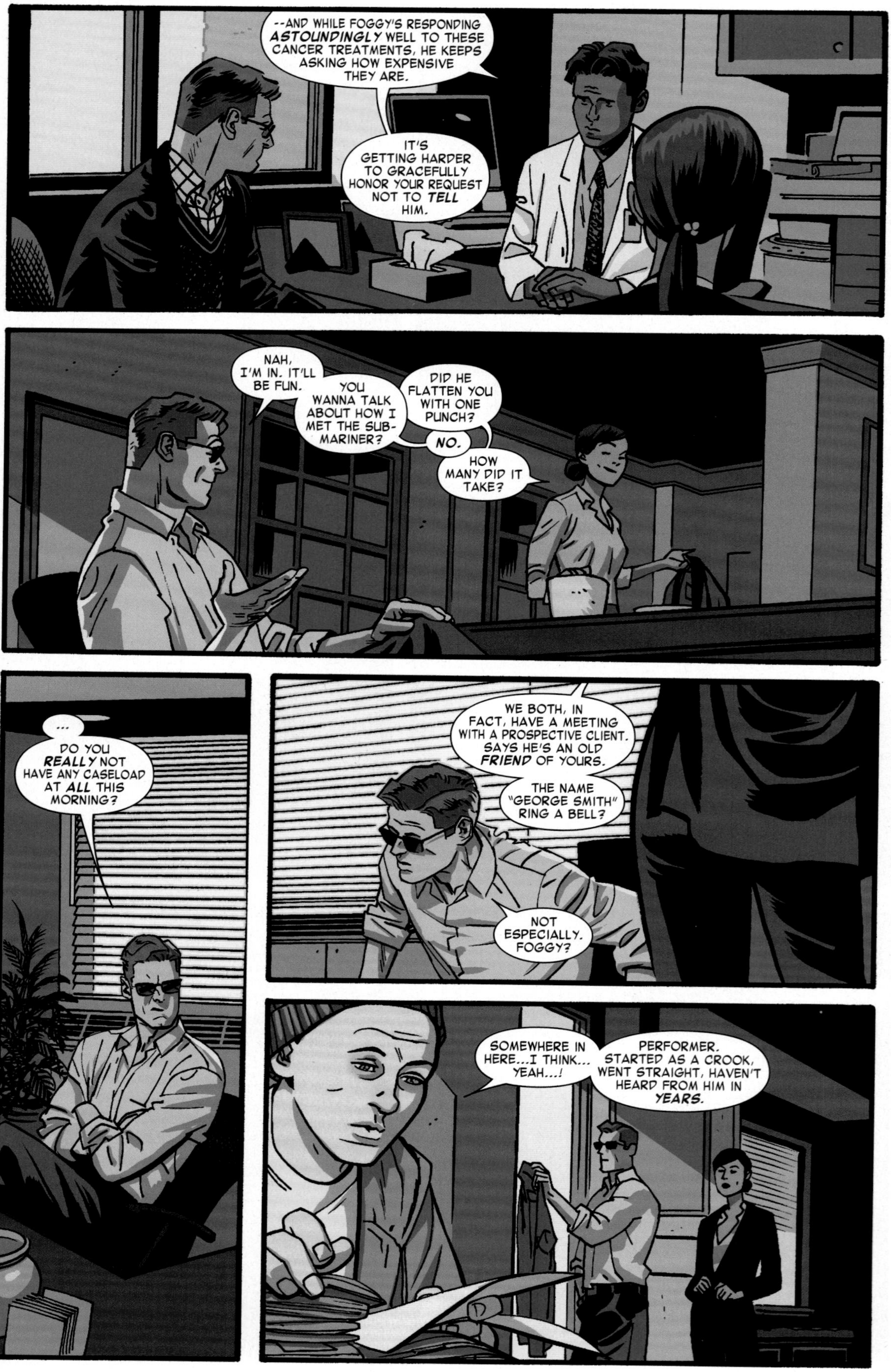
--AND WHILE FOGGY'S RESPONDING ASTOUNDINGLY WELL TO THESE CANCER TREATMENTS, HE KEEPS ASKING HOW EXPENSIVE THEY ARE.
IT'S GETTING HARDER TO GRACEFULLY HONOR YOUR REQUEST NOT TO TELL HIM.
NAH, I'M IN. IT'LL BE FUN.
YOU WANNA TALK ABOUT HOW I MET THE SUB-MARINER?
DID HE FLATTEN YOU WITH ONE PUNCH?
NO.
HOW MANY DID IT TAKE?
...
DO YOU REALLY NOT HAVE ANY CASELOAD AT ALL THIS MORNING?
WE BOTH, IN FACT, HAVE A MEETING WITH A PROSPECTIVE CLIENT. SAYS HE'S AN OLD FRIEND OF YOURS.
THE NAME "GEORGE SMITH" RING A BELL?
NOT ESPECIALLY. FOGGY?
SOMEWHERE IN HERE...I THINK... YEAH...!
PERFORMER. STARTED AS A CROOK, WENT STRAIGHT, HAVEN'T HEARD FROM HIM IN YEARS.

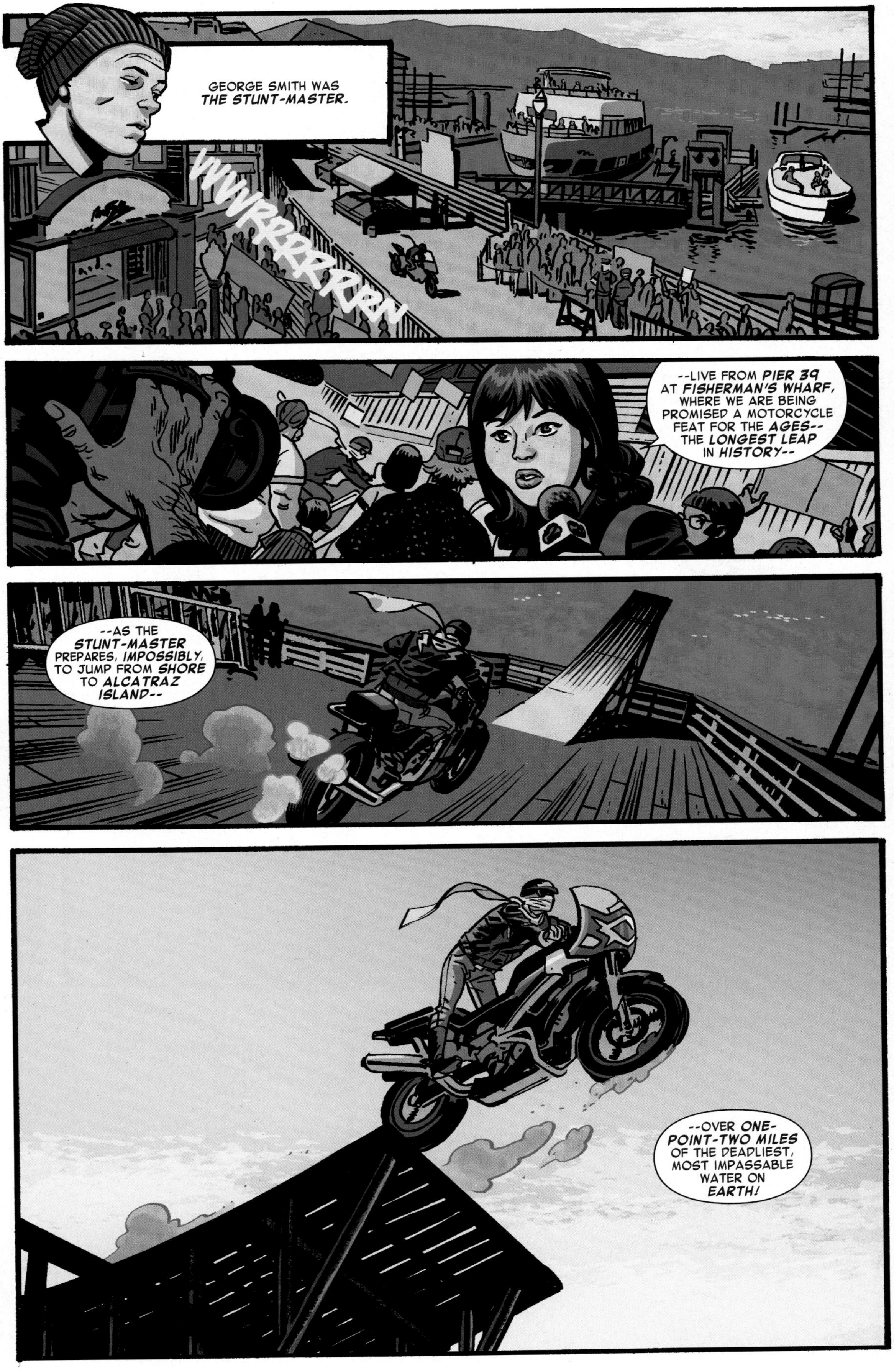
GEORGE SMITH WAS THE STUNT-MASTER.
WWVRRRRRRRN
--LIVE FROM PIER 39 AT FISHERMAN'S WHARF, WHERE WE ARE BEING PROMISED A MOTORCYCLE FEAT FOR THE AGES-- THE LONGEST LEAP IN HISTORY--
--AS THE STUNT-MASTER PREPARES, IMPOSSIBLY, TO JUMP FROM SHORE TO ALCATRAZ ISLAND--
--OVER ONE-POINT-TWO MILES OF THE DEADLIEST, MOST IMPASSABLE WATER ON EARTH!

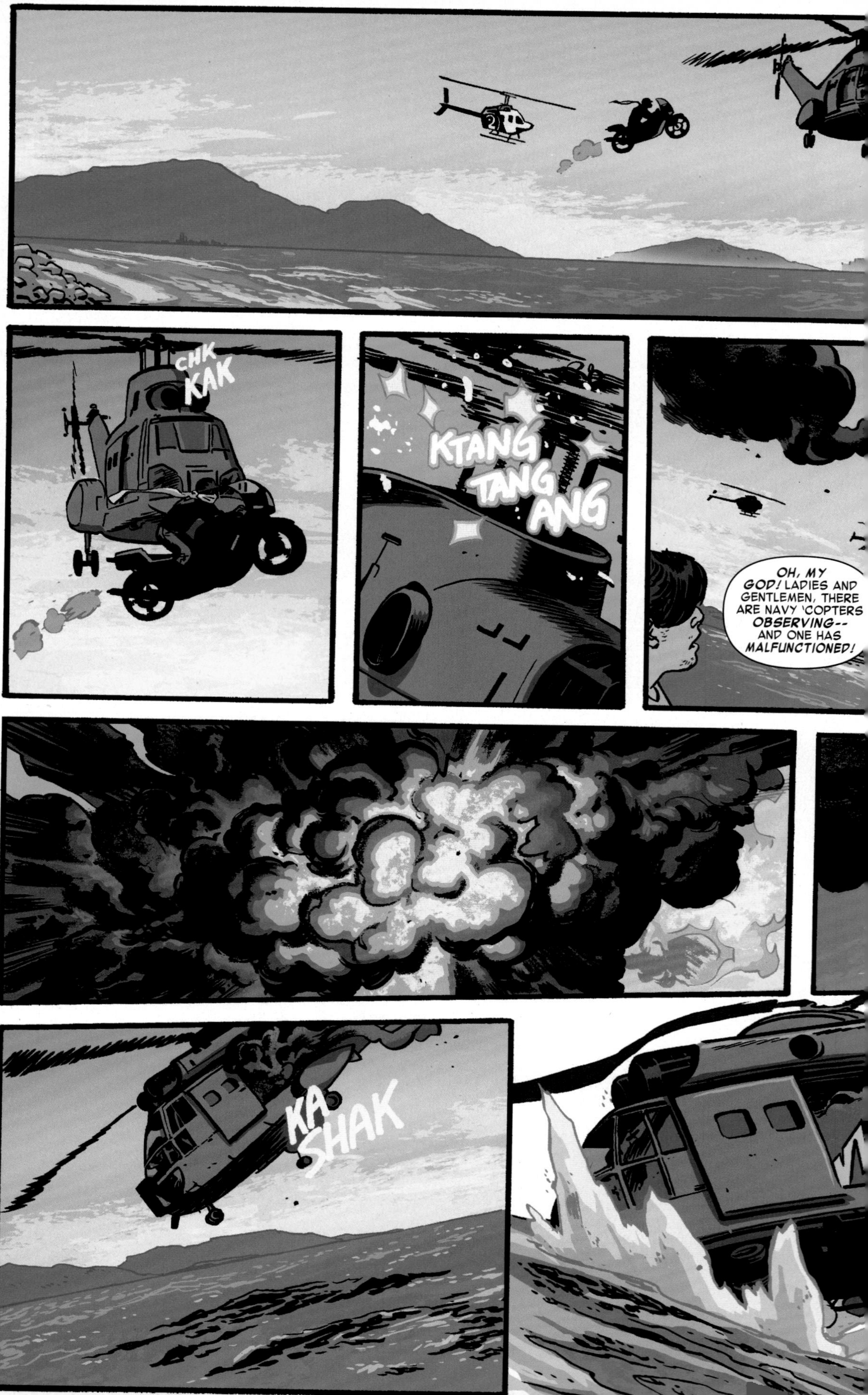
CHK
KAK
KTANG
TANG
ANG
OH, MY GOD! LADIES AND GENTLEMEN, THERE ARE NAVY 'COPTERS OBSERVING-- AND ONE HAS MALFUNCTIONED!
KA
SHAK

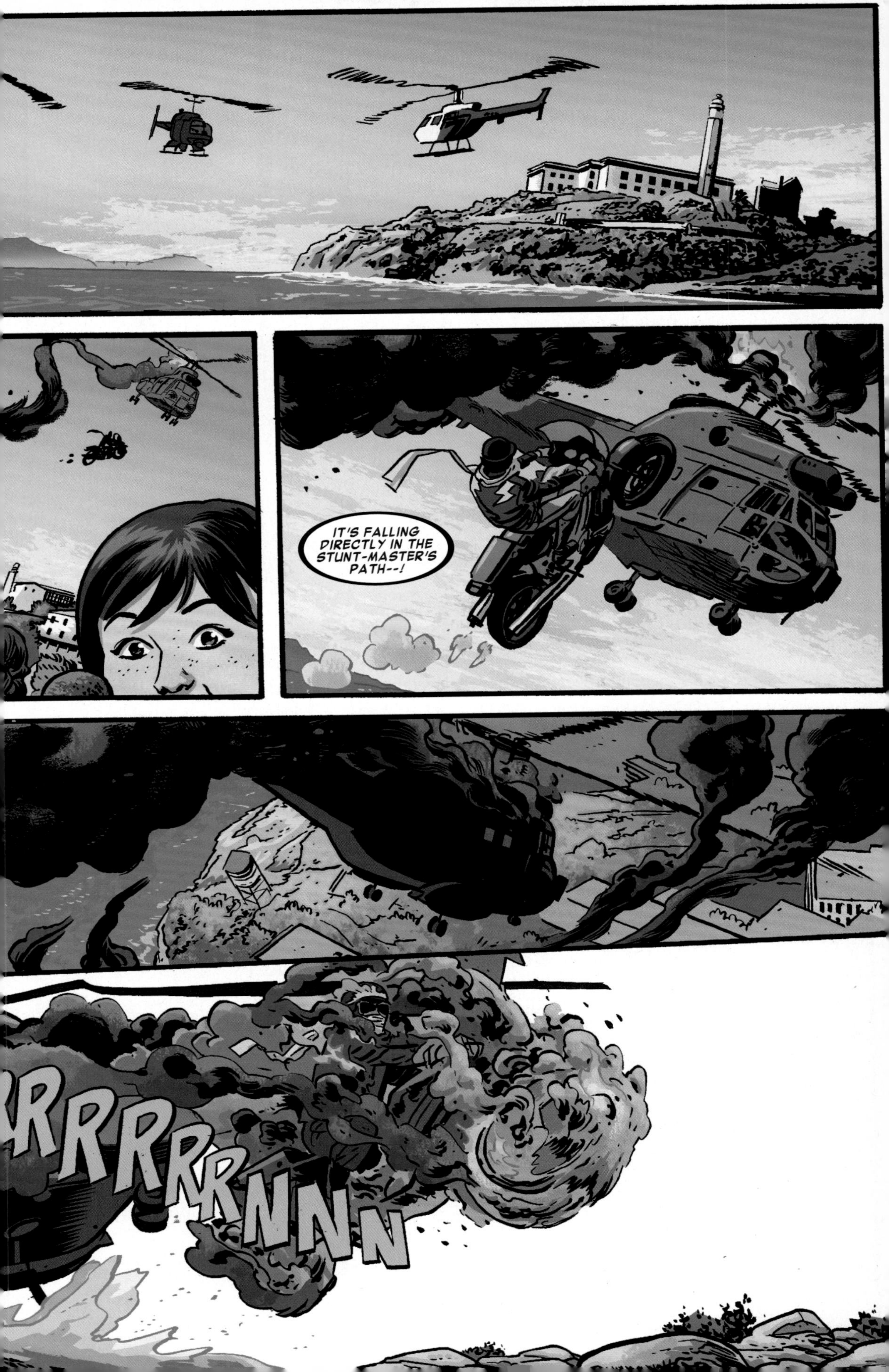
IT'S FALLING DIRECTLY IN THE STUNT-MASTER'S PATH--!
RRRRRRNNNN

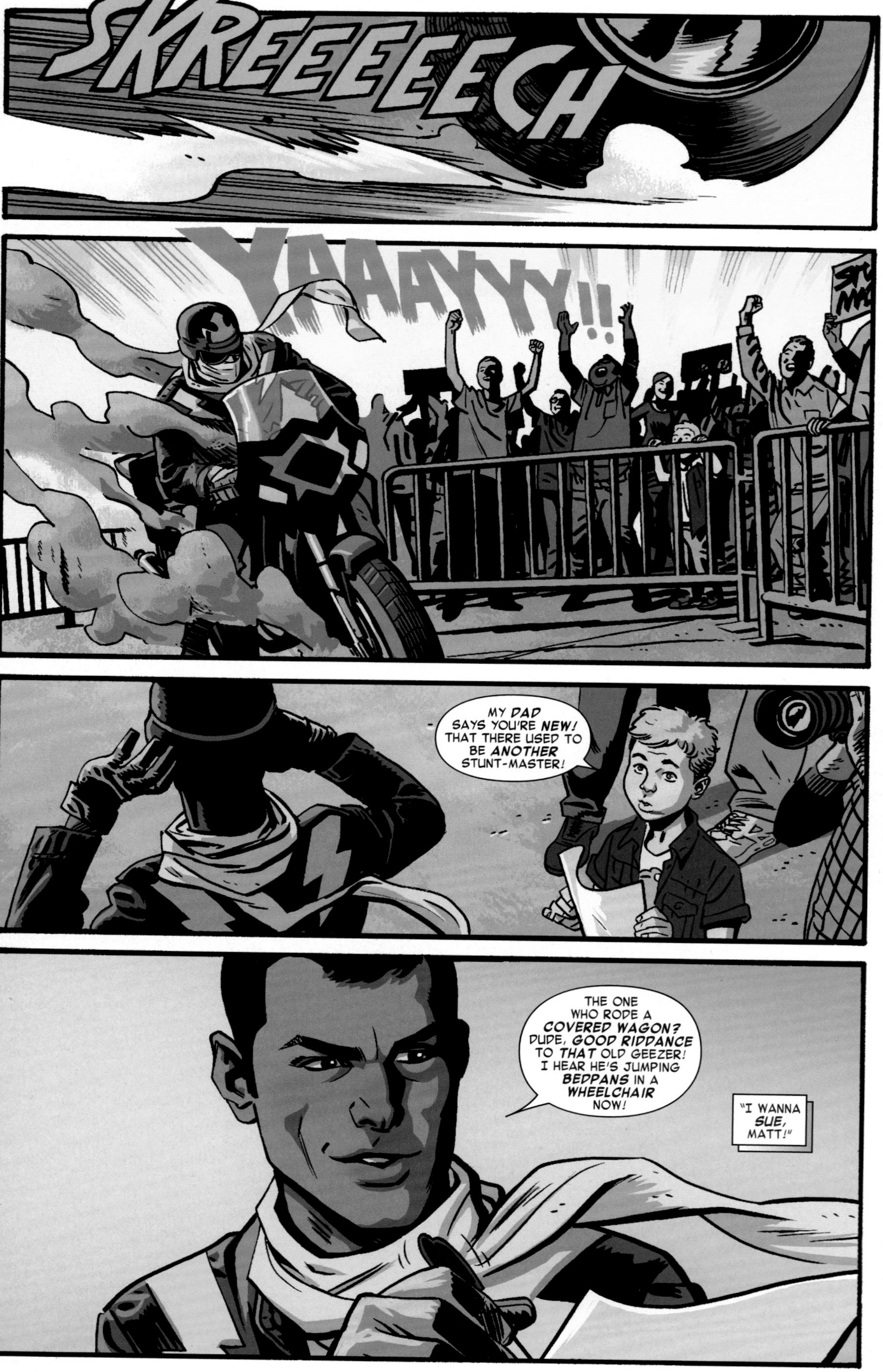
SKREEEEEECH
YAAAYYY!!
MY DAD SAYS YOU'RE NEW! THAT THERE USED TO BE ANOTHER STUNT-MASTER!
THE ONE WHO RODE A COVERED WAGON? DUDE, GOOD RIDDANCE TO THAT OLD GEEZER! I HEAR HE'S JUMPING BEDPANS IN A WHEELCHAIR NOW!
"I WANNA SUE, MATT!"

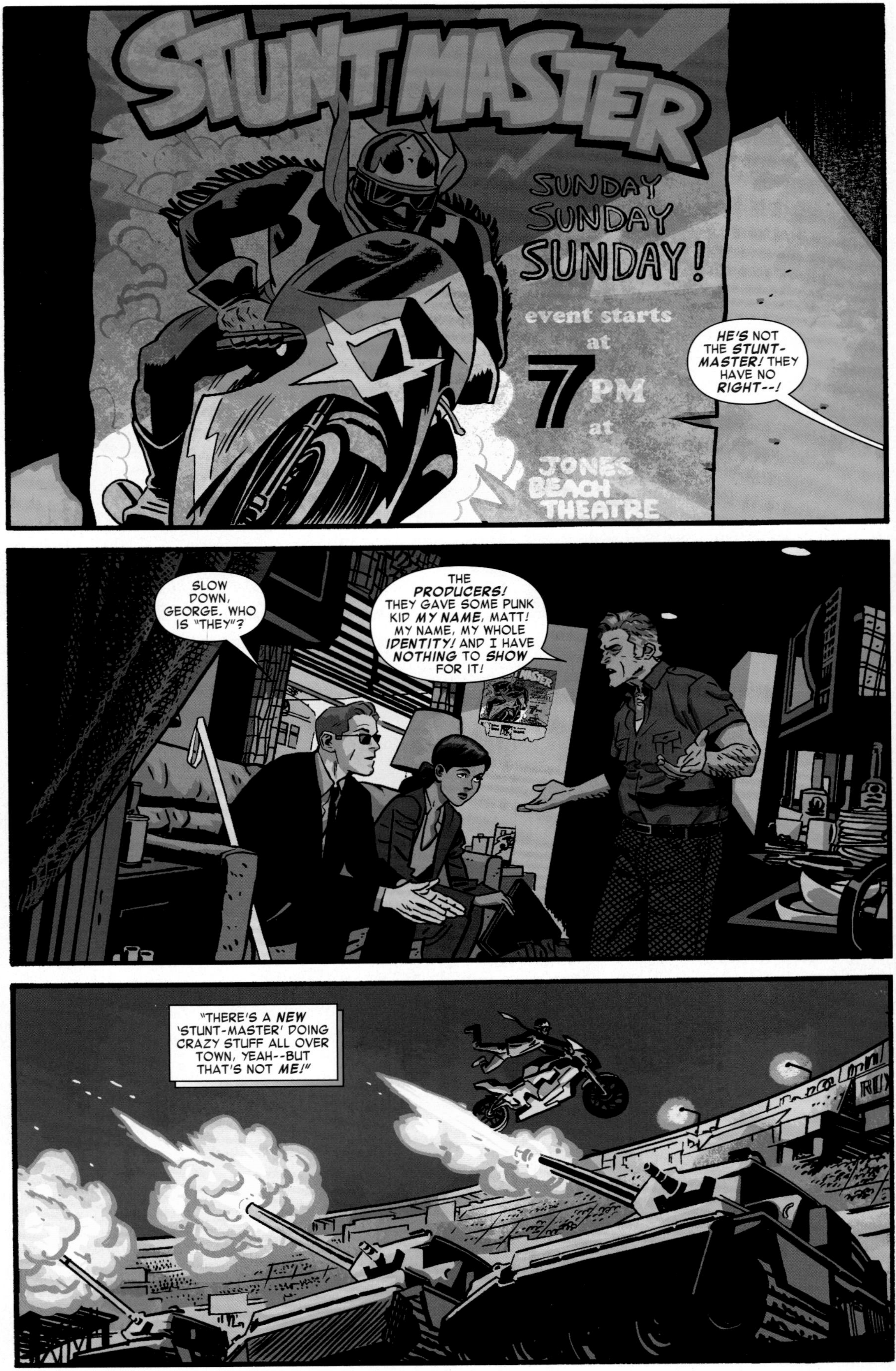
STUNT MASTER
SUNDAY SUNDAY SUNDAY!
event starts at 7 PM at JONES BEACH THEATRE
HE'S NOT THE STUNT-MASTER! THEY HAVE NO RIGHT--!
SLOW DOWN, GEORGE. WHO IS "THEY"?
THE PRODUCERS! THEY GAVE SOME PUNK KID MY NAME, MATT! MY NAME, MY WHOLE IDENTITY! AND I HAVE NOTHING TO SHOW FOR IT!
"THERE'S A NEW 'STUNT-MASTER' DOING CRAZY STUFF ALL OVER TOWN, YEAH--BUT THAT'S NOT ME!"

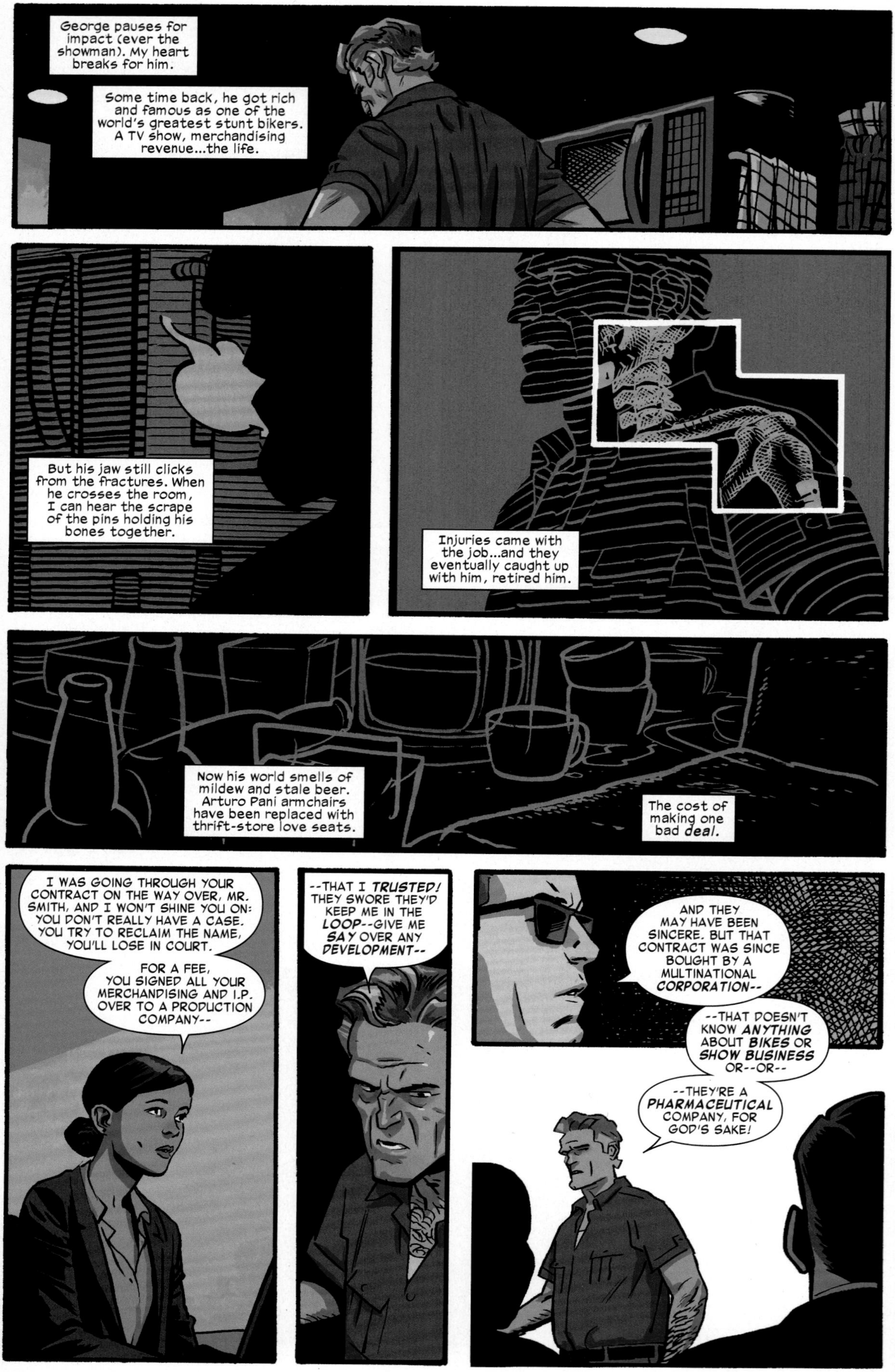
George pauses for impact (ever the showman). My heart breaks for him.
Some time back, he got rich and famous as one of the world's greatest stunt bikers. A TV show, merchandising revenue...the life.
But his jaw still clicks from the fractures. When he crosses the room, I can hear the scrape of the pins holding his bones together.
Injuries came with the job...and they eventually caught up with him, retired him.
Now his world smells of mildew and stale beer. Arturo Pani armchairs have been replaced with thrift-store love seats.
The cost of making one bad *deal.*
I WAS GOING THROUGH YOUR CONTRACT ON THE WAY OVER, MR. SMITH, AND I WON'T SHINE YOU ON: YOU DON'T REALLY HAVE A CASE. YOU TRY TO RECLAIM THE NAME, YOU'LL LOSE IN COURT.
FOR A FEE, YOU SIGNED ALL YOUR MERCHANDISING AND I.P. OVER TO A PRODUCTION COMPANY--
--THAT I ***TRUSTED!*** THEY SWORE THEY'D KEEP ME IN THE ***LOOP***--GIVE ME ***SAY*** OVER ANY ***DEVELOPMENT***--
AND THEY MAY HAVE BEEN SINCERE. BUT THAT CONTRACT WAS SINCE BOUGHT BY A MULTINATIONAL ***CORPORATION***--
--THAT DOESN'T KNOW ***ANYTHING*** ABOUT ***BIKES*** OR ***SHOW BUSINESS*** OR--OR--
--THEY'RE A ***PHARMACEUTICAL*** COMPANY, FOR GOD'S SAKE!

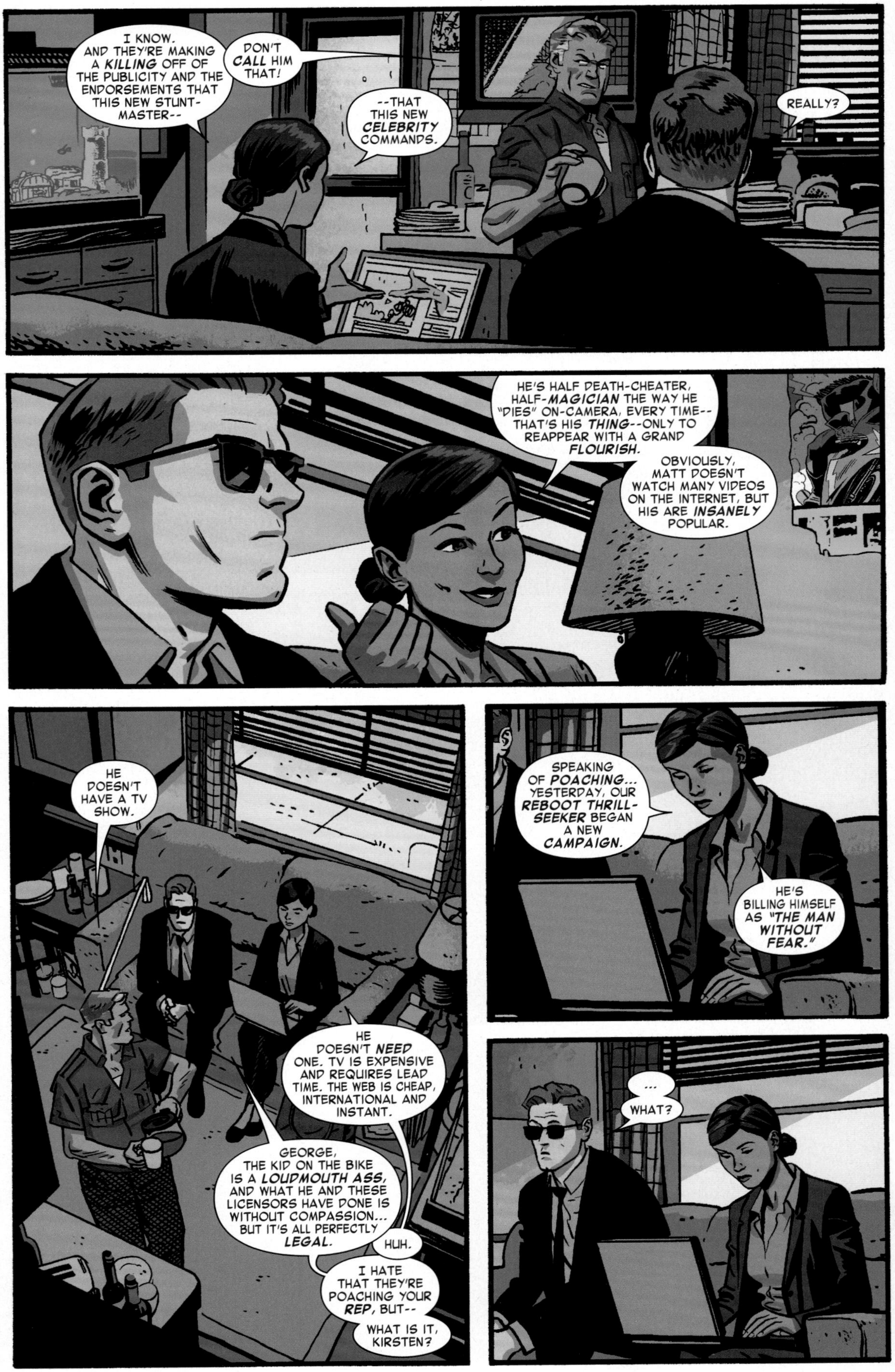
I KNOW. AND THEY'RE MAKING A KILLING OFF OF THE PUBLICITY AND THE ENDORSEMENTS THAT THIS NEW STUNT-MASTER--
DON'T CALL HIM THAT!
--THAT THIS NEW CELEBRITY COMMANDS.
REALLY?
HE'S HALF DEATH-CHEATER, HALF-MAGICIAN THE WAY HE "DIES" ON-CAMERA, EVERY TIME--THAT'S HIS THING--ONLY TO REAPPEAR WITH A GRAND FLOURISH.
OBVIOUSLY, MATT DOESN'T WATCH MANY VIDEOS ON THE INTERNET, BUT HIS ARE INSANELY POPULAR.
HE DOESN'T HAVE A TV SHOW.
HE DOESN'T NEED ONE. TV IS EXPENSIVE AND REQUIRES LEAD TIME. THE WEB IS CHEAP, INTERNATIONAL AND INSTANT.
GEORGE, THE KID ON THE BIKE IS A LOUDMOUTH ASS, AND WHAT HE AND THESE LICENSORS HAVE DONE IS WITHOUT COMPASSION... BUT IT'S ALL PERFECTLY LEGAL.
HUH.
I HATE THAT THEY'RE POACHING YOUR REP, BUT--
WHAT IS IT, KIRSTEN?
SPEAKING OF POACHING... YESTERDAY, OUR REBOOT THRILL-SEEKER BEGAN A NEW CAMPAIGN.
HE'S BILLING HIMSELF AS "THE MAN WITHOUT FEAR."
...
WHAT?

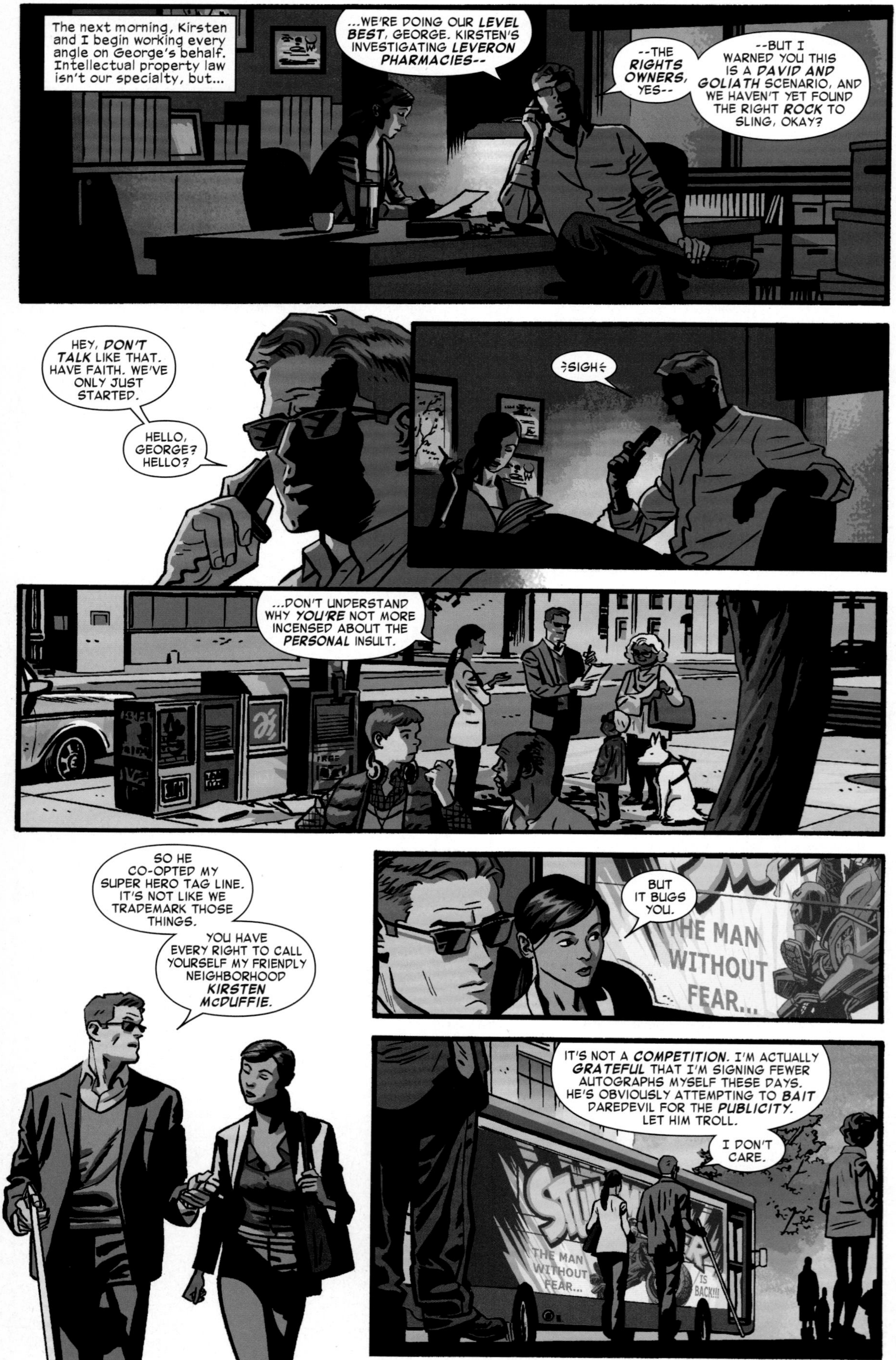
The next morning, Kirsten and I begin working every angle on George's behalf. Intellectual property law isn't our specialty, but...
...WE'RE DOING OUR LEVEL BEST, GEORGE. KIRSTEN'S INVESTIGATING LEVERON PHARMACIES--
--THE RIGHTS OWNERS, YES--
--BUT I WARNED YOU THIS IS A DAVID AND GOLIATH SCENARIO, AND WE HAVEN'T YET FOUND THE RIGHT ROCK TO SLING, OKAY?
HEY, DON'T TALK LIKE THAT. HAVE FAITH. WE'VE ONLY JUST STARTED.
HELLO, GEORGE? HELLO?
SIGH
...DON'T UNDERSTAND WHY YOU'RE NOT MORE INCENSED ABOUT THE PERSONAL INSULT.
SO HE CO-OPTED MY SUPER HERO TAG LINE. IT'S NOT LIKE WE TRADEMARK THOSE THINGS.
YOU HAVE EVERY RIGHT TO CALL YOURSELF MY FRIENDLY NEIGHBORHOOD KIRSTEN McDUFFIE.
BUT IT BUGS YOU.
THE MAN WITHOUT FEAR...
IT'S NOT A COMPETITION. I'M ACTUALLY GRATEFUL THAT I'M SIGNING FEWER AUTOGRAPHS MYSELF THESE DAYS. HE'S OBVIOUSLY ATTEMPTING TO BAIT DAREDEVIL FOR THE PUBLICITY. LET HIM TROLL.
I DON'T CARE.
THE MAN WITHOUT FEAR...
IS BACK!!!

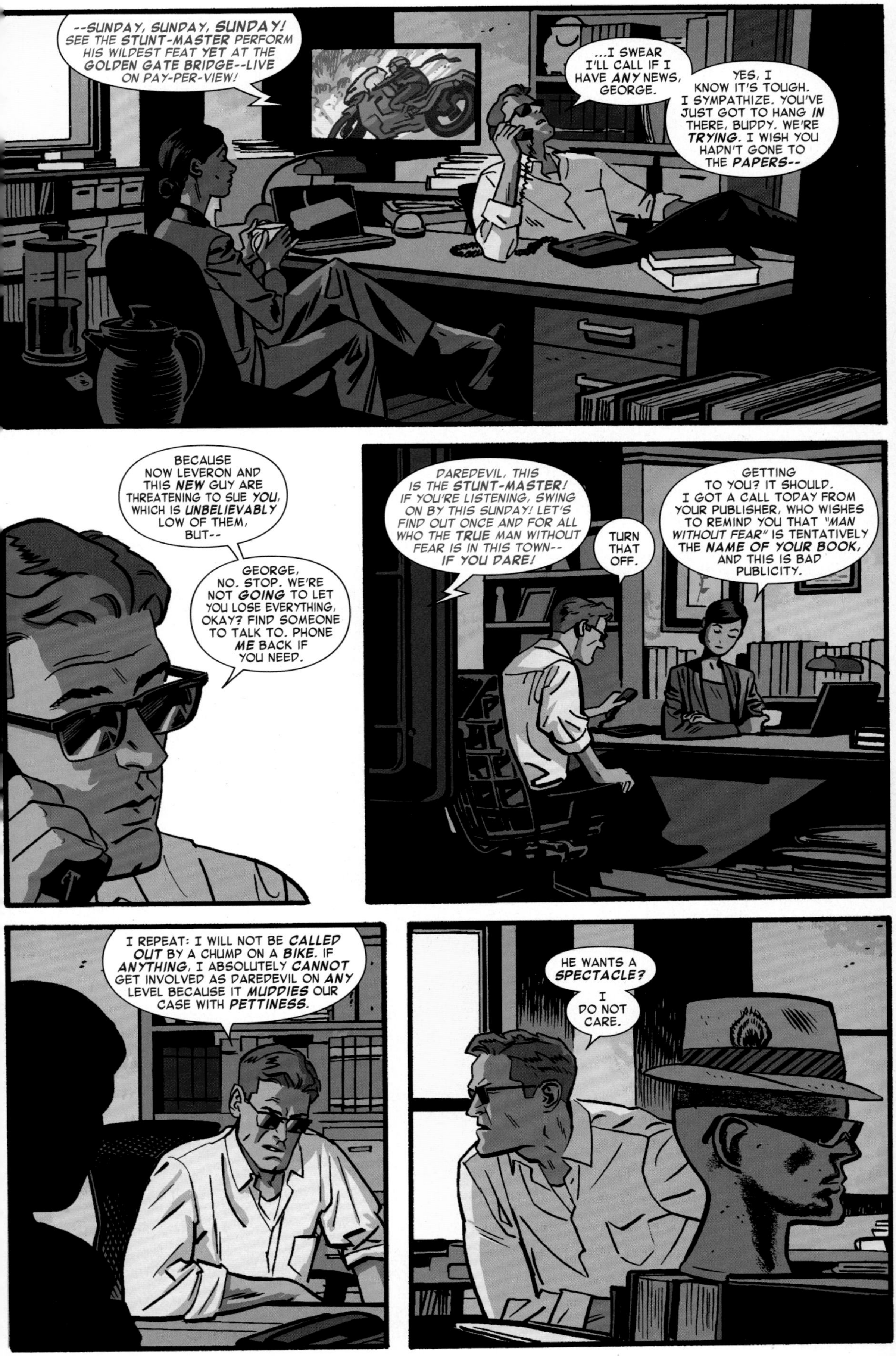

--SUNDAY, SUNDAY, SUNDAY! SEE THE STUNT-MASTER PERFORM HIS WILDEST FEAT YET AT THE GOLDEN GATE BRIDGE--LIVE ON PAY-PER-VIEW!
...I SWEAR I'LL CALL IF I HAVE ANY NEWS, GEORGE.
YES, I KNOW IT'S TOUGH. I SYMPATHIZE. YOU'VE JUST GOT TO HANG IN THERE, BUDDY. WE'RE TRYING. I WISH YOU HADN'T GONE TO THE PAPERS--
BECAUSE NOW LEVERON AND THIS NEW GUY ARE THREATENING TO SUE YOU, WHICH IS UNBELIEVABLY LOW OF THEM, BUT--
GEORGE, NO. STOP. WE'RE NOT GOING TO LET YOU LOSE EVERYTHING, OKAY? FIND SOMEONE TO TALK TO. PHONE ME BACK IF YOU NEED.
DAREDEVIL, THIS IS THE STUNT-MASTER! IF YOU'RE LISTENING, SWING ON BY THIS SUNDAY! LET'S FIND OUT ONCE AND FOR ALL WHO THE TRUE MAN WITHOUT FEAR IS IN THIS TOWN-- IF YOU DARE!
TURN THAT OFF.
GETTING TO YOU? IT SHOULD. I GOT A CALL TODAY FROM YOUR PUBLISHER, WHO WISHES TO REMIND YOU THAT "MAN WITHOUT FEAR" IS TENTATIVELY THE NAME OF YOUR BOOK, AND THIS IS BAD PUBLICITY.
I REPEAT: I WILL NOT BE CALLED OUT BY A CHUMP ON A BIKE. IF ANYTHING, I ABSOLUTELY CANNOT GET INVOLVED AS DAREDEVIL ON ANY LEVEL BECAUSE IT MUDDIES OUR CASE WITH PETTINESS.
HE WANTS A SPECTACLE?
I DO NOT CARE.

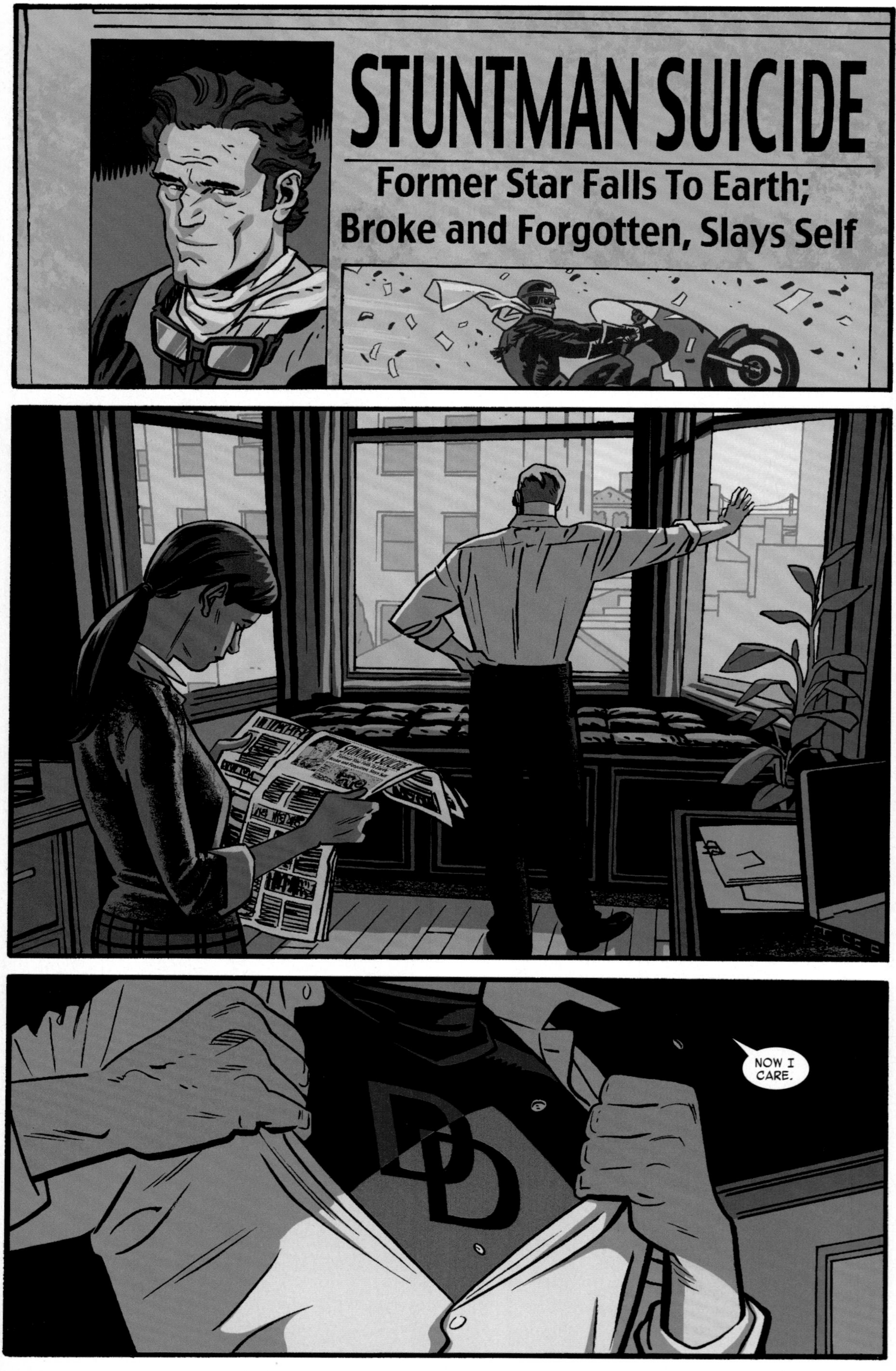
STUNTMAN SUICIDE
Former Star Falls To Earth;
Broke and Forgotten, Slays Self
NOW I CARE.

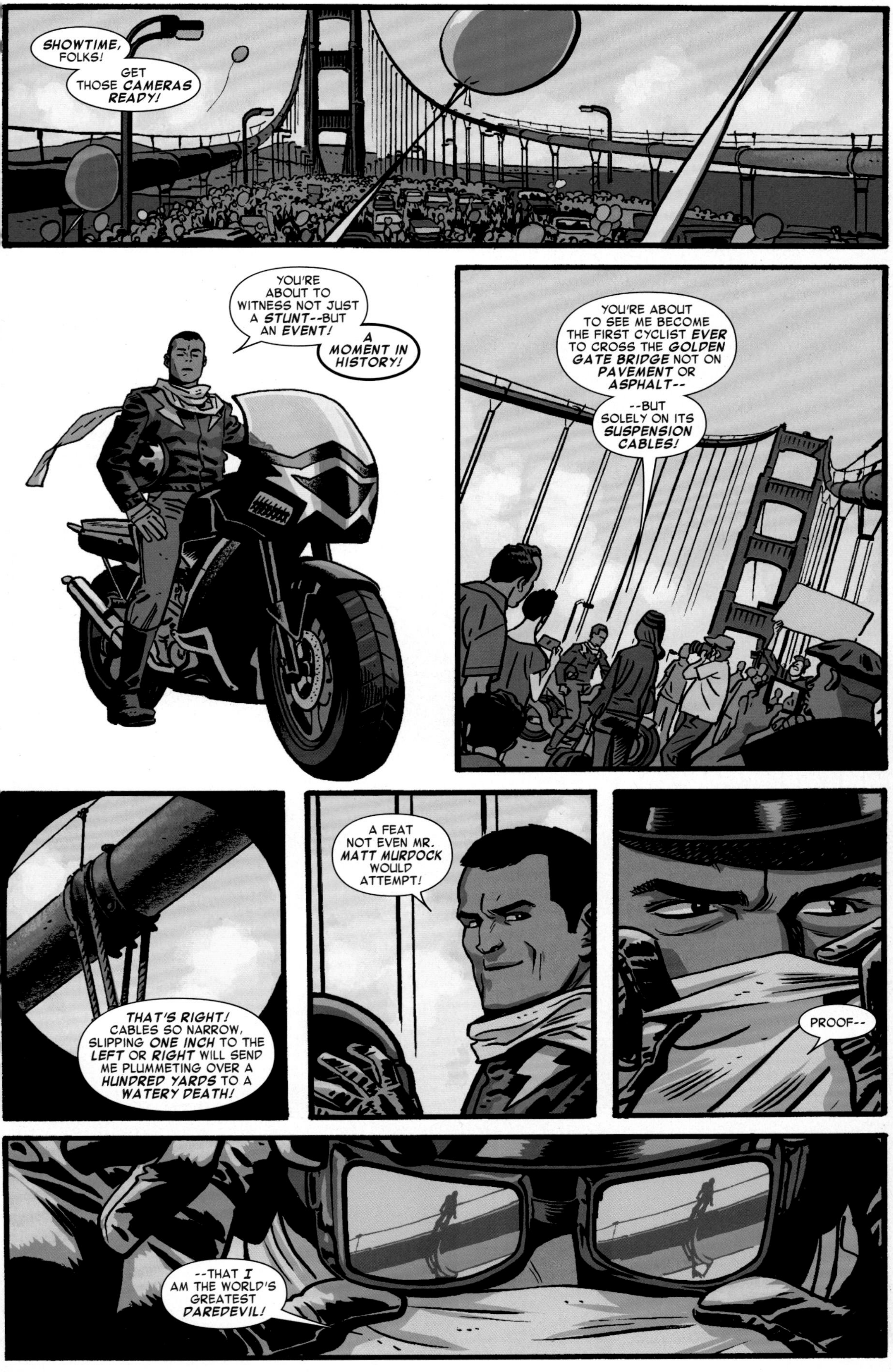
SHOWTIME, FOLKS!
GET THOSE CAMERAS READY!
YOU'RE ABOUT TO WITNESS NOT JUST A STUNT--BUT AN EVENT!
A MOMENT IN HISTORY!
YOU'RE ABOUT TO SEE ME BECOME THE FIRST CYCLIST EVER TO CROSS THE GOLDEN GATE BRIDGE NOT ON PAVEMENT OR ASPHALT--
--BUT SOLELY ON ITS SUSPENSION CABLES!
THAT'S RIGHT! CABLES SO NARROW, SLIPPING ONE INCH TO THE LEFT OR RIGHT WILL SEND ME PLUMMETING OVER A HUNDRED YARDS TO A WATERY DEATH!
A FEAT NOT EVEN MR. MATT MURDOCK WOULD ATTEMPT!
PROOF--
--THAT I AM THE WORLD'S GREATEST DAREDEVIL!

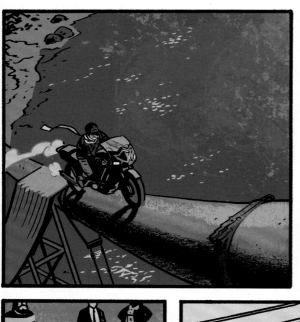

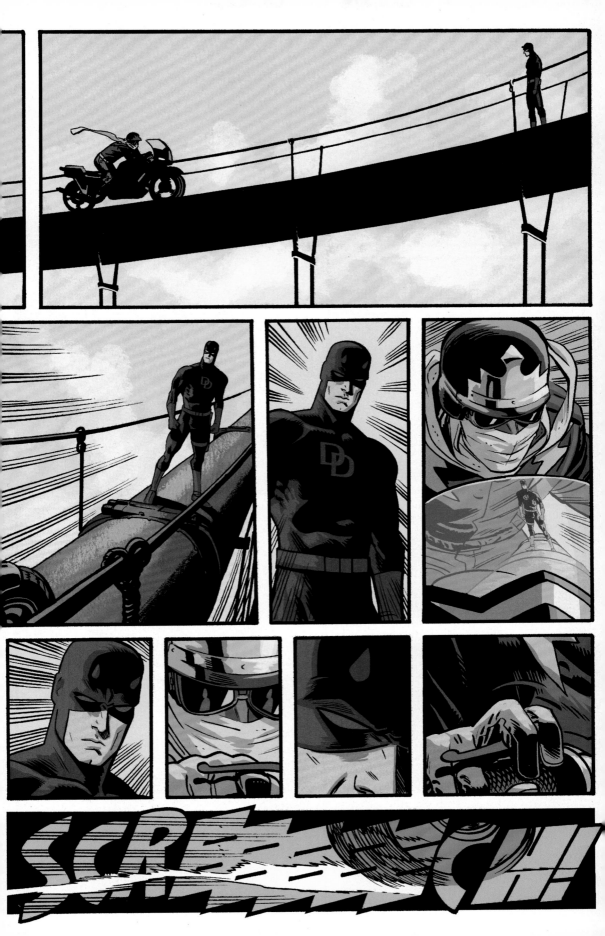

SCREECH!

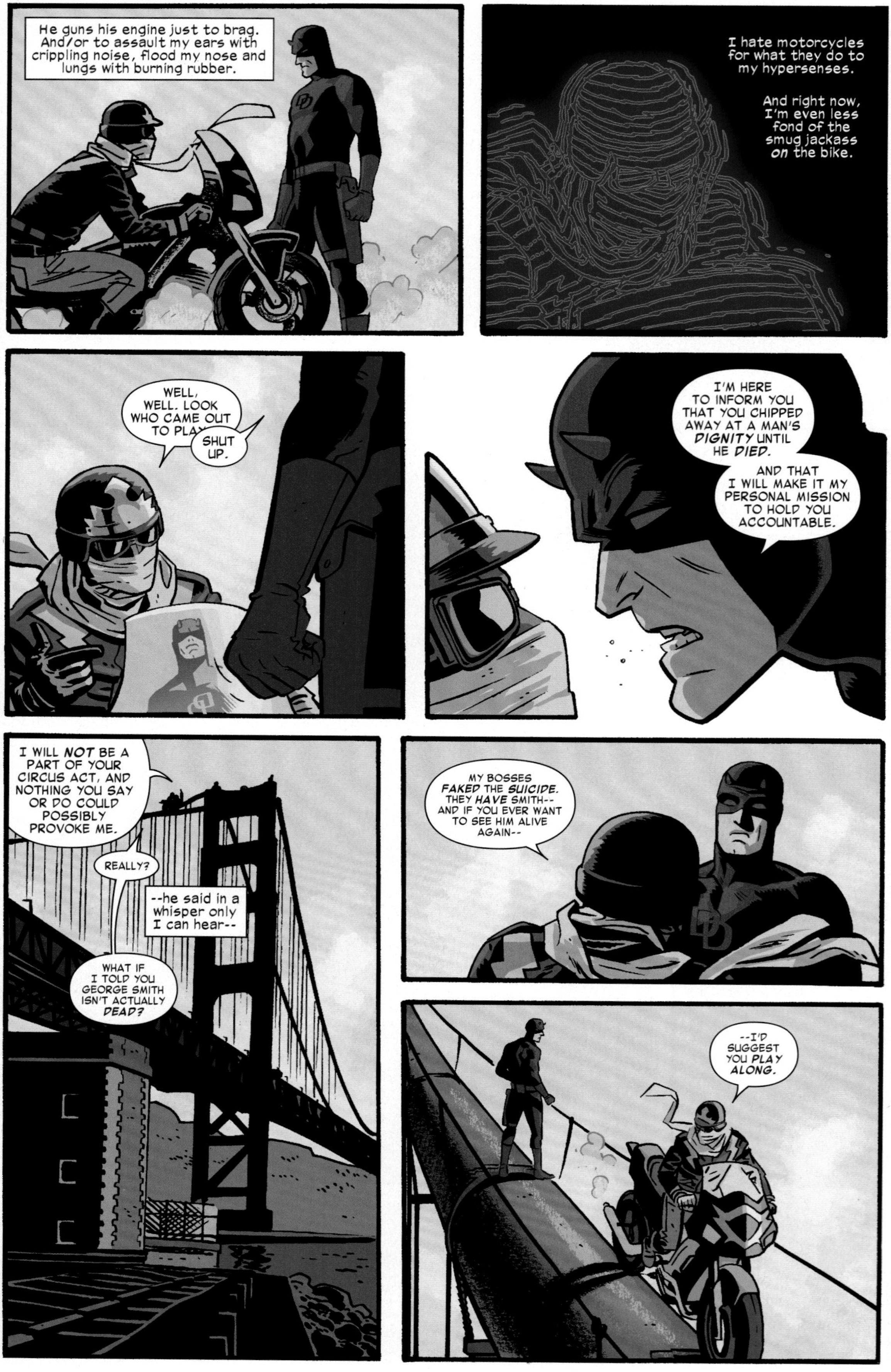
He guns his engine just to brag. And/or to assault my ears with crippling noise, flood my nose and lungs with burning rubber.
I hate motorcycles for what they do to my hypersenses.
And right now, I'm even less fond of the smug jackass *on* the bike.
WELL, WELL. LOOK WHO CAME OUT TO PLAY
SHUT UP.
I'M HERE TO INFORM YOU THAT YOU CHIPPED AWAY AT A MAN'S *DIGNITY* UNTIL HE *DIED.*
AND THAT I WILL MAKE IT MY PERSONAL MISSION TO HOLD YOU ACCOUNTABLE.
I WILL *NOT* BE A PART OF YOUR CIRCUS ACT, AND NOTHING YOU SAY OR DO COULD POSSIBLY PROVOKE ME.
REALLY?
--he said in a whisper only I can hear--
WHAT IF I TOLD YOU GEORGE SMITH ISN'T ACTUALLY *DEAD?*
MY BOSSES *FAKED* THE *SUICIDE.* THEY *HAVE* SMITH-- AND IF YOU EVER WANT TO SEE HIM ALIVE AGAIN--
--I'D SUGGEST YOU *PLAY ALONG.*

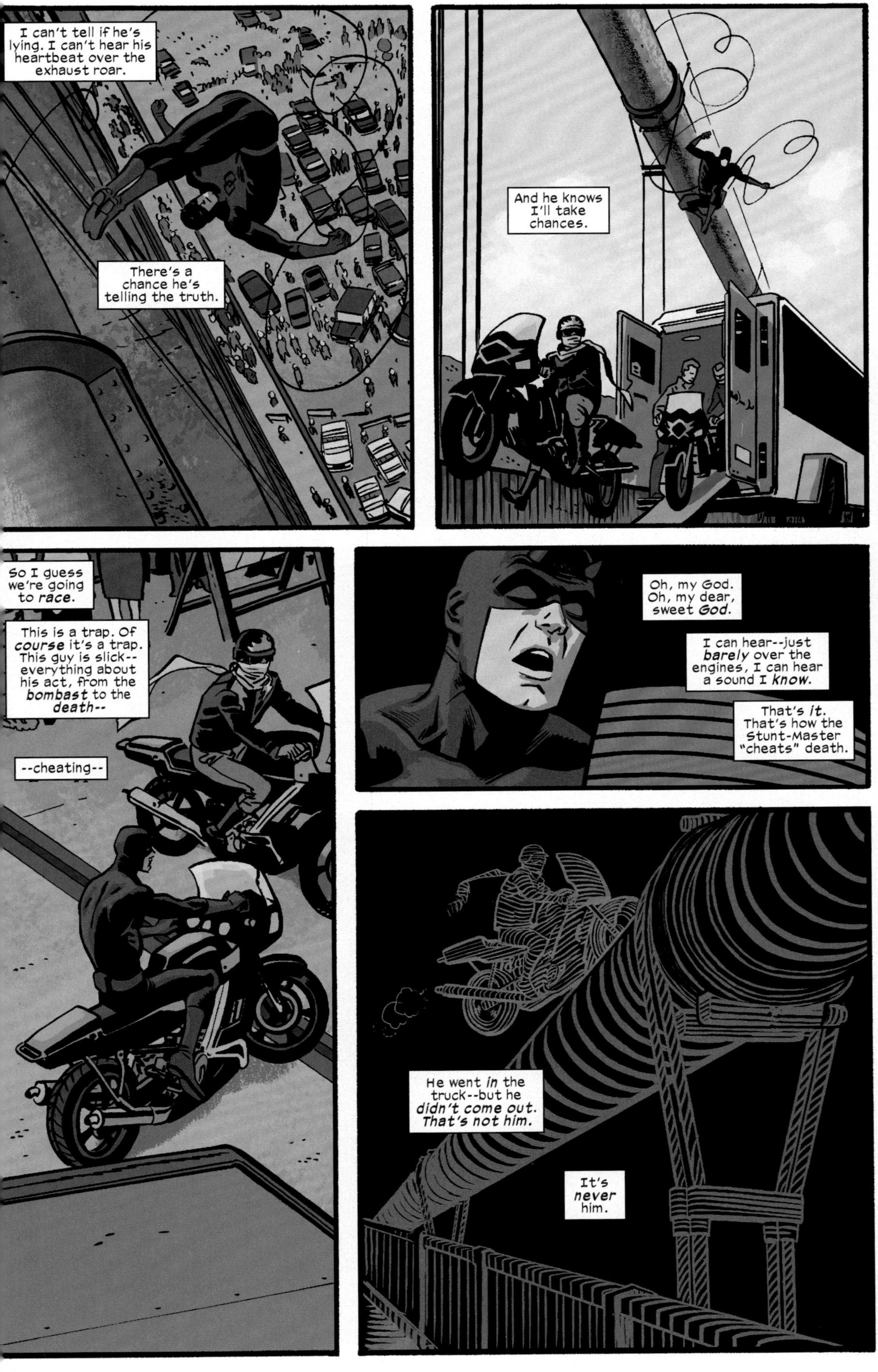
I can't tell if he's lying. I can't hear his heartbeat over the exhaust roar.
There's a chance he's telling the truth.
And he knows I'll take chances.
So I guess we're going to *race*.
This is a trap. Of *course* it's a trap. This guy is slick-- everything about his act, from the *bombast* to the *death*--
--cheating--
Oh, my God. Oh, my dear, sweet *God*.
I can hear--just *barely* over the engines, I can hear a sound I *know*.
That's *it*. That's how the Stunt-Master "cheats" death.
He went *in* the truck--but he *didn't come out. That's not him.*
It's *never* him.

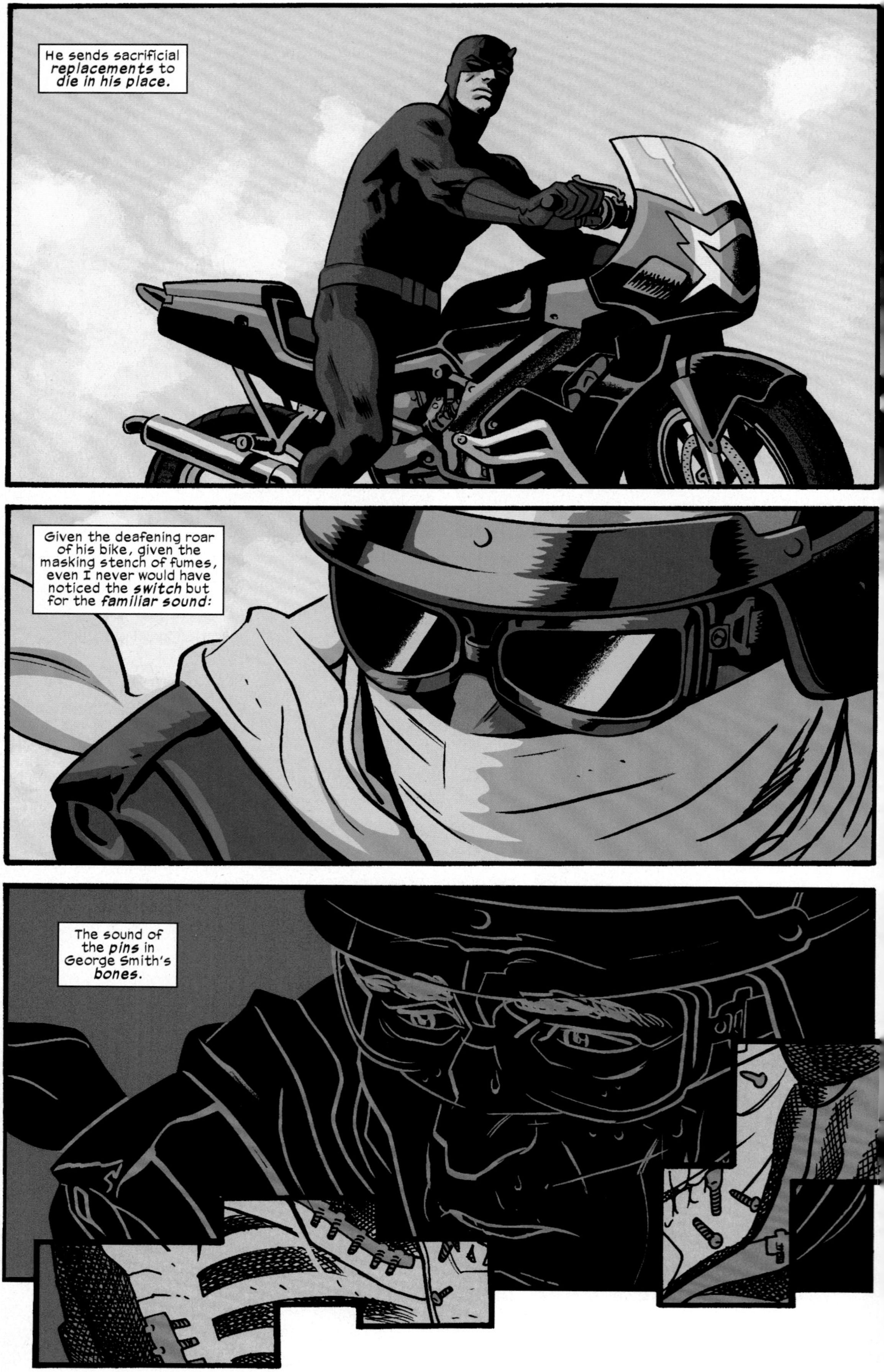
He sends sacrificial replacements to die in his place.
Given the deafening roar of his bike, given the masking stench of fumes, even I never would have noticed the switch but for the familiar sound:
The sound of the pins in George Smith's bones.

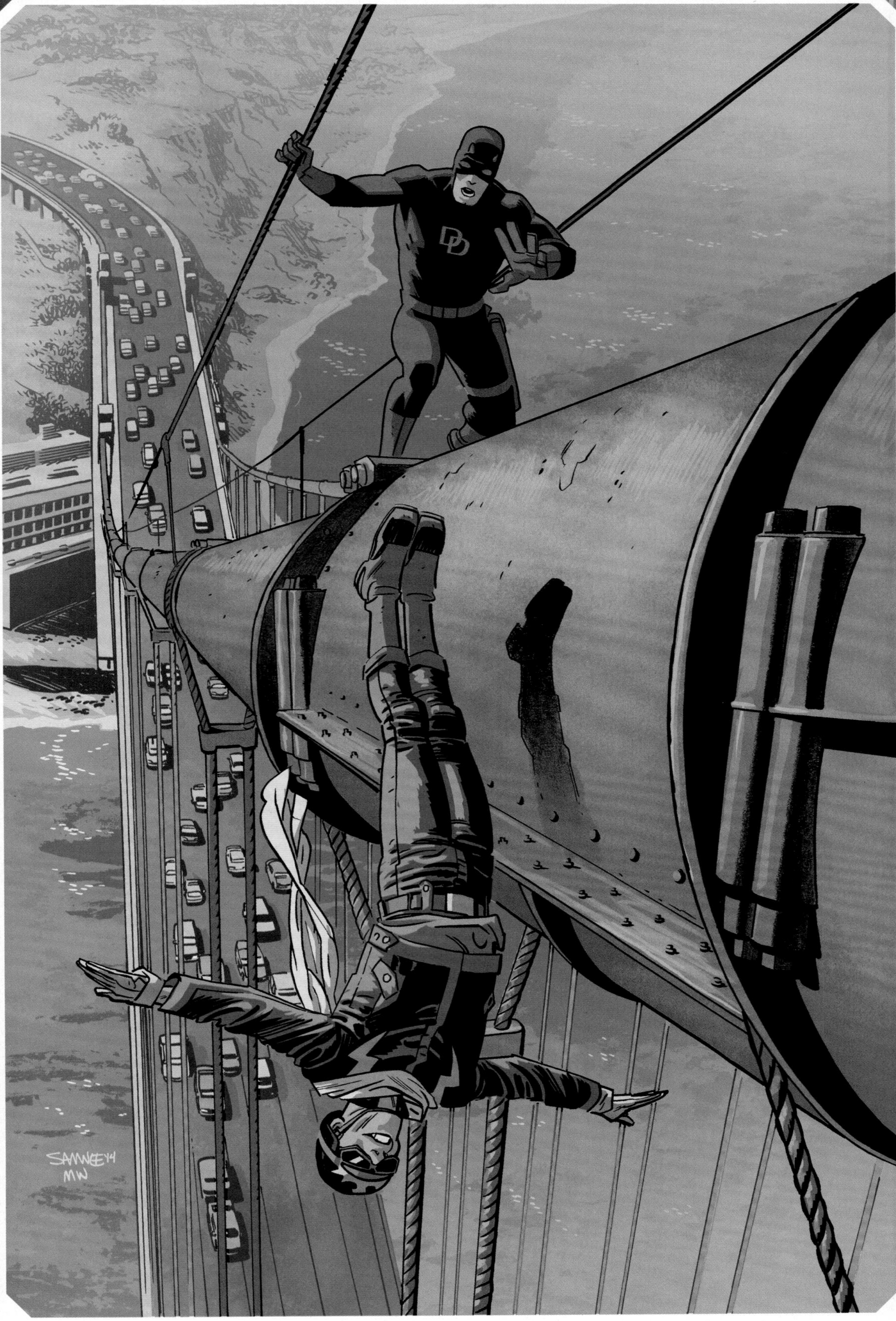
SAMNEE'14
MW

DAREDEVIL #12

On occasion, I have to convince people that I'm not suicidal.

This will reassure no one.

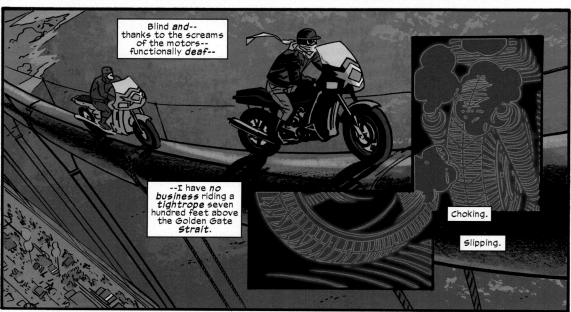

Blind and-- thanks to the screams of the motors-- functionally *deaf*--

--I have *no business* riding a *tightrope* seven hundred feet above the Golden Gate *strait*.

Choking.

Slipping.

Cycle's *vibrations* make my radar sense practically *useless*.

I never dreamed this would be so utterly impossible. But if I don't catch up to the man in *front* of me...

...he's going to *die*.

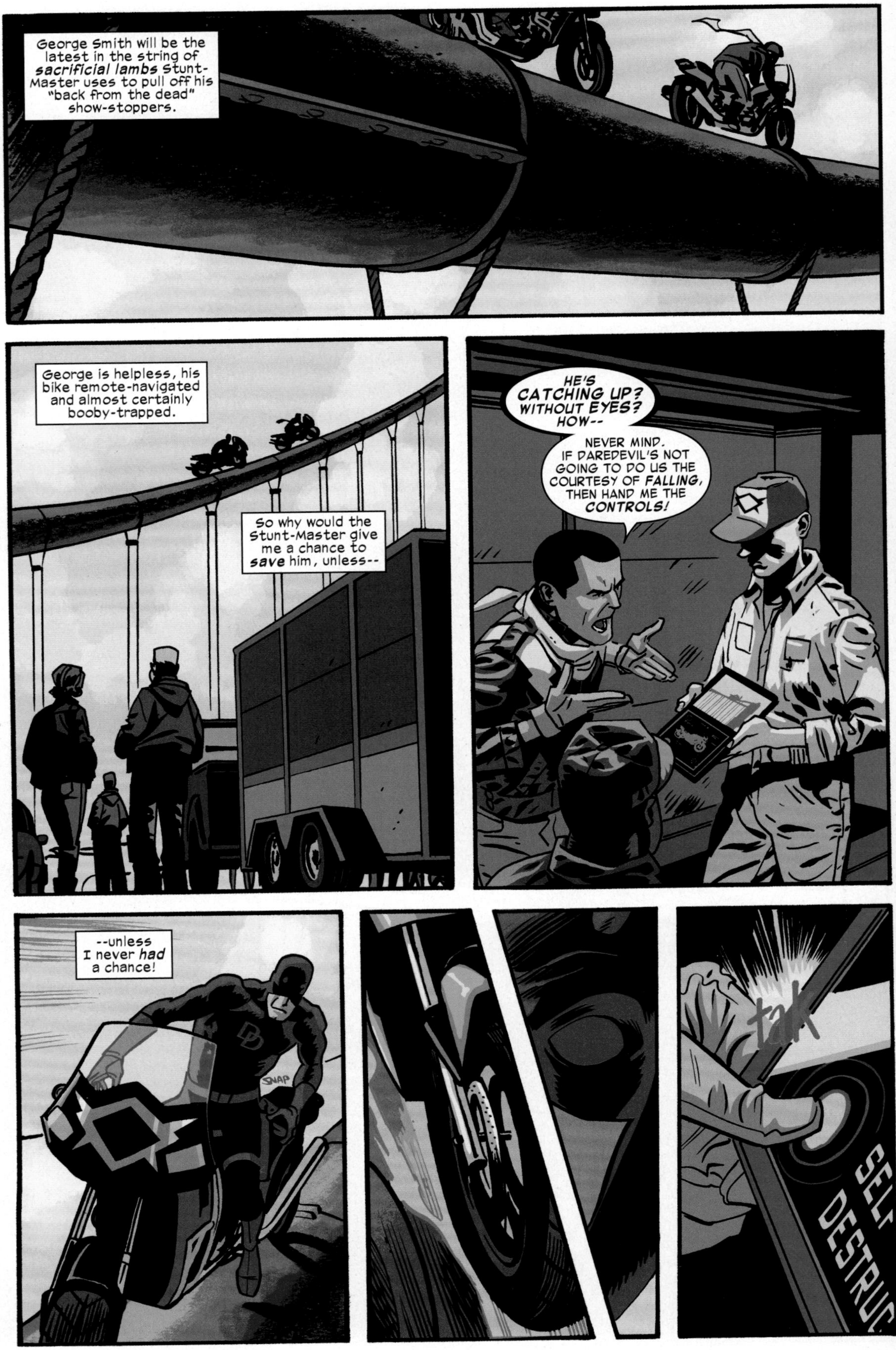
George Smith will be the latest in the string of sacrificial lambs Stunt-Master uses to pull off his "back from the dead" show-stoppers.
George is helpless, his bike remote-navigated and almost certainly booby-trapped.
So why would the Stunt-Master give me a chance to save him, unless--
HE'S CATCHING UP? WITHOUT EYES? HOW--
NEVER MIND. IF DAREDEVIL'S NOT GOING TO DO US THE COURTESY OF FALLING, THEN HAND ME THE CONTROLS!
--unless I never had a chance!
SNAP
tak
SELF DESTRUC

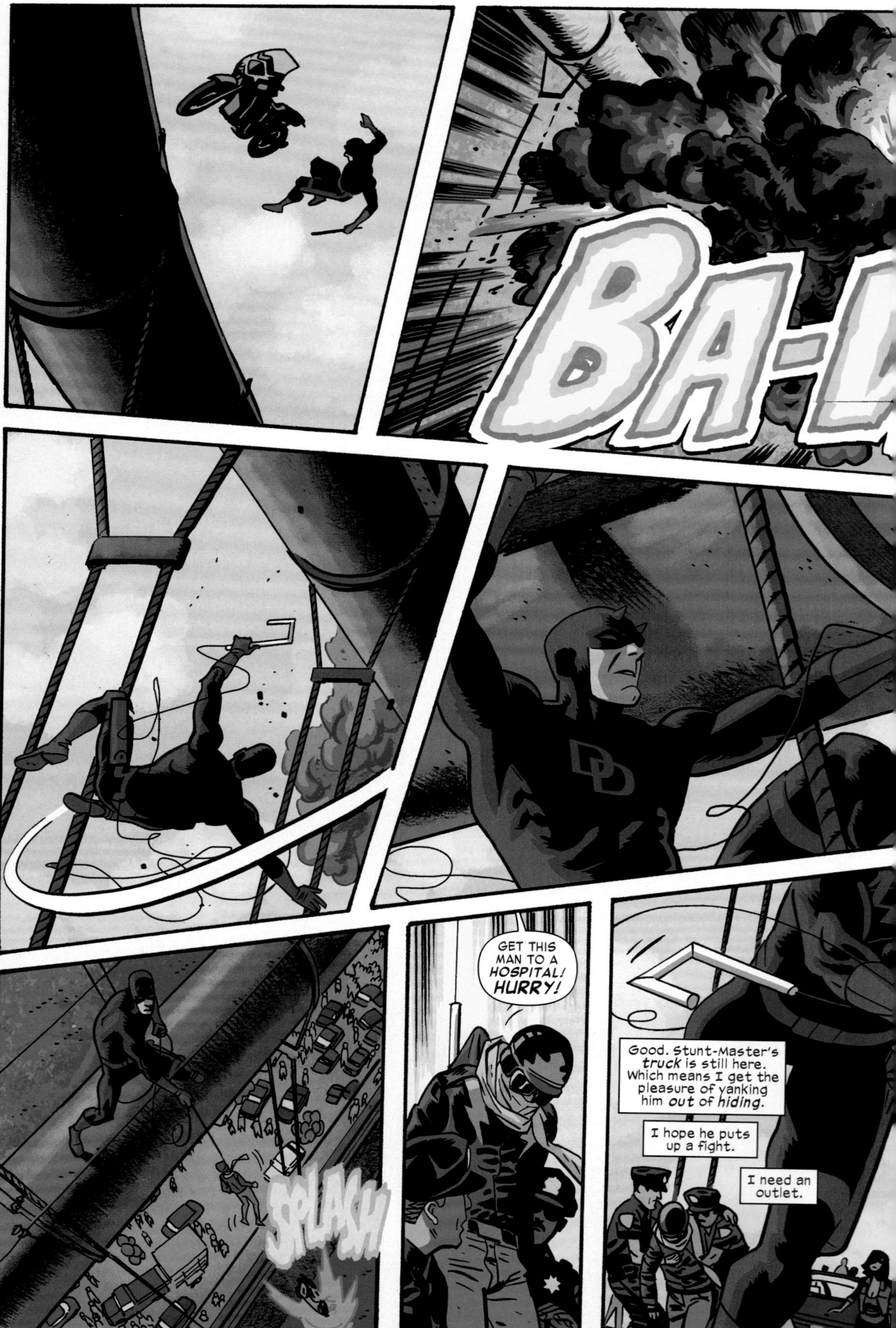
BA-
GET THIS MAN TO A HOSPITAL! HURRY!
Good. Stunt-Master's truck is still here. Which means I get the pleasure of yanking him out of hiding.
I hope he puts up a fight.
I need an outlet.
SPLASH

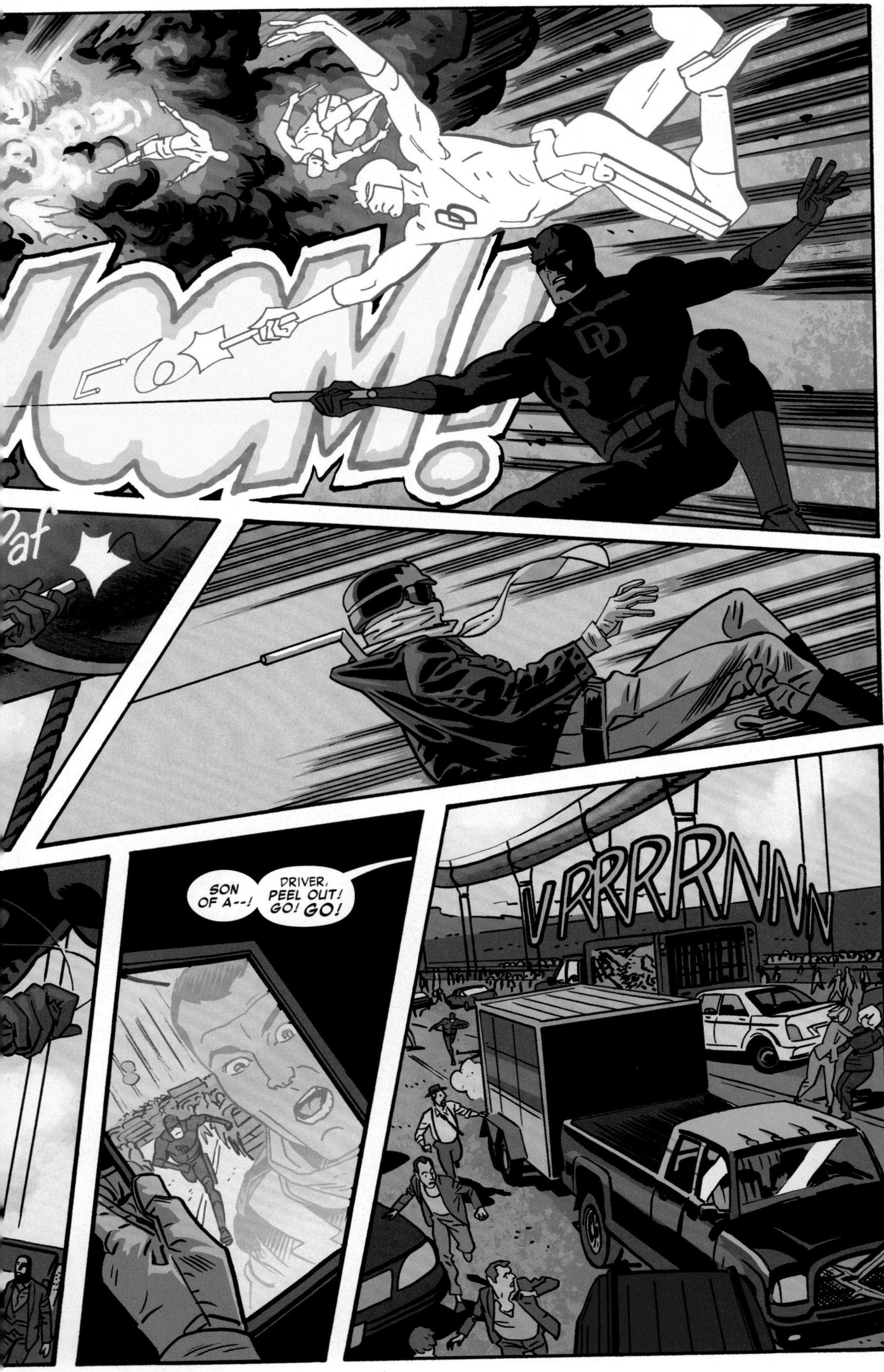

Paf
SON OF A--!
DRIVER, PEEL OUT! GO! GO!
VRRRRNNNN

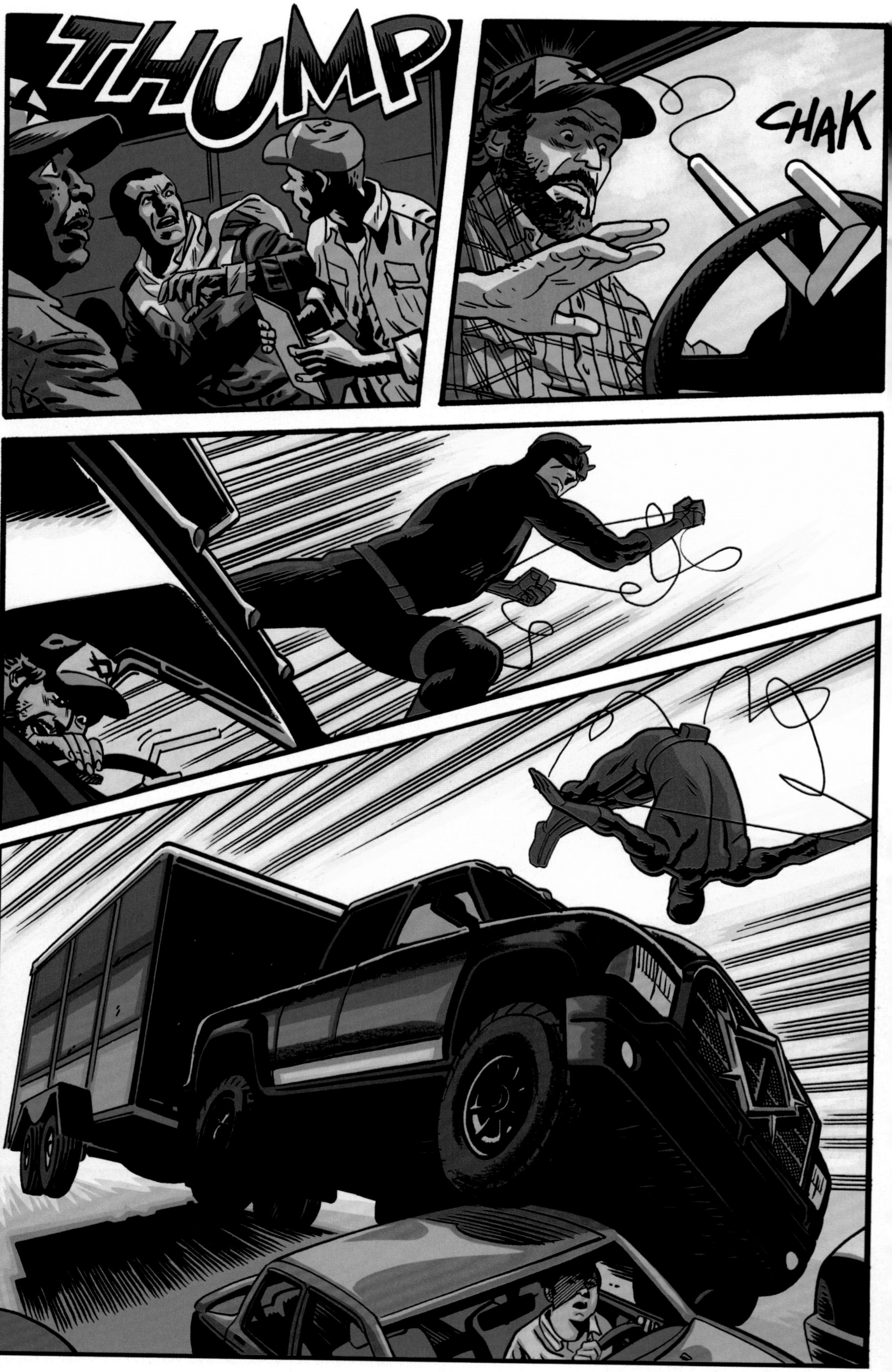
THUMP
CHAK

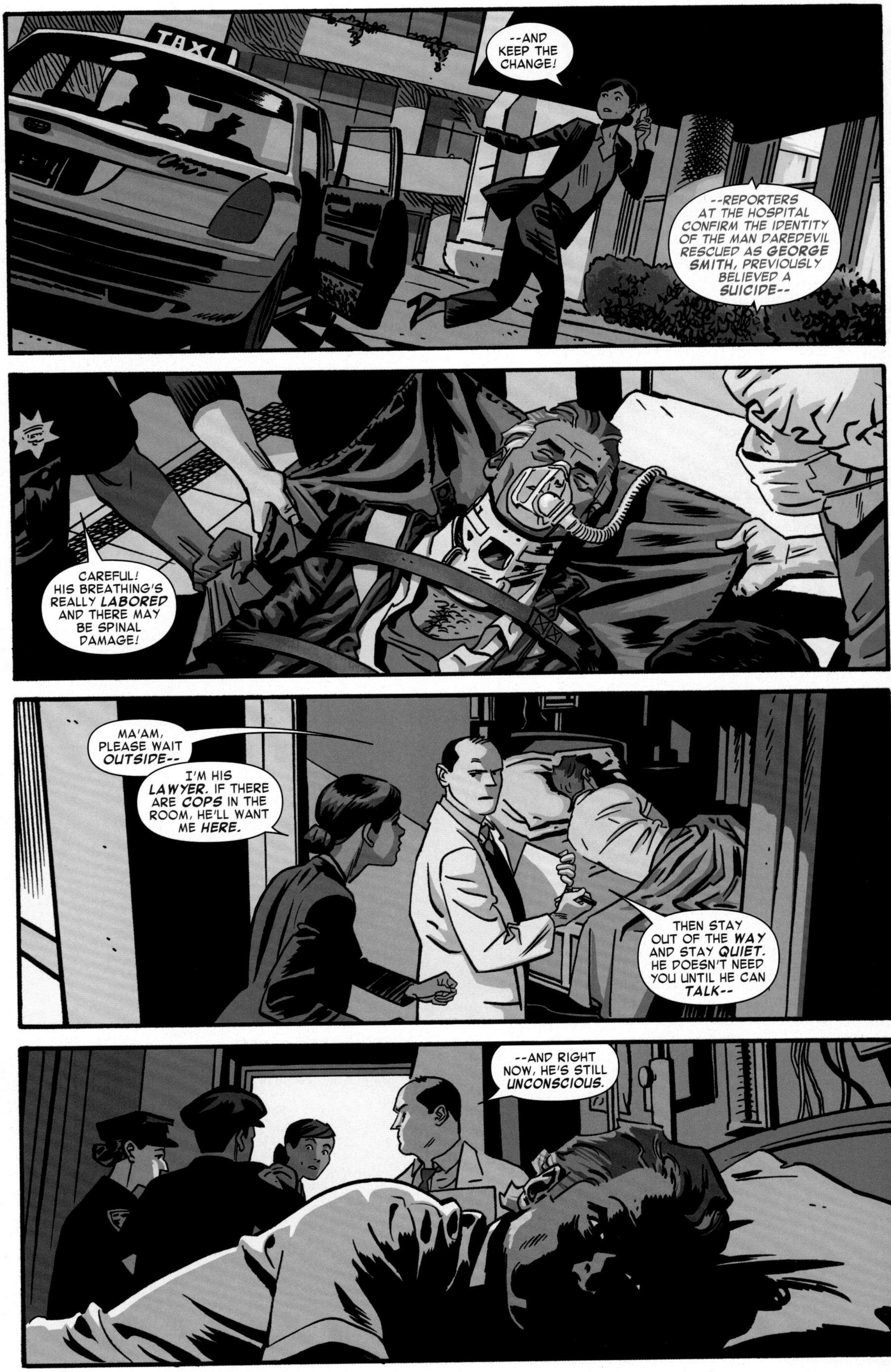
--AND KEEP THE CHANGE!
--REPORTERS AT THE HOSPITAL CONFIRM THE IDENTITY OF THE MAN DAREDEVIL RESCUED AS GEORGE SMITH, PREVIOUSLY BELIEVED A SUICIDE--
CAREFUL! HIS BREATHING'S REALLY LABORED AND THERE MAY BE SPINAL DAMAGE!
MA'AM, PLEASE WAIT OUTSIDE--
I'M HIS LAWYER. IF THERE ARE COPS IN THE ROOM, HE'LL WANT ME HERE.
THEN STAY OUT OF THE WAY AND STAY QUIET. HE DOESN'T NEED YOU UNTIL HE CAN TALK--
--AND RIGHT NOW, HE'S STILL UNCONSCIOUS.

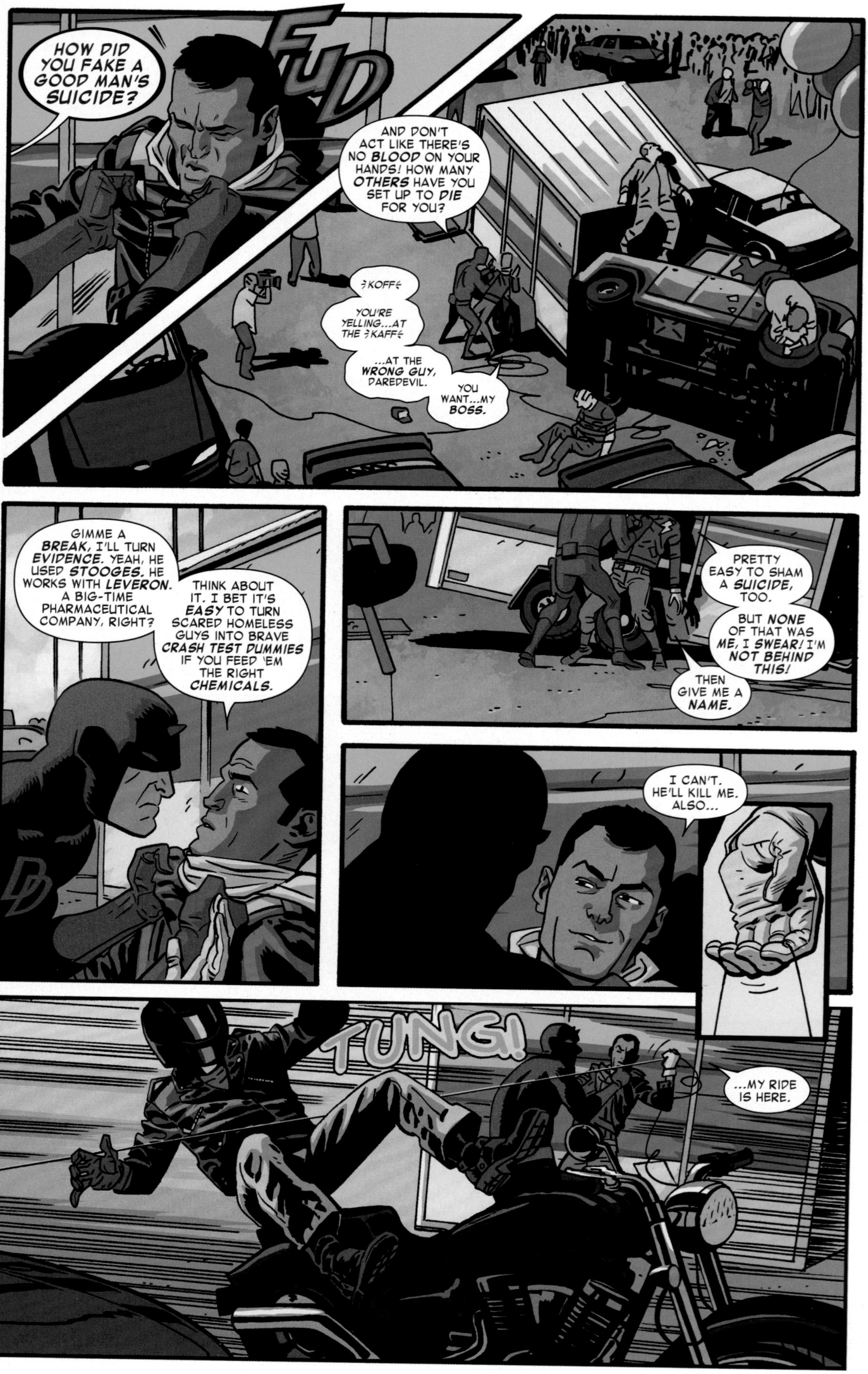
HOW DID YOU FAKE A GOOD MAN'S SUICIDE?
FUD
AND DON'T ACT LIKE THERE'S NO BLOOD ON YOUR HANDS! HOW MANY OTHERS HAVE YOU SET UP TO DIE FOR YOU?
KOFF
YOU'RE YELLING...AT THE KAFF
...AT THE WRONG GUY, DAREDEVIL.
YOU WANT...MY BOSS.
GIMME A BREAK, I'LL TURN EVIDENCE. YEAH, HE USED STOOGES. HE WORKS WITH LEVERON. A BIG-TIME PHARMACEUTICAL COMPANY, RIGHT?
THINK ABOUT IT. I BET IT'S EASY TO TURN SCARED HOMELESS GUYS INTO BRAVE CRASH TEST DUMMIES IF YOU FEED 'EM THE RIGHT CHEMICALS.
PRETTY EASY TO SHAM A SUICIDE, TOO.
BUT NONE OF THAT WAS ME, I SWEAR! I'M NOT BEHIND THIS!
THEN GIVE ME A NAME.
I CAN'T. HE'LL KILL ME. ALSO...
TUNG!
...MY RIDE IS HERE.

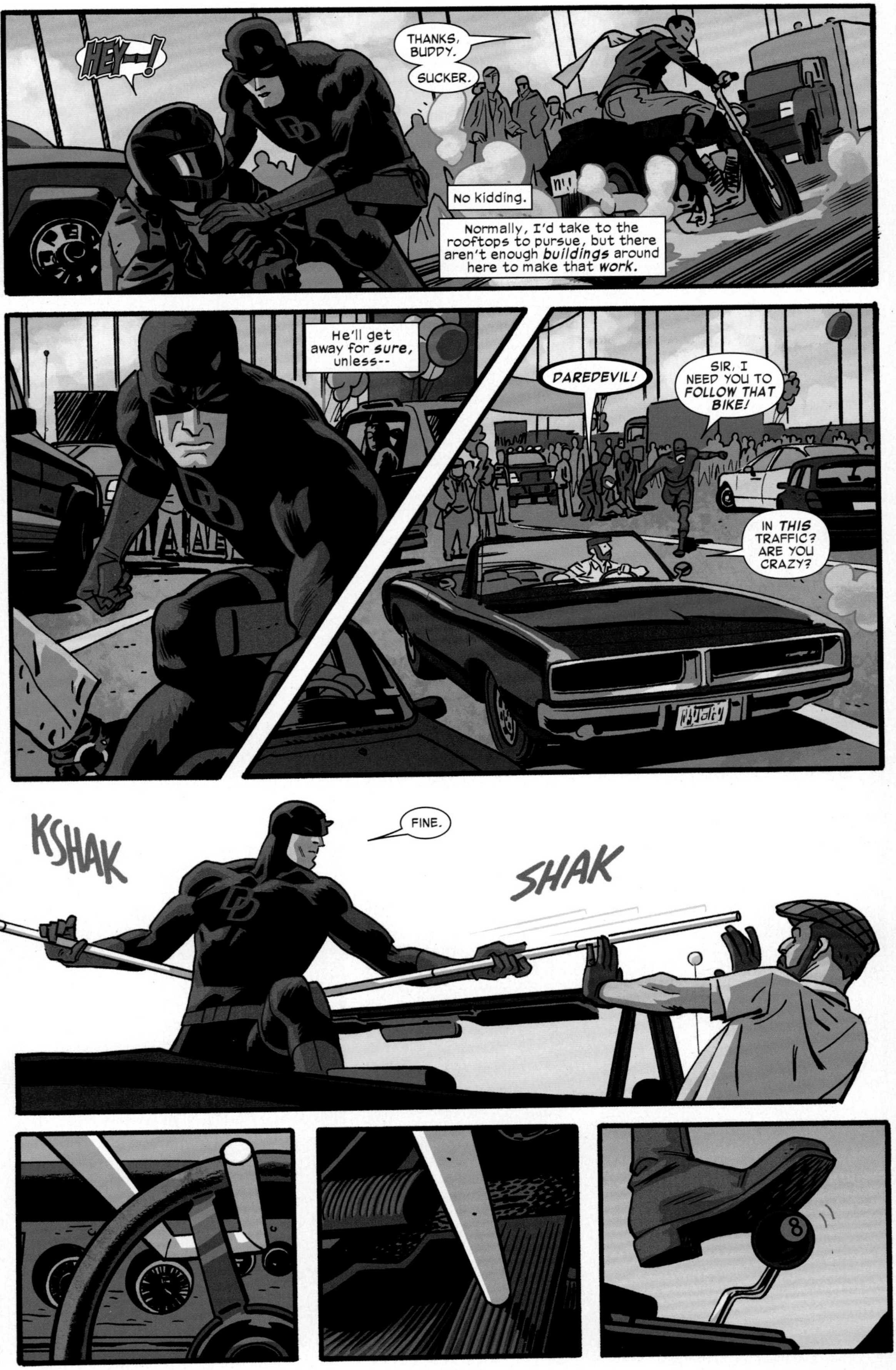
HEY--!
THANKS, BUDDY.
SUCKER.
No kidding.
Normally, I'd take to the rooftops to pursue, but there aren't enough *buildings* around here to make that *work.*
He'll get away for *sure,* unless--
DAREDEVIL!
SIR, I NEED YOU TO FOLLOW THAT BIKE!
IN THIS TRAFFIC? ARE YOU CRAZY?
KSHAK
FINE.
SHAK

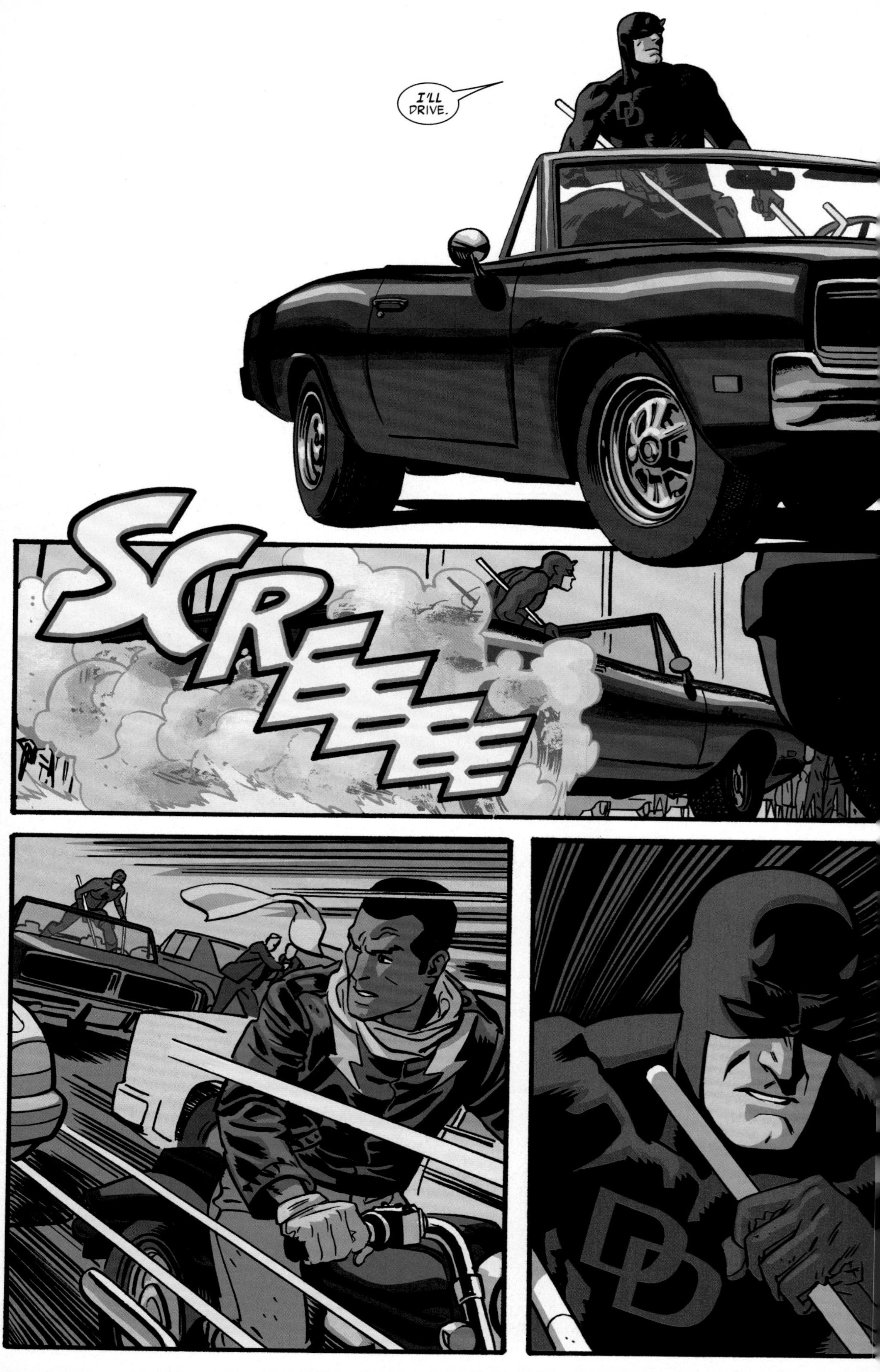
I'LL DRIVE.
SCREEEEEE

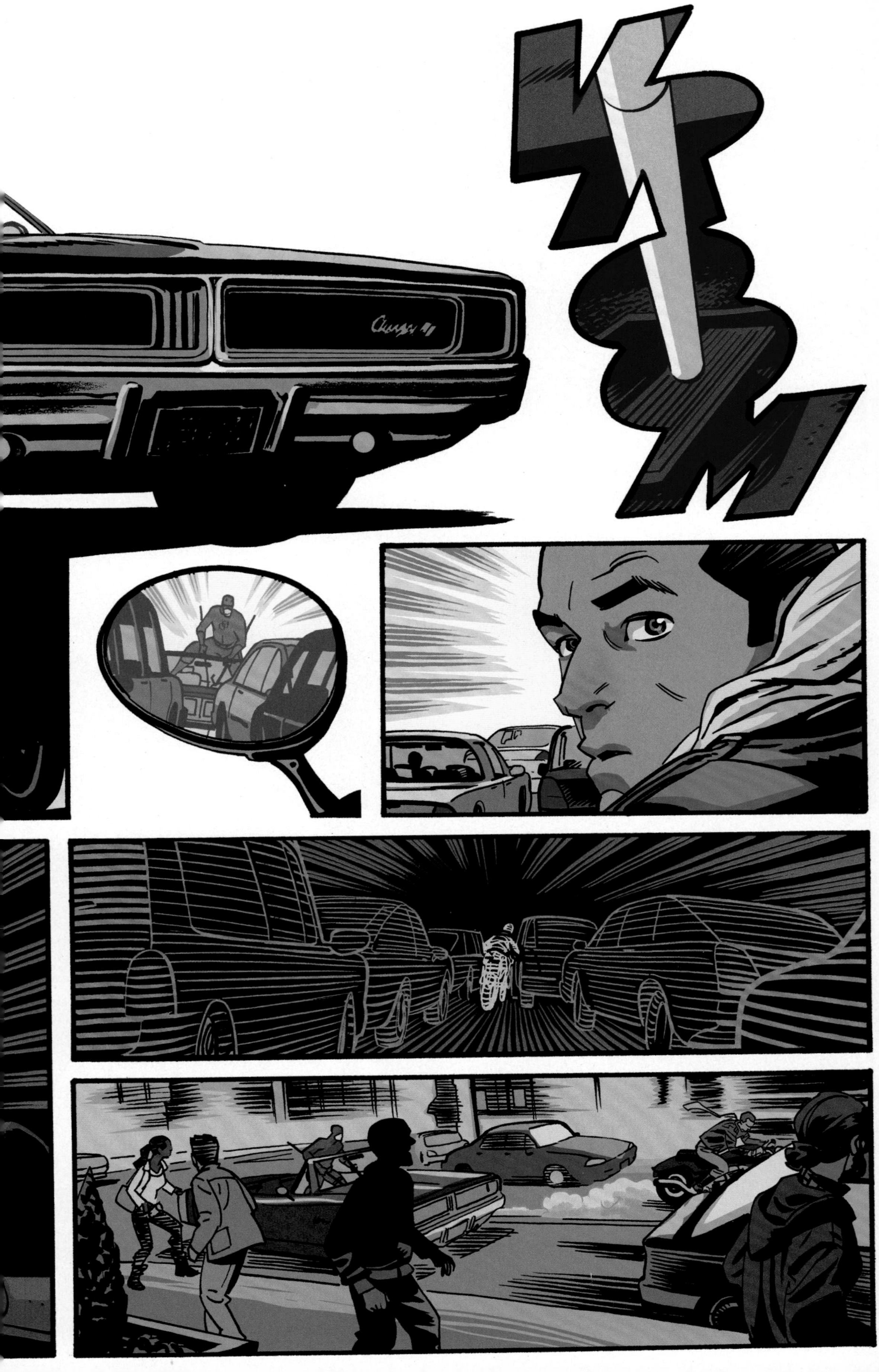

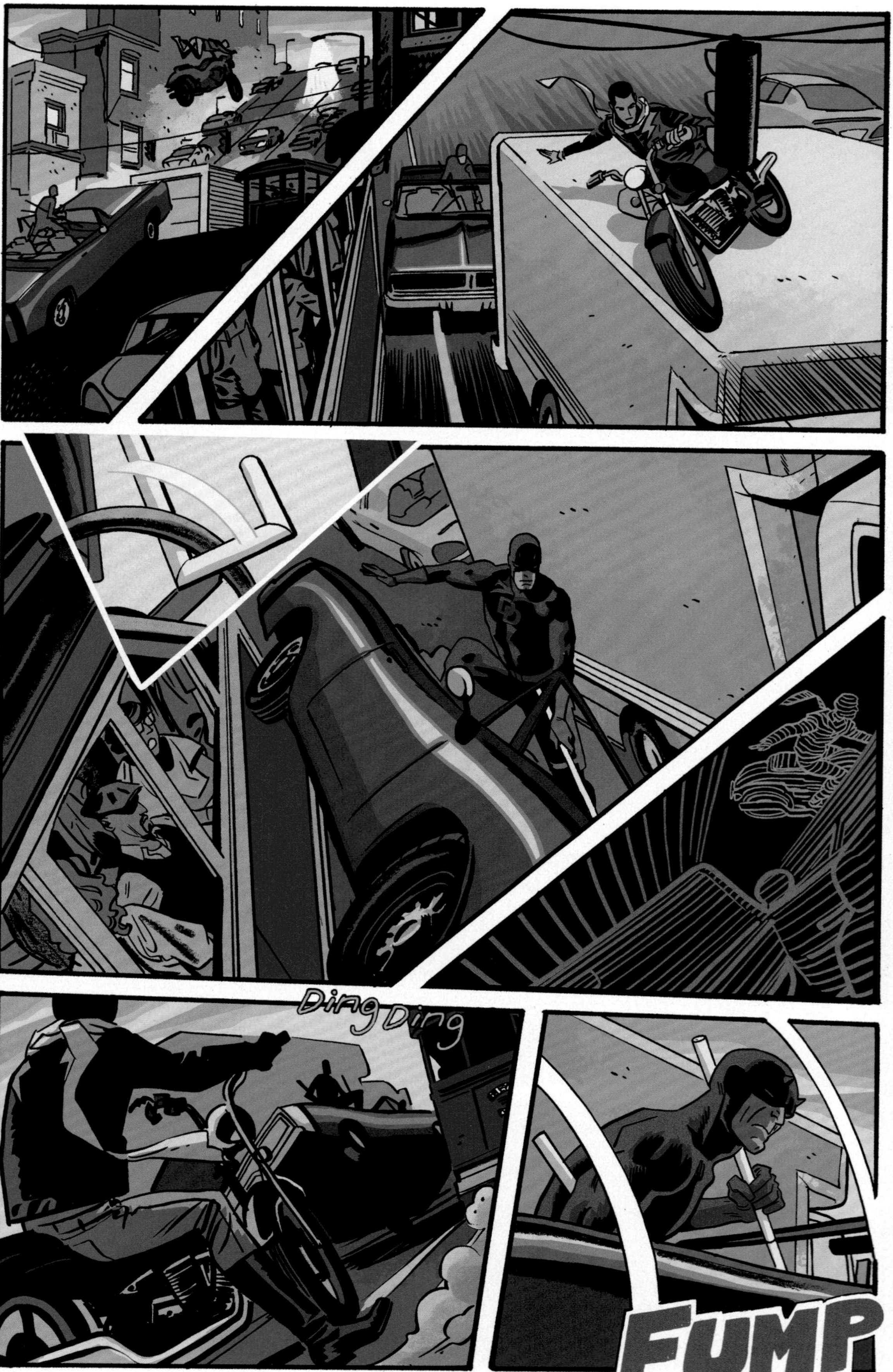
Ding Ding
FUMP

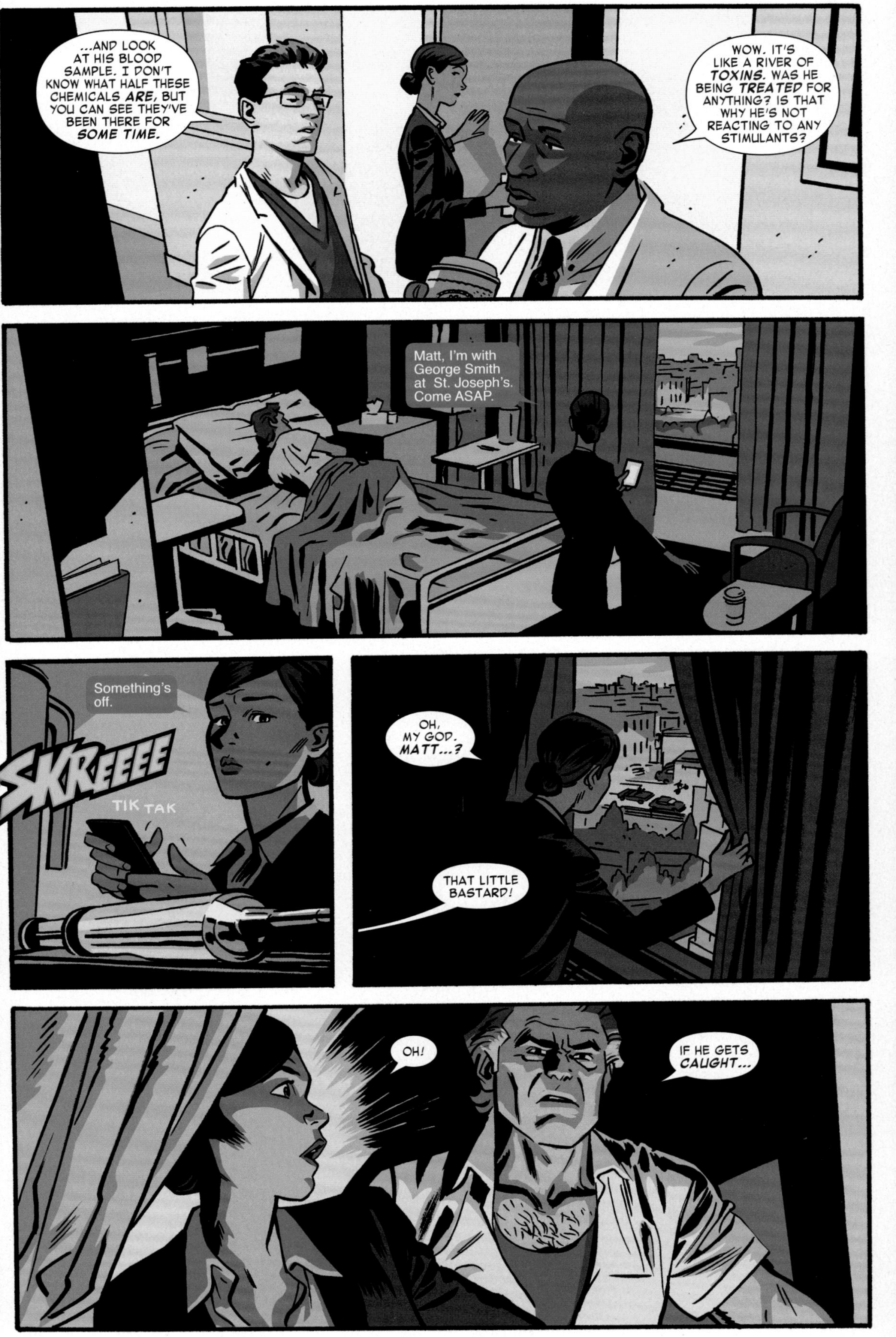
...AND LOOK AT HIS BLOOD SAMPLE. I DON'T KNOW WHAT HALF THESE CHEMICALS ARE, BUT YOU CAN SEE THEY'VE BEEN THERE FOR SOME TIME.
WOW. IT'S LIKE A RIVER OF TOXINS. WAS HE BEING TREATED FOR ANYTHING? IS THAT WHY HE'S NOT REACTING TO ANY STIMULANTS?
Matt, I'm with George Smith at St. Joseph's. Come ASAP.
Something's off.
SKREEEE
TIK TAK
OH, MY GOD. MATT...?
THAT LITTLE BASTARD!
OH!
IF HE GETS CAUGHT...

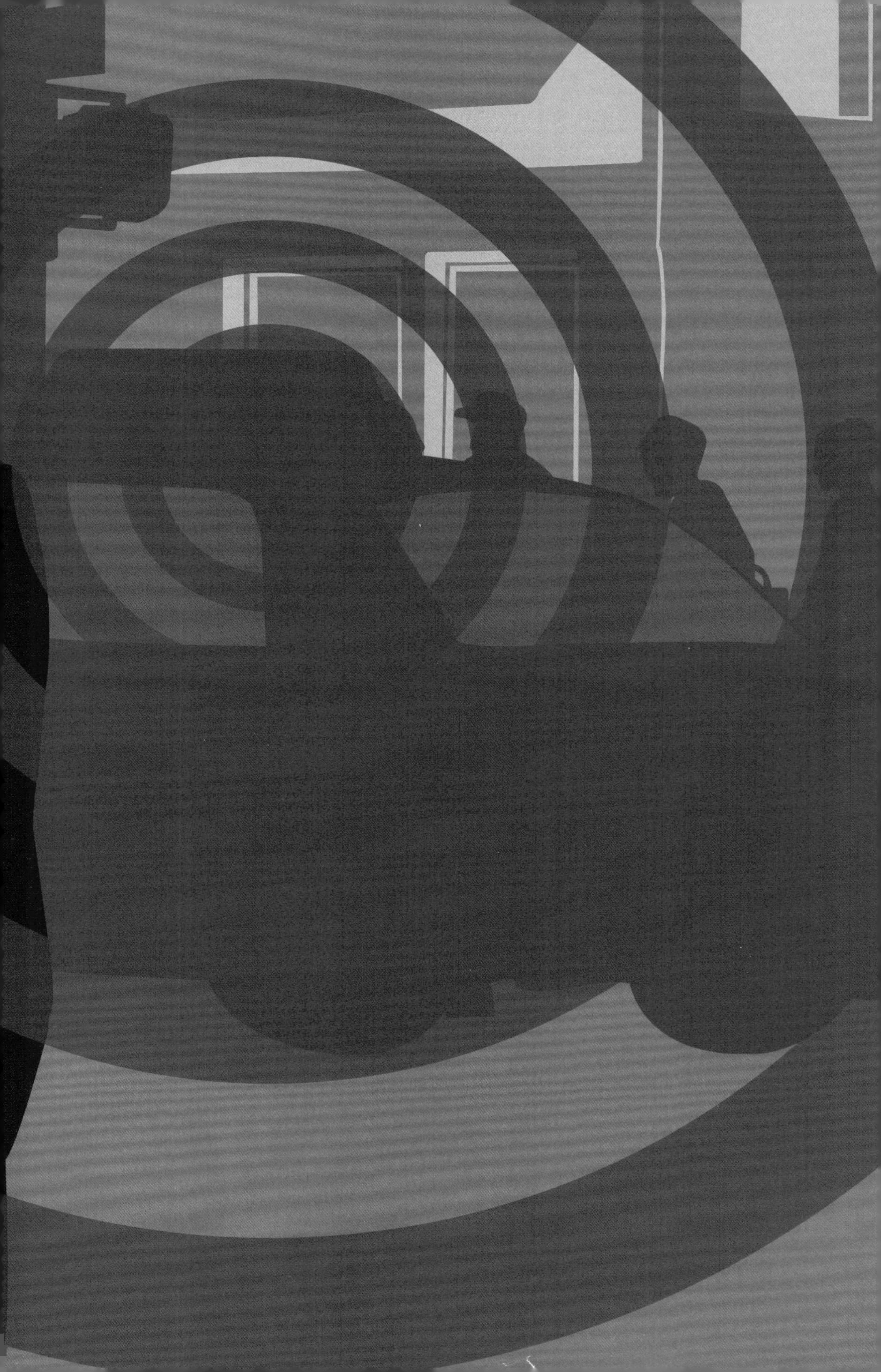

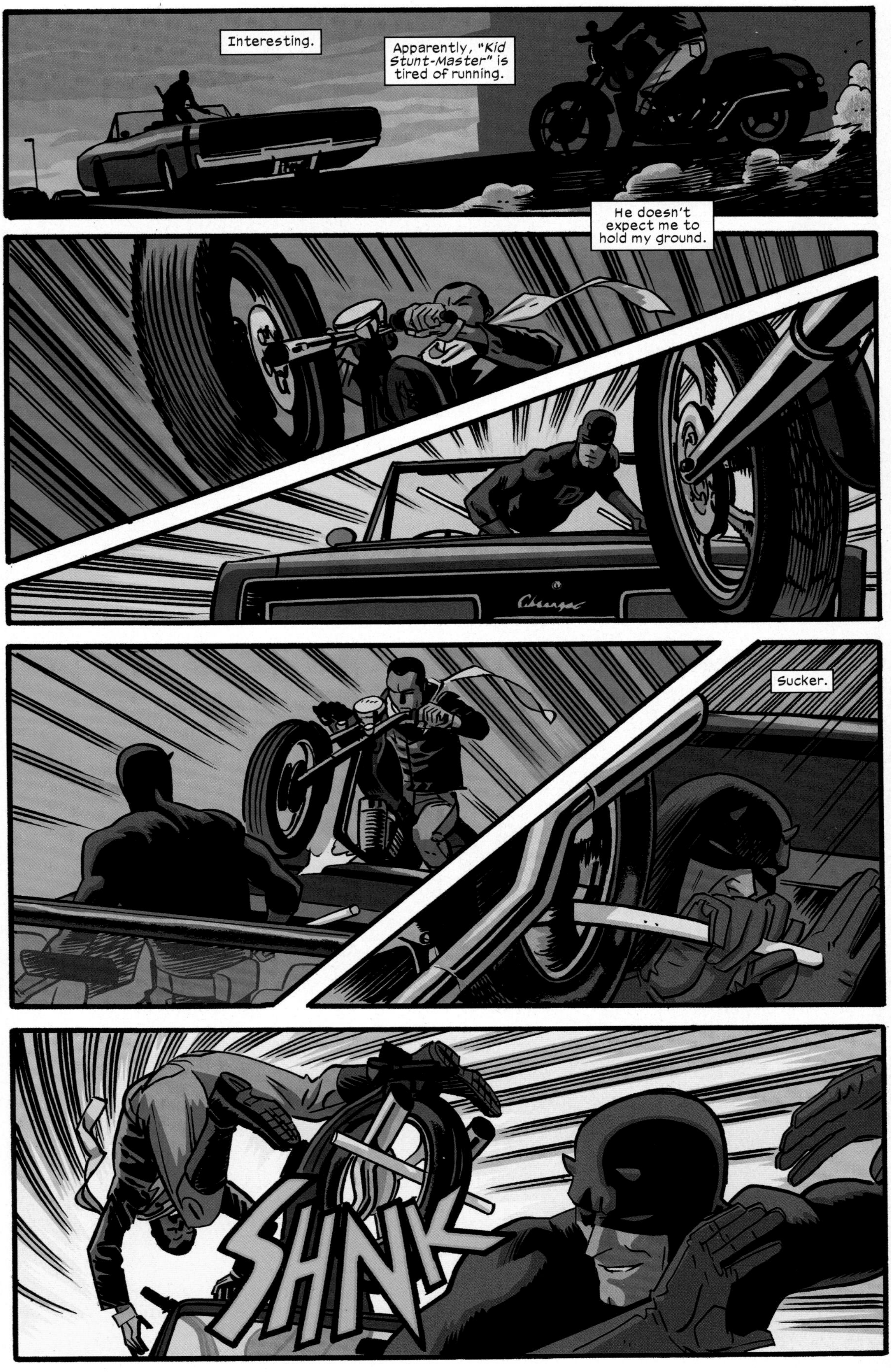
Interesting.
Apparently, "Kid Stunt-Master" is tired of running.
He doesn't expect me to hold my ground.
Sucker.
SHNK

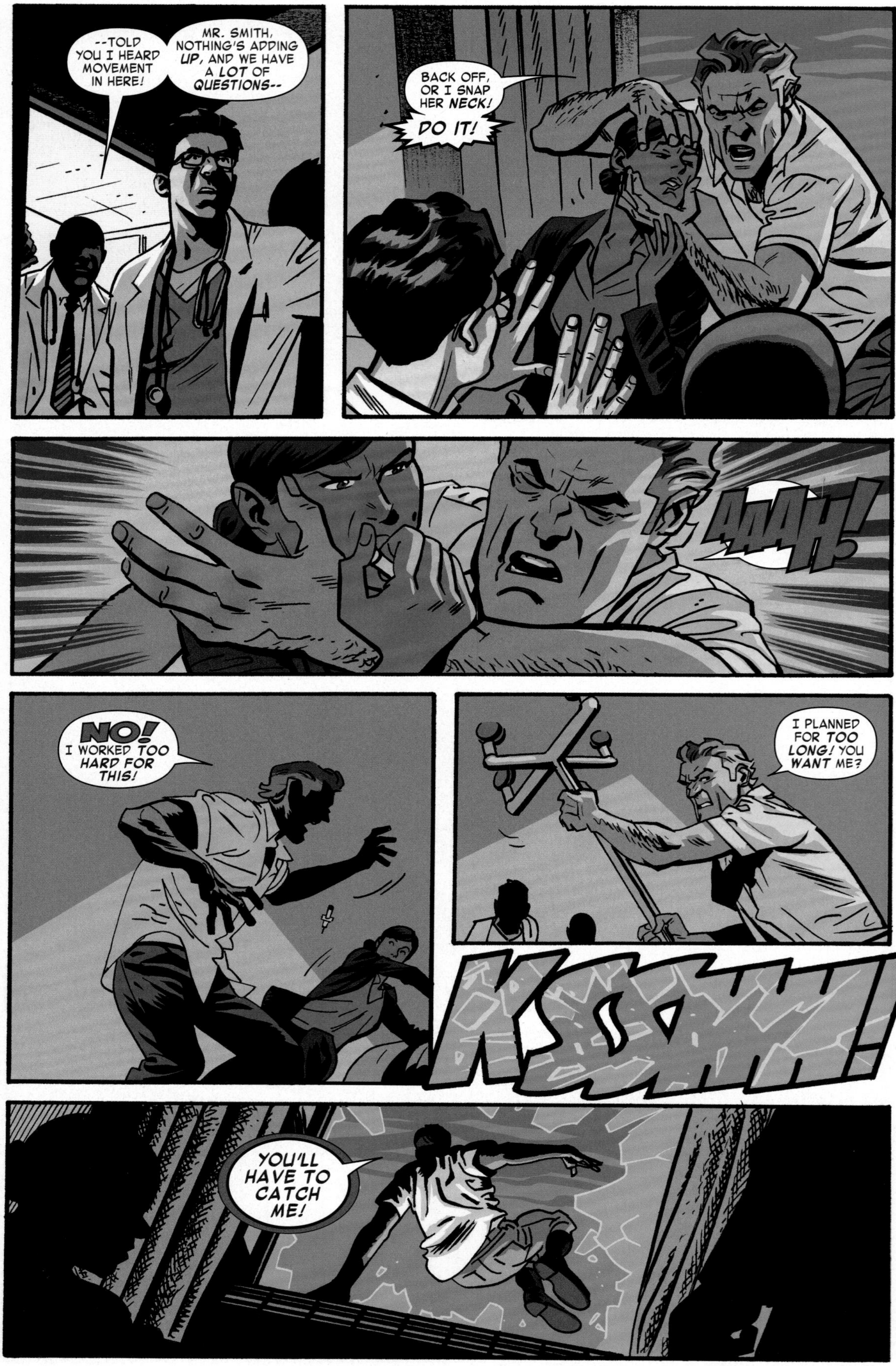

--TOLD YOU I HEARD MOVEMENT IN HERE!
MR. SMITH, NOTHING'S ADDING UP, AND WE HAVE A LOT OF QUESTIONS--
BACK OFF, OR I SNAP HER NECK!
DO IT!
AAAAH!
NO! I WORKED TOO HARD FOR THIS!
I PLANNED FOR TOO LONG! YOU WANT ME?
KSSHH!
YOU'LL HAVE TO CATCH ME!

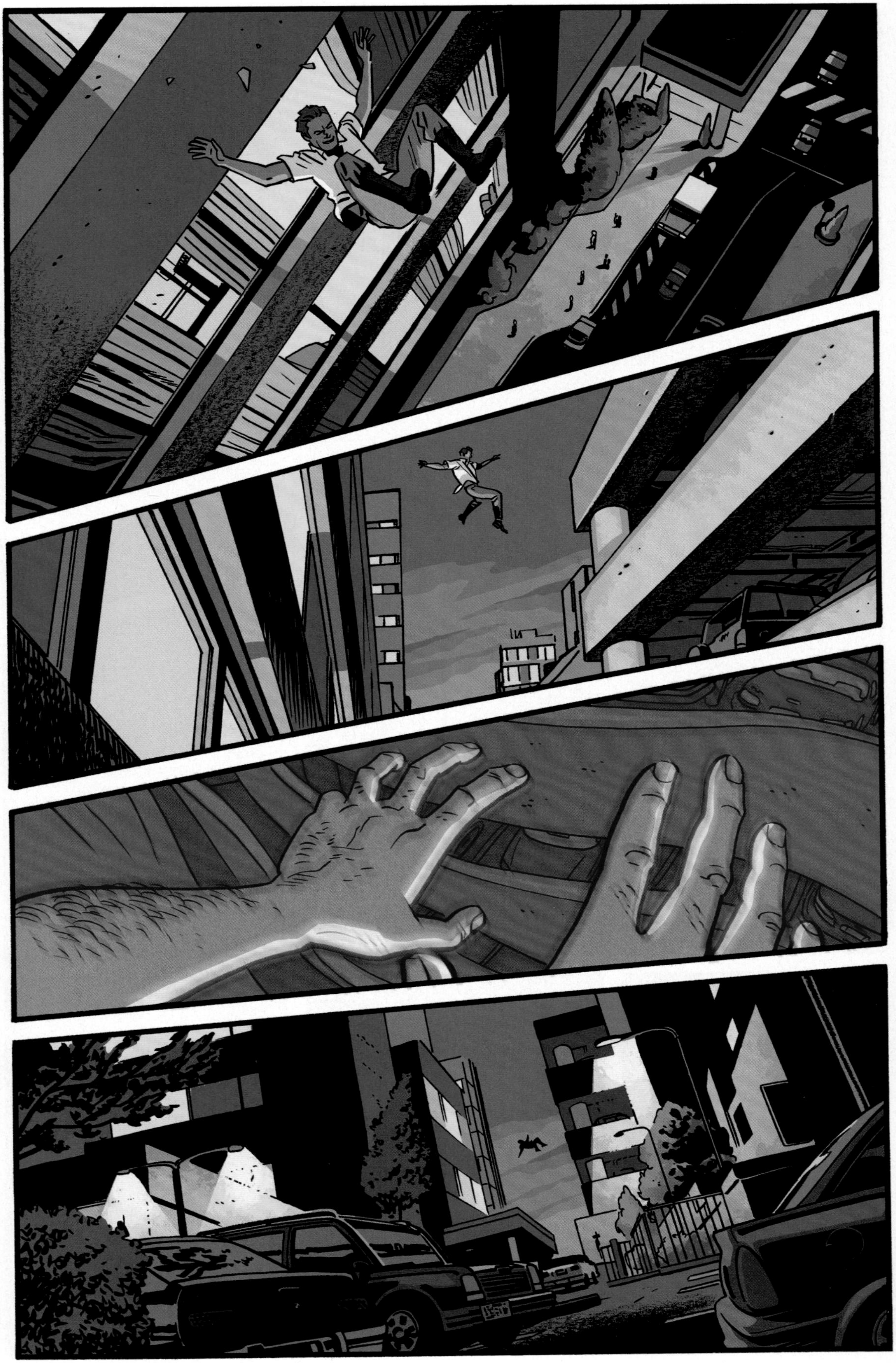

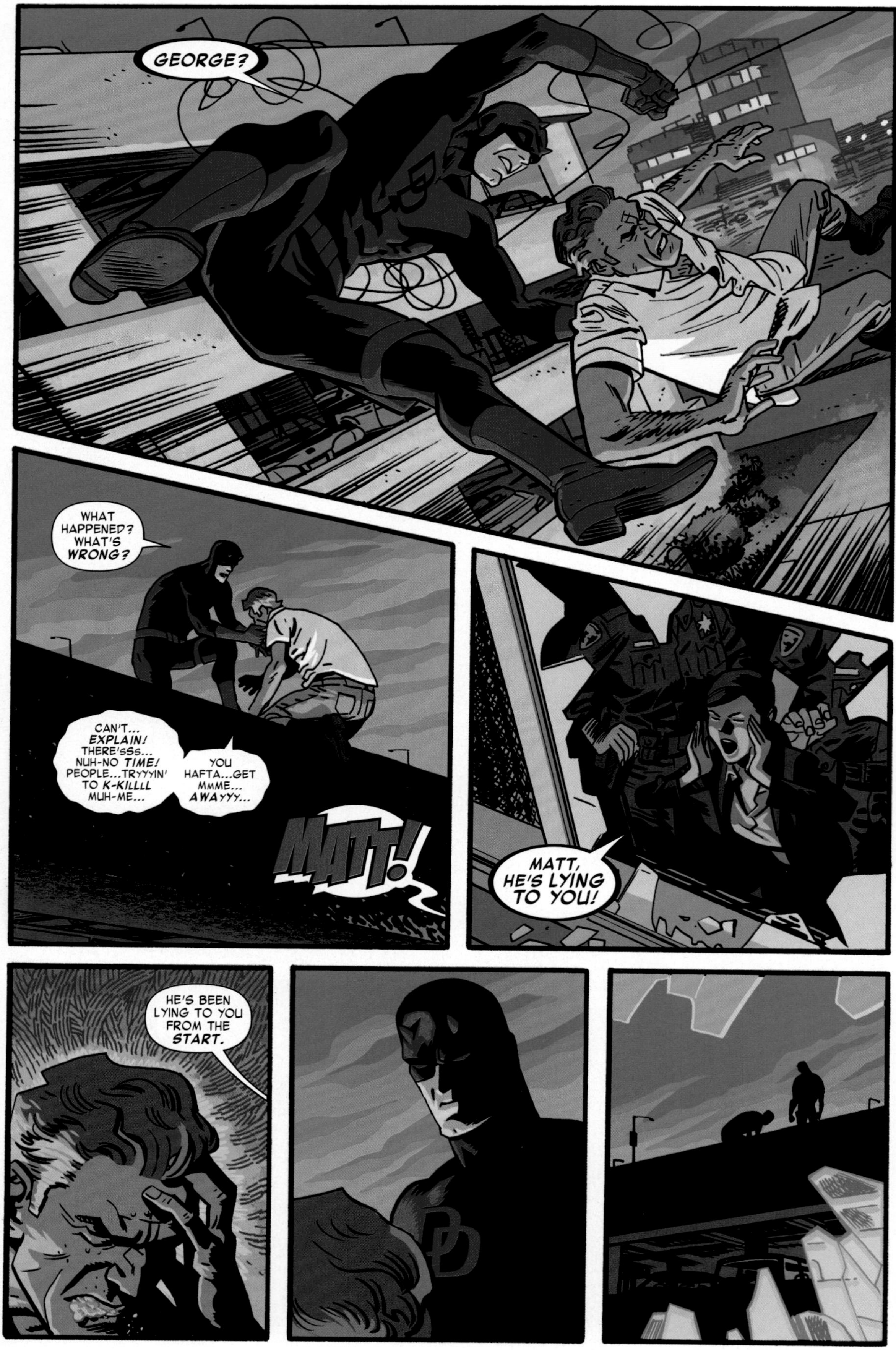
GEORGE?
WHAT HAPPENED? WHAT'S WRONG?
CAN'T... EXPLAIN! THERE'SSS... NUH-NO TIME! PEOPLE...TRYYYIN' TO K-KILLLL MUH-ME...
YOU HAFTA...GET MMME... AWAYYY...
MATT!
MATT, HE'S LYING TO YOU!
HE'S BEEN LYING TO YOU FROM THE START.

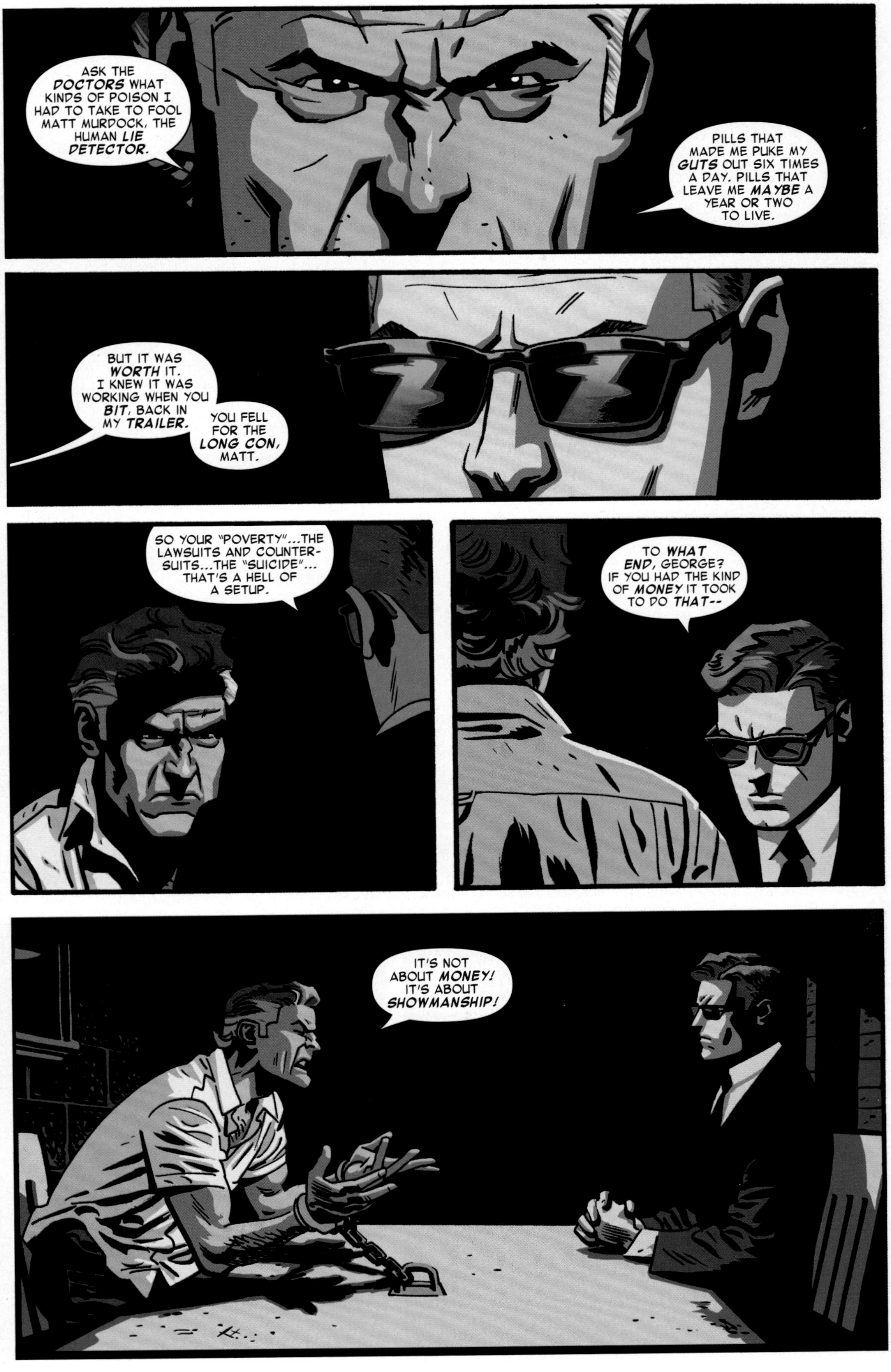
ASK THE DOCTORS WHAT KINDS OF POISON I HAD TO TAKE TO FOOL MATT MURDOCK, THE HUMAN LIE DETECTOR.
PILLS THAT MADE ME PUKE MY GUTS OUT SIX TIMES A DAY. PILLS THAT LEAVE ME MAYBE A YEAR OR TWO TO LIVE.
BUT IT WAS WORTH IT. I KNEW IT WAS WORKING WHEN YOU BIT, BACK IN MY TRAILER.
YOU FELL FOR THE LONG CON, MATT.
SO YOUR "POVERTY"...THE LAWSUITS AND COUNTER-SUITS...THE "SUICIDE"... THAT'S A HELL OF A SETUP.
TO WHAT END, GEORGE? IF YOU HAD THE KIND OF MONEY IT TOOK TO DO THAT--
IT'S NOT ABOUT MONEY! IT'S ABOUT SHOWMANSHIP!

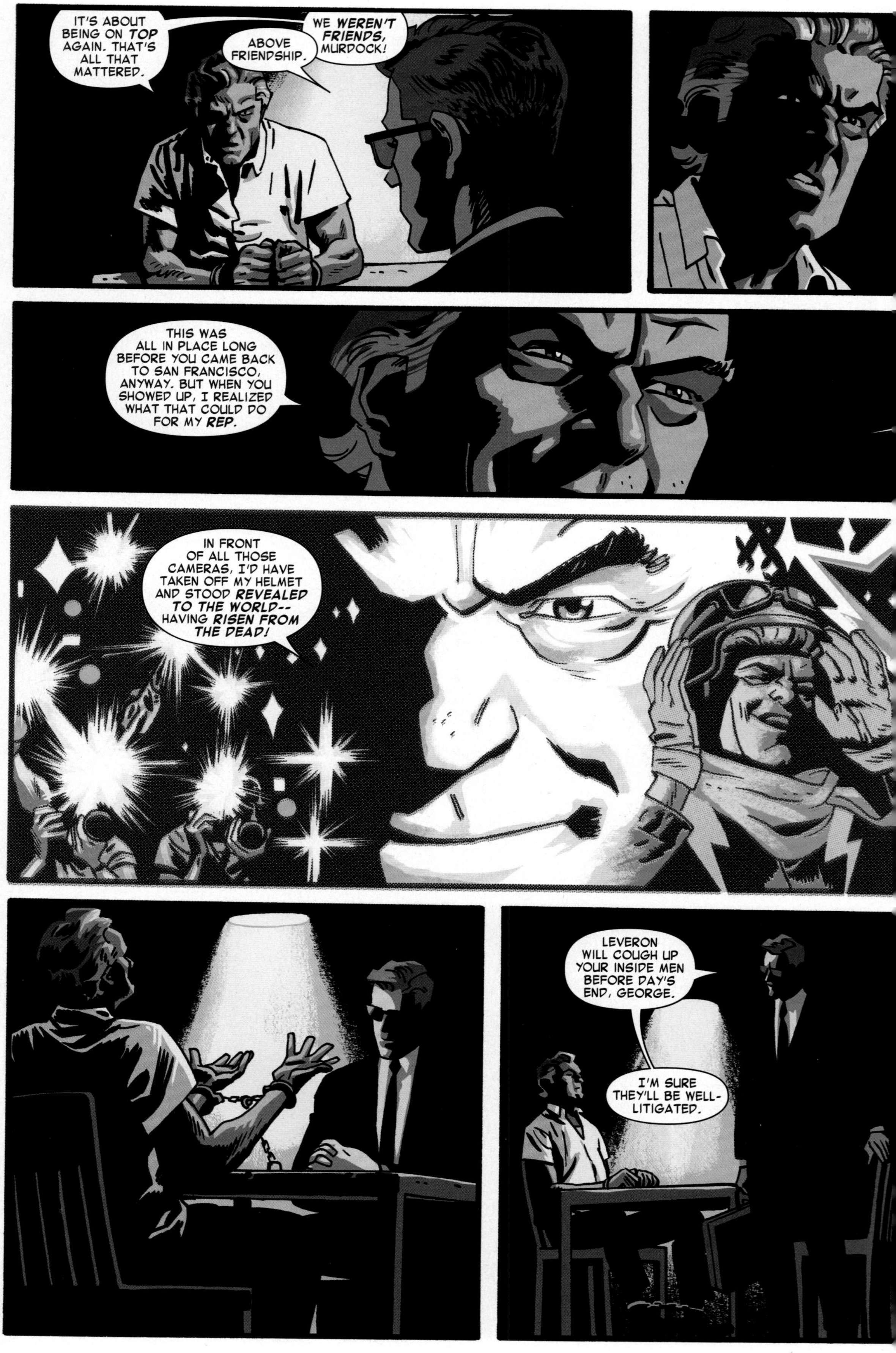
IT'S ABOUT BEING ON TOP AGAIN. THAT'S ALL THAT MATTERED.
WE WEREN'T FRIENDS, MURDOCK!
ABOVE FRIENDSHIP.
THIS WAS ALL IN PLACE LONG BEFORE YOU CAME BACK TO SAN FRANCISCO, ANYWAY. BUT WHEN YOU SHOWED UP, I REALIZED WHAT THAT COULD DO FOR MY REP.
IN FRONT OF ALL THOSE CAMERAS, I'D HAVE TAKEN OFF MY HELMET AND STOOD REVEALED TO THE WORLD-- HAVING RISEN FROM THE DEAD!
LEVERON WILL COUGH UP YOUR INSIDE MEN BEFORE DAY'S END, GEORGE.
I'M SURE THEY'LL BE WELL-LITIGATED.

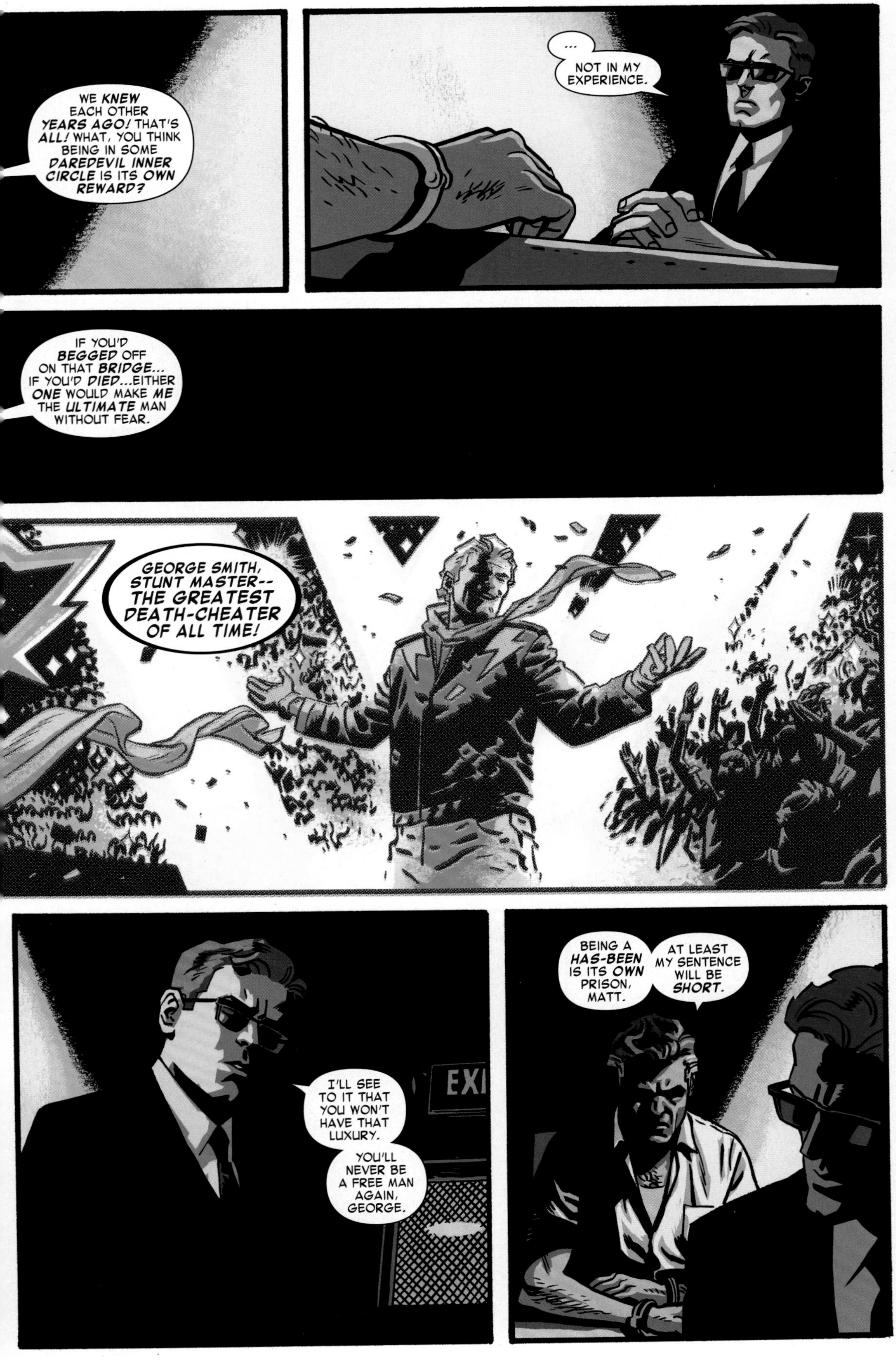
WE KNEW EACH OTHER YEARS AGO! THAT'S ALL! WHAT, YOU THINK BEING IN SOME DAREDEVIL INNER CIRCLE IS ITS OWN REWARD?
...
NOT IN MY EXPERIENCE.
IF YOU'D BEGGED OFF ON THAT BRIDGE... IF YOU'D DIED...EITHER ONE WOULD MAKE ME THE ULTIMATE MAN WITHOUT FEAR.
GEORGE SMITH, STUNT MASTER-- THE GREATEST DEATH-CHEATER OF ALL TIME!
I'LL SEE TO IT THAT YOU WON'T HAVE THAT LUXURY.
YOU'LL NEVER BE A FREE MAN AGAIN, GEORGE.
EXI
BEING A HAS-BEEN IS ITS OWN PRISON, MATT.
AT LEAST MY SENTENCE WILL BE SHORT.

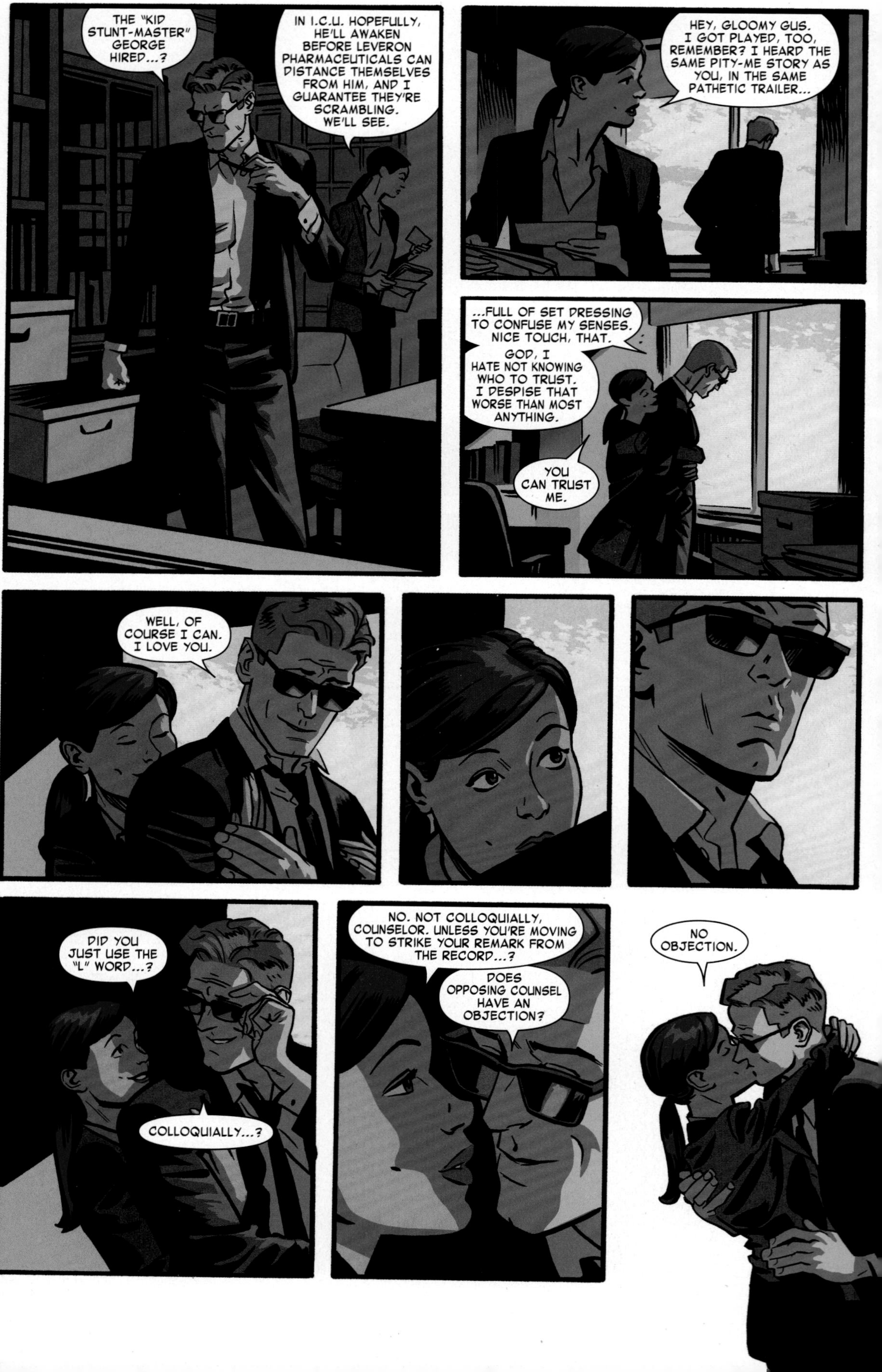

THE "KID STUNT-MASTER" GEORGE HIRED...?
IN I.C.U. HOPEFULLY, HE'LL AWAKEN BEFORE LEVERON PHARMACEUTICALS CAN DISTANCE THEMSELVES FROM HIM, AND I GUARANTEE THEY'RE SCRAMBLING. WE'LL SEE.
HEY, GLOOMY GUS. I GOT PLAYED, TOO, REMEMBER? I HEARD THE SAME PITY-ME STORY AS YOU, IN THE SAME PATHETIC TRAILER...
...FULL OF SET DRESSING TO CONFUSE MY SENSES. NICE TOUCH, THAT.
GOD, I HATE NOT KNOWING WHO TO TRUST. I DESPISE THAT WORSE THAN MOST ANYTHING.
YOU CAN TRUST ME.
WELL, OF COURSE I CAN. I LOVE YOU.
DID YOU JUST USE THE "L" WORD...?
COLLOQUIALLY...?
NO. NOT COLLOQUIALLY, COUNSELOR. UNLESS YOU'RE MOVING TO STRIKE YOUR REMARK FROM THE RECORD...?
DOES OPPOSING COUNSEL HAVE AN OBJECTION?
NO OBJECTION.

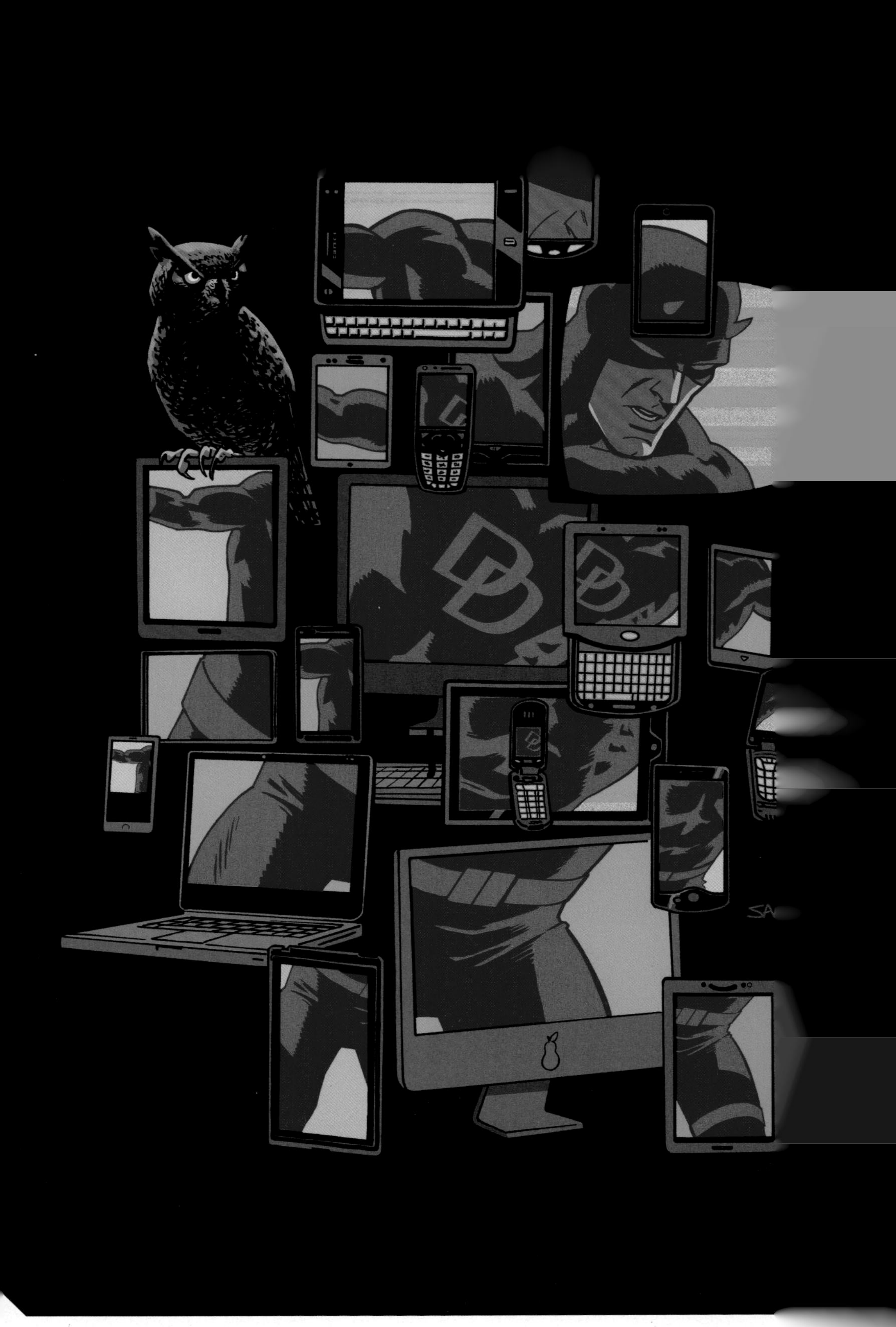

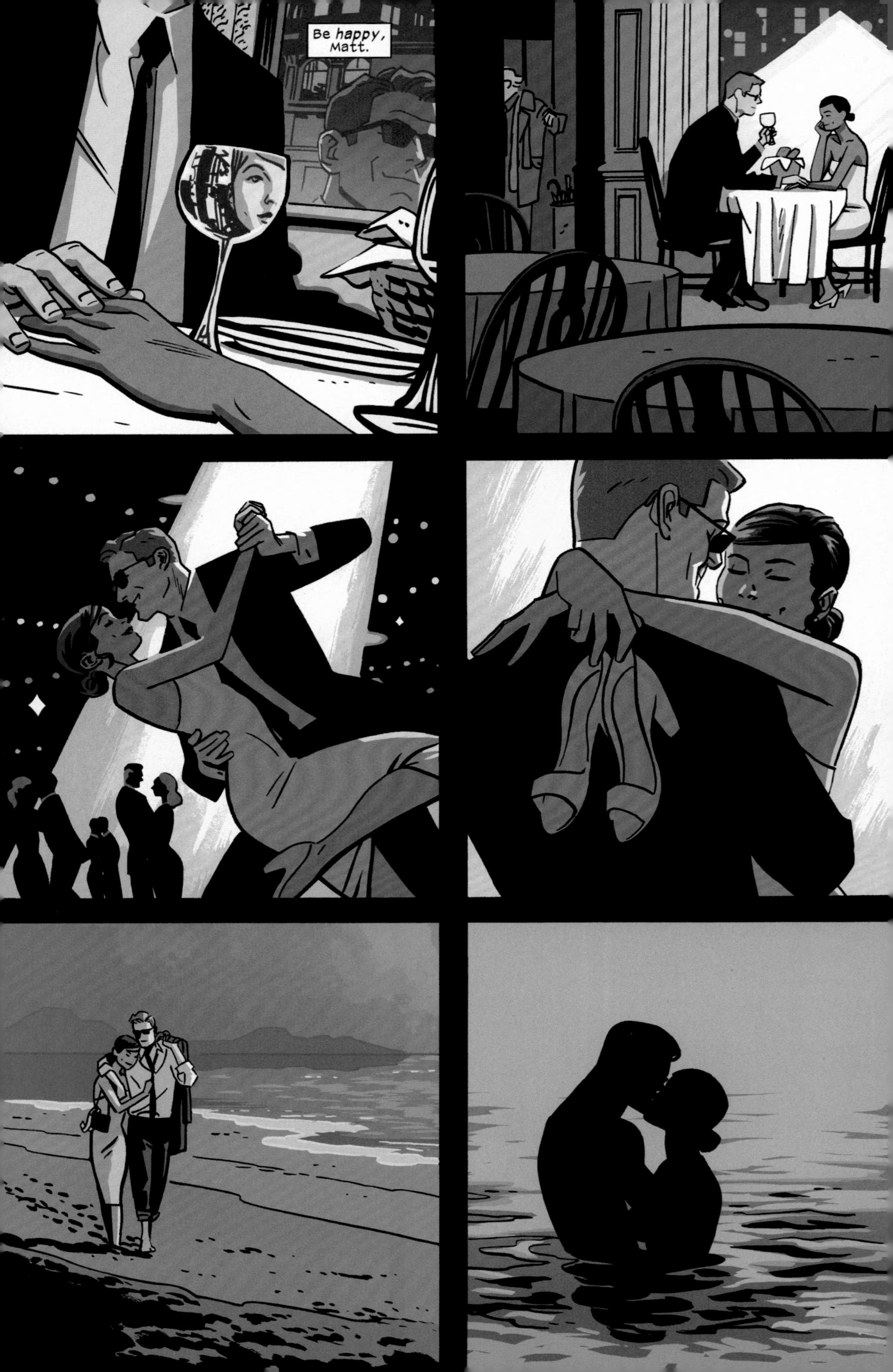
Be happy, Matt.

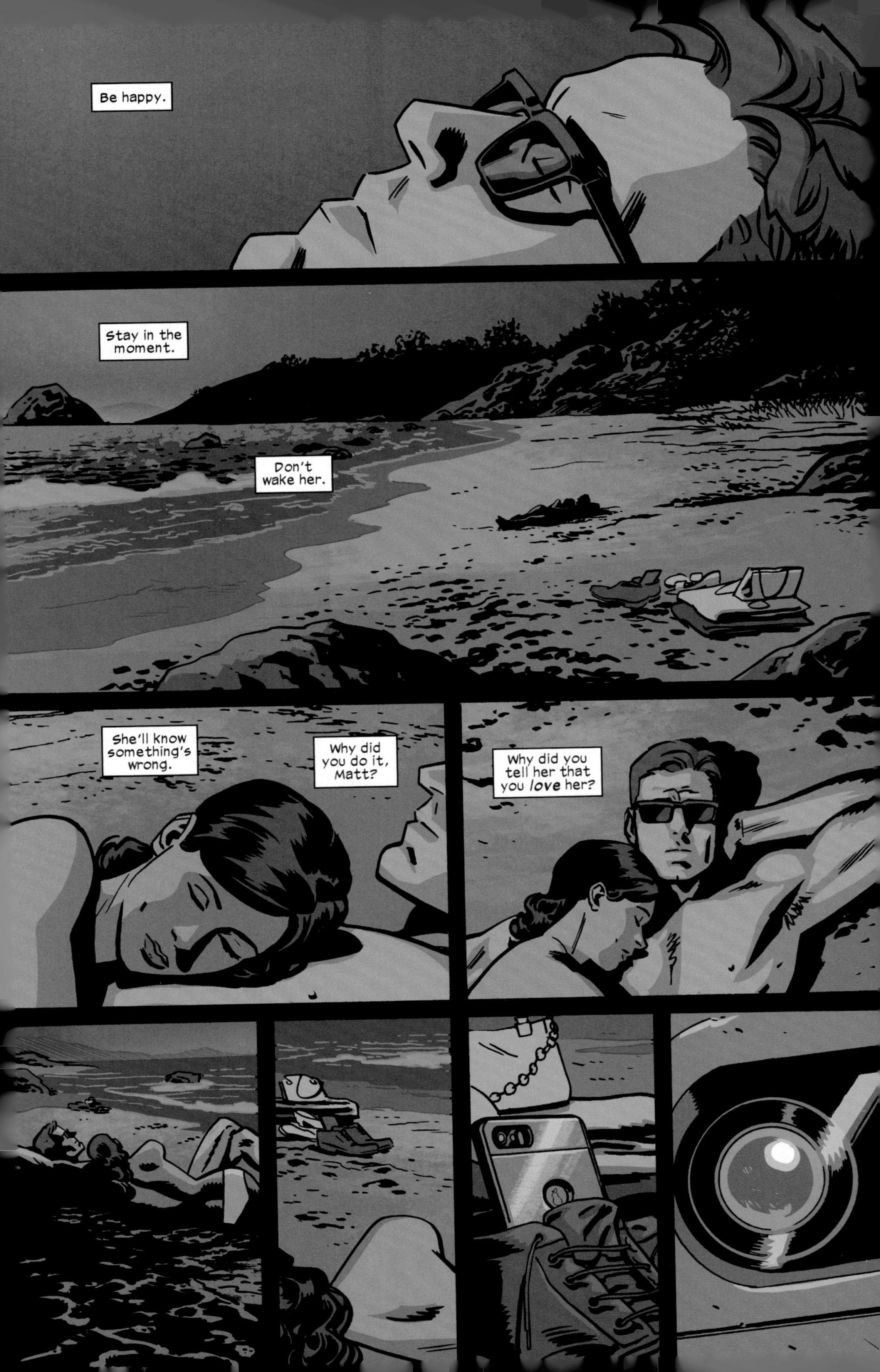
Be happy.
Stay in the moment.
Don't wake her.
She'll know something's wrong.
Why did you do it, Matt?
Why did you tell her that you *love* her?

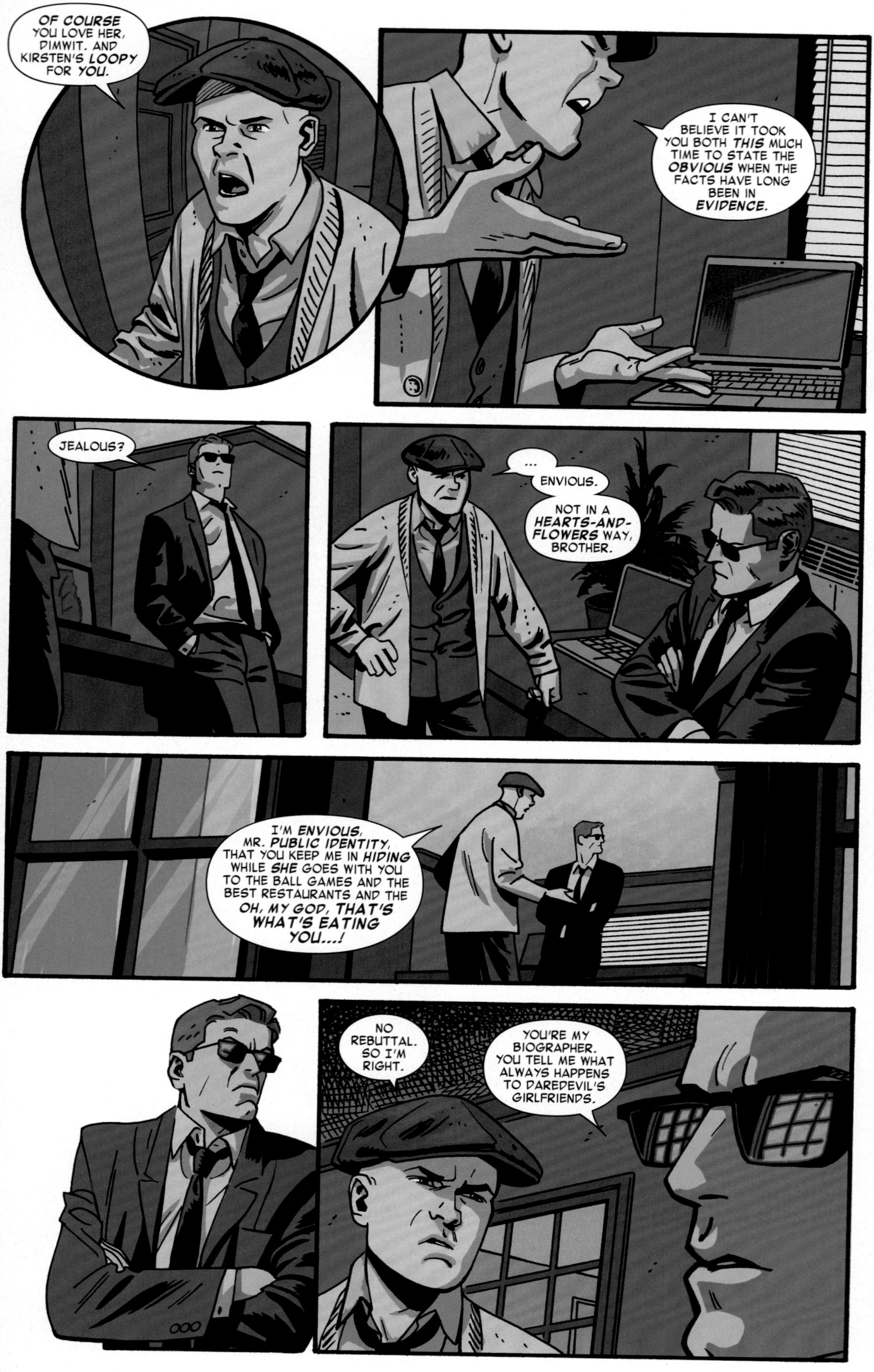
OF COURSE YOU LOVE HER, DIMWIT. AND KIRSTEN'S LOOPY FOR YOU.
I CAN'T BELIEVE IT TOOK YOU BOTH THIS MUCH TIME TO STATE THE OBVIOUS WHEN THE FACTS HAVE LONG BEEN IN EVIDENCE.
JEALOUS?
...
ENVIOUS.
NOT IN A HEARTS-AND-FLOWERS WAY, BROTHER.
I'M ENVIOUS, MR. PUBLIC IDENTITY, THAT YOU KEEP ME IN HIDING WHILE SHE GOES WITH YOU TO THE BALL GAMES AND THE BEST RESTAURANTS AND THE OH, MY GOD, THAT'S WHAT'S EATING YOU...!
NO REBUTTAL. SO I'M RIGHT.
YOU'RE MY BIOGRAPHER. YOU TELL ME WHAT ALWAYS HAPPENS TO DAREDEVIL'S GIRLFRIENDS.

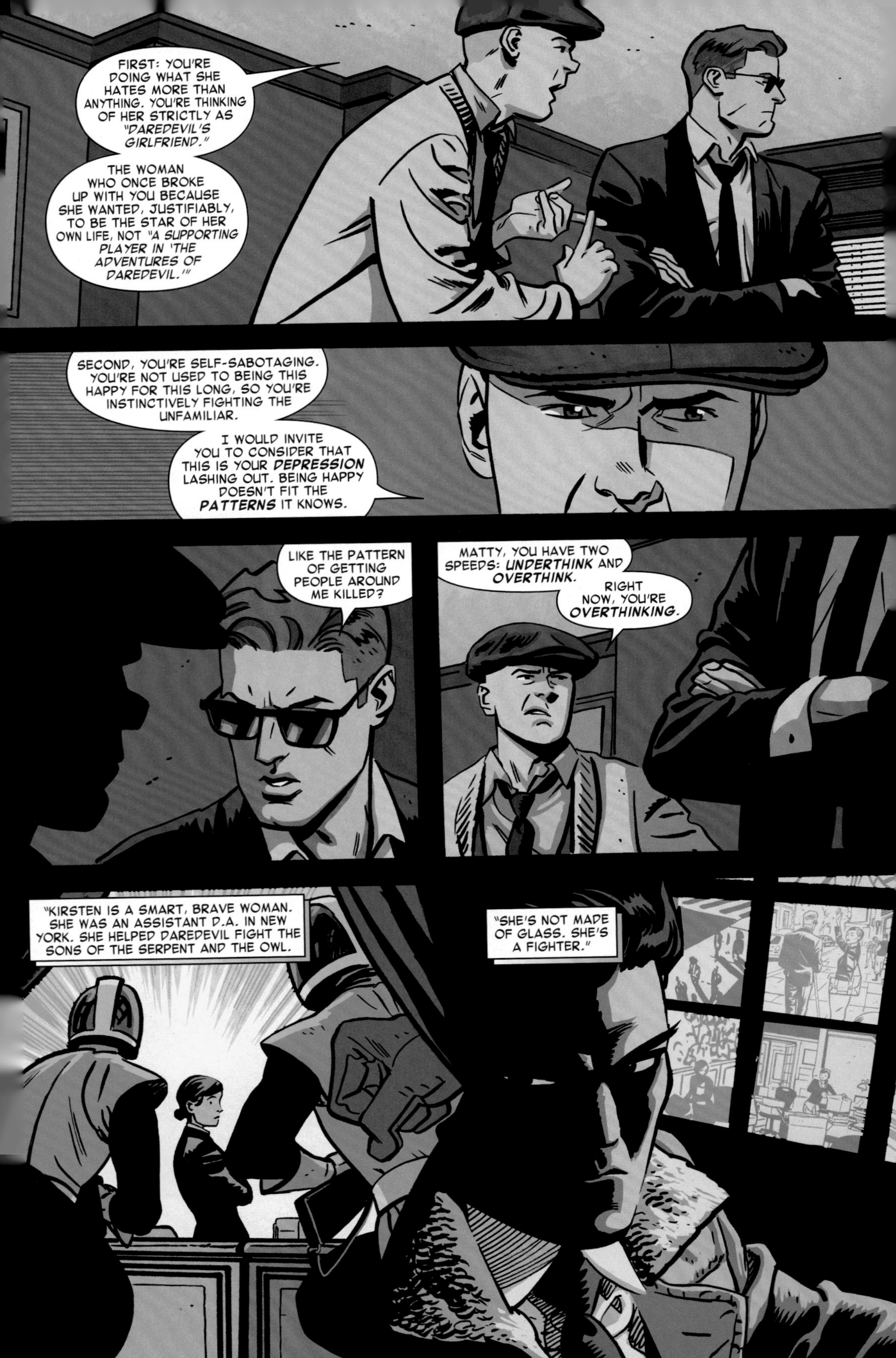

FIRST: YOU'RE DOING WHAT SHE HATES MORE THAN ANYTHING. YOU'RE THINKING OF HER STRICTLY AS "DAREDEVIL'S GIRLFRIEND."
THE WOMAN WHO ONCE BROKE UP WITH YOU BECAUSE SHE WANTED, JUSTIFIABLY, TO BE THE STAR OF HER OWN LIFE, NOT "A SUPPORTING PLAYER IN 'THE ADVENTURES OF DAREDEVIL.'"
SECOND, YOU'RE SELF-SABOTAGING. YOU'RE NOT USED TO BEING THIS HAPPY FOR THIS LONG, SO YOU'RE INSTINCTIVELY FIGHTING THE UNFAMILIAR.
I WOULD INVITE YOU TO CONSIDER THAT THIS IS YOUR DEPRESSION LASHING OUT. BEING HAPPY DOESN'T FIT THE PATTERNS IT KNOWS.
LIKE THE PATTERN OF GETTING PEOPLE AROUND ME KILLED?
MATTY, YOU HAVE TWO SPEEDS: UNDERTHINK AND OVERTHINK.
RIGHT NOW, YOU'RE OVERTHINKING.
"KIRSTEN IS A SMART, BRAVE WOMAN. SHE WAS AN ASSISTANT D.A. IN NEW YORK. SHE HELPED DAREDEVIL FIGHT THE SONS OF THE SERPENT AND THE OWL.
"SHE'S NOT MADE OF GLASS. SHE'S A FIGHTER."

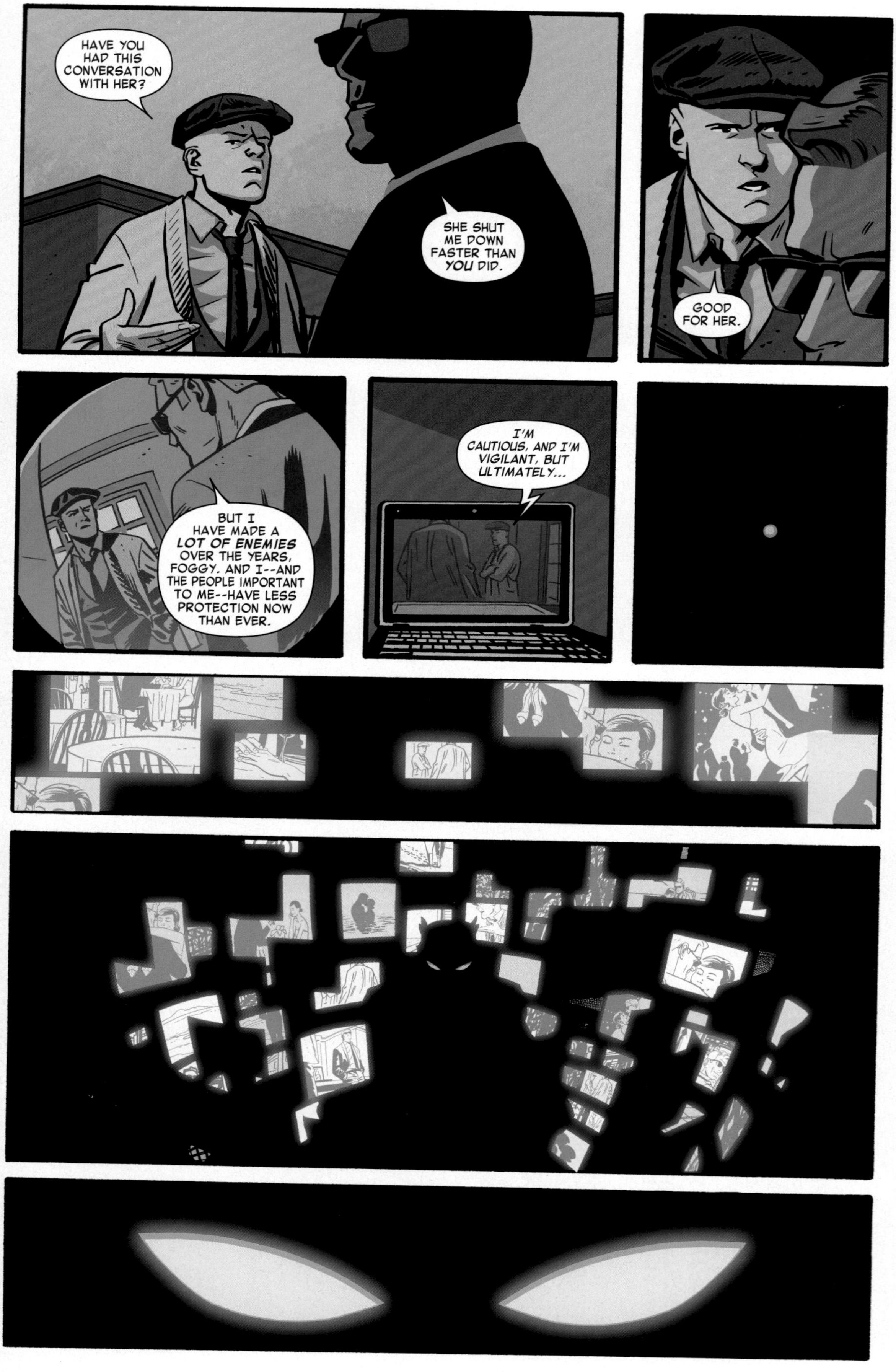
HAVE YOU HAD THIS CONVERSATION WITH HER?
SHE SHUT ME DOWN FASTER THAN *YOU* DID.
GOOD FOR HER.
BUT I HAVE MADE A ***LOT OF ENEMIES*** OVER THE YEARS, FOGGY. AND I--AND THE PEOPLE IMPORTANT TO ME--HAVE LESS PROTECTION NOW THAN EVER.
I'M CAUTIOUS, AND I'M VIGILANT, BUT ULTIMATELY...

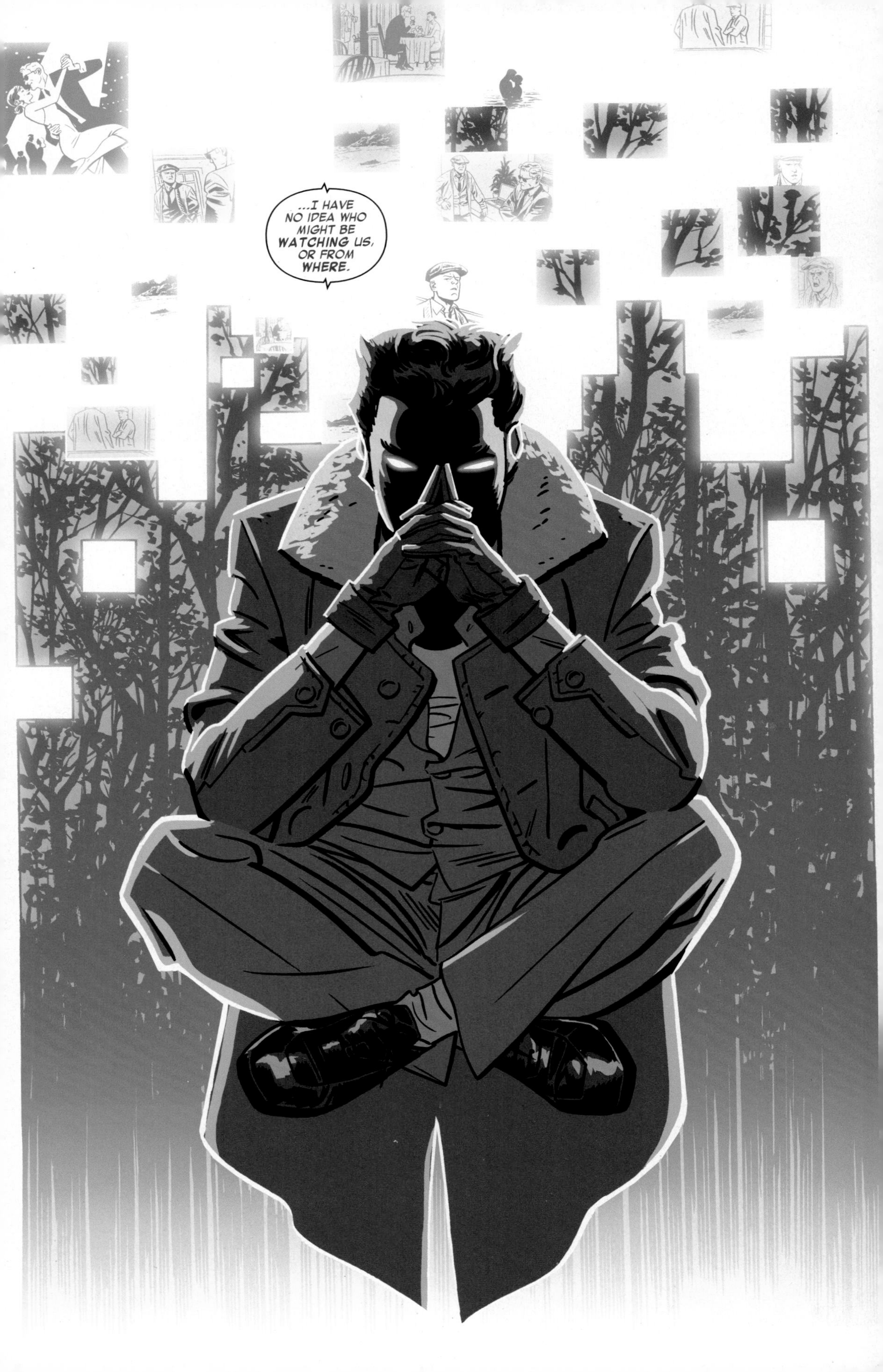
...I HAVE NO IDEA WHO MIGHT BE WATCHING US, OR FROM WHERE.

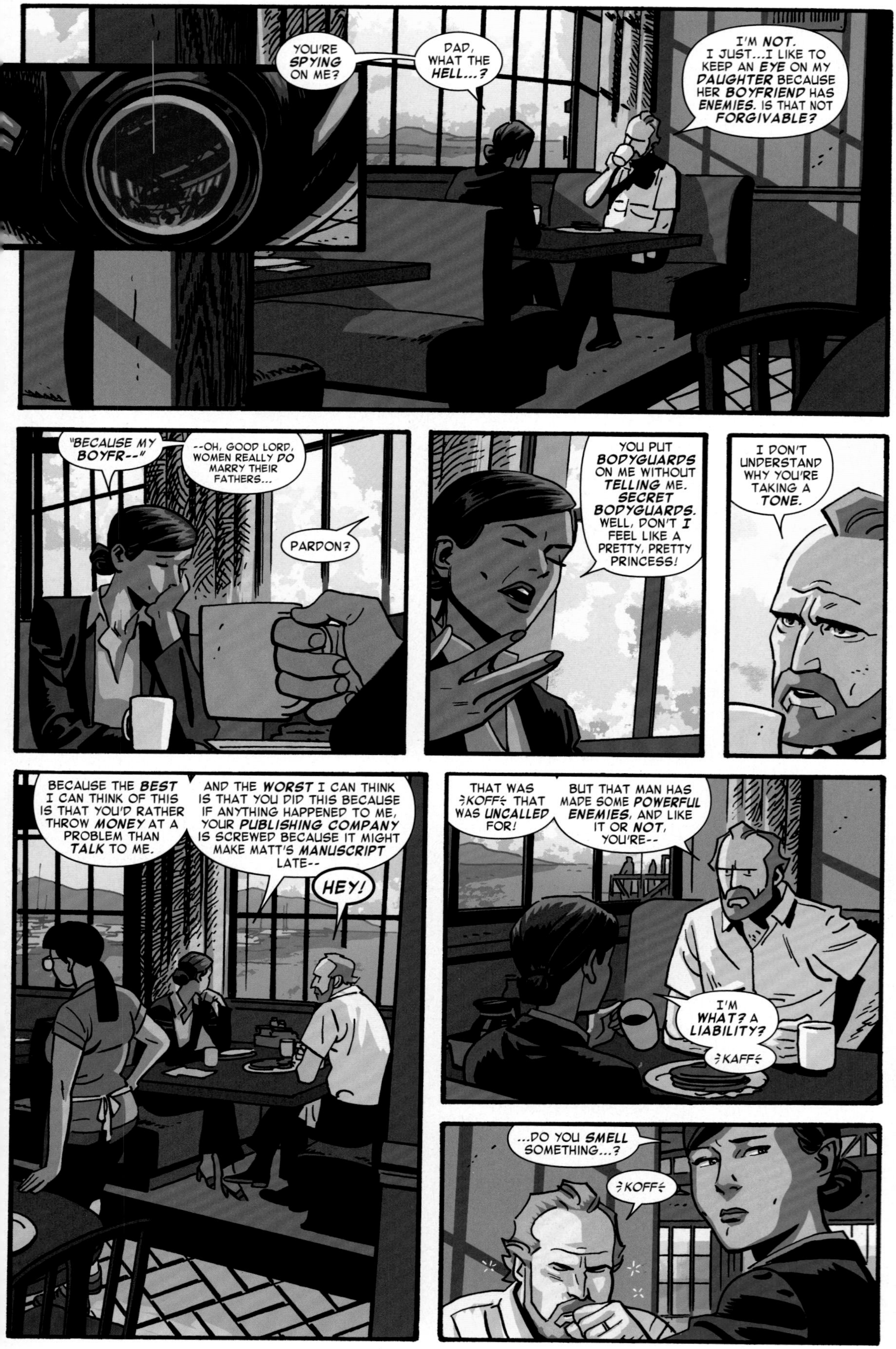
YOU'RE SPYING ON ME?
DAD, WHAT THE HELL...?
I'M NOT. I JUST...I LIKE TO KEEP AN EYE ON MY DAUGHTER BECAUSE HER BOYFRIEND HAS ENEMIES. IS THAT NOT FORGIVABLE?
"BECAUSE MY BOYFR--"
--OH, GOOD LORD, WOMEN REALLY DO MARRY THEIR FATHERS...
PARDON?
YOU PUT BODYGUARDS ON ME WITHOUT TELLING ME. SECRET BODYGUARDS. WELL, DON'T I FEEL LIKE A PRETTY, PRETTY PRINCESS!
I DON'T UNDERSTAND WHY YOU'RE TAKING A TONE.
BECAUSE THE BEST I CAN THINK OF THIS IS THAT YOU'D RATHER THROW MONEY AT A PROBLEM THAN TALK TO ME.
AND THE WORST I CAN THINK IS THAT YOU DID THIS BECAUSE IF ANYTHING HAPPENED TO ME, YOUR PUBLISHING COMPANY IS SCREWED BECAUSE IT MIGHT MAKE MATT'S MANUSCRIPT LATE--
HEY!
THAT WAS KOFF THAT WAS UNCALLED FOR!
BUT THAT MAN HAS MADE SOME POWERFUL ENEMIES, AND LIKE IT OR NOT, YOU'RE--
I'M WHAT? A LIABILITY?
KAFF
...DO YOU SMELL SOMETHING...?
KOFF

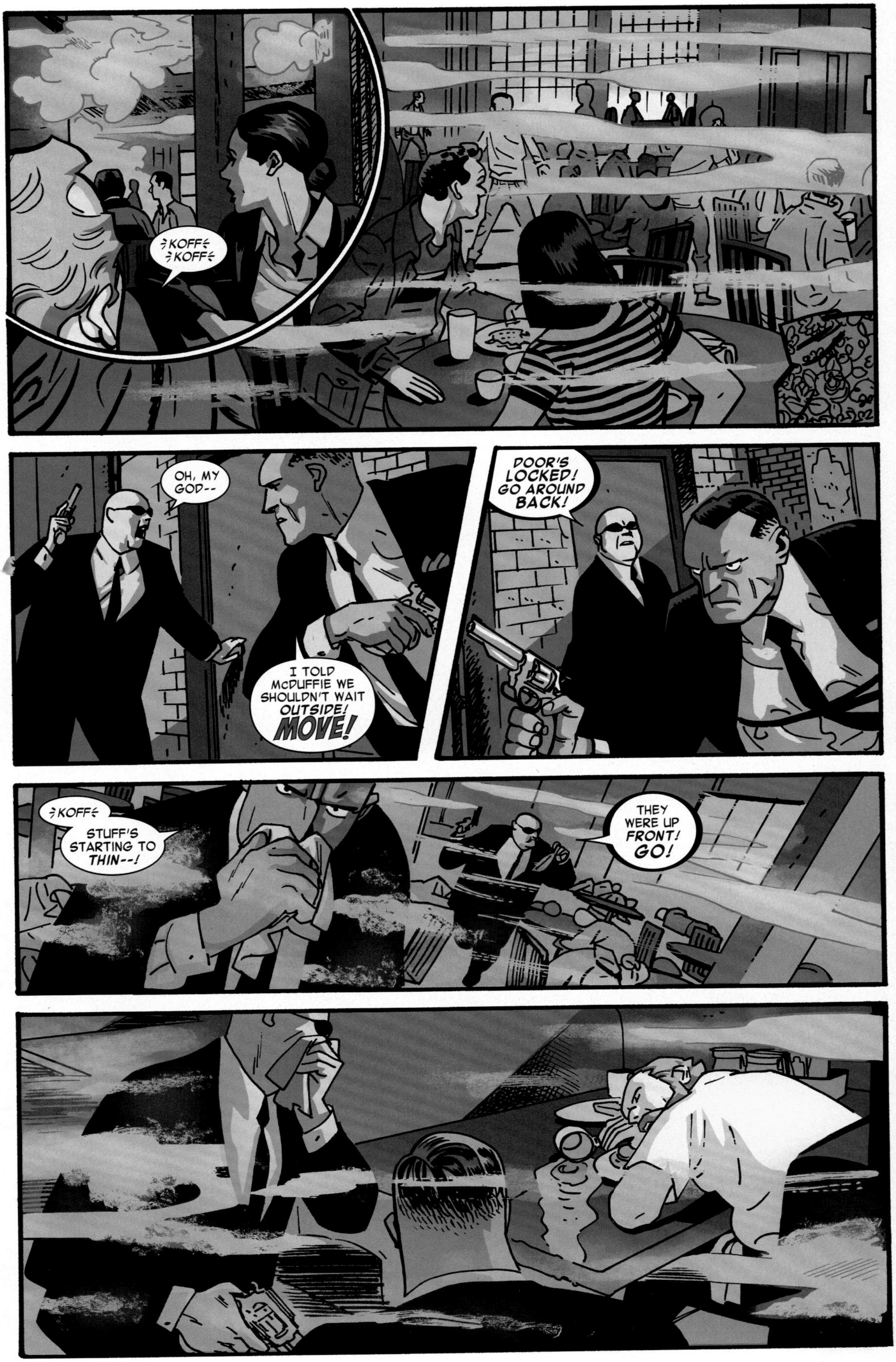

KOFF KOFF
OH, MY GOD--
I TOLD McDUFFIE WE SHOULDN'T WAIT OUTSIDE! MOVE!
DOOR'S LOCKED! GO AROUND BACK!
KOFF
STUFF'S STARTING TO THIN--!
THEY WERE UP FRONT! GO!

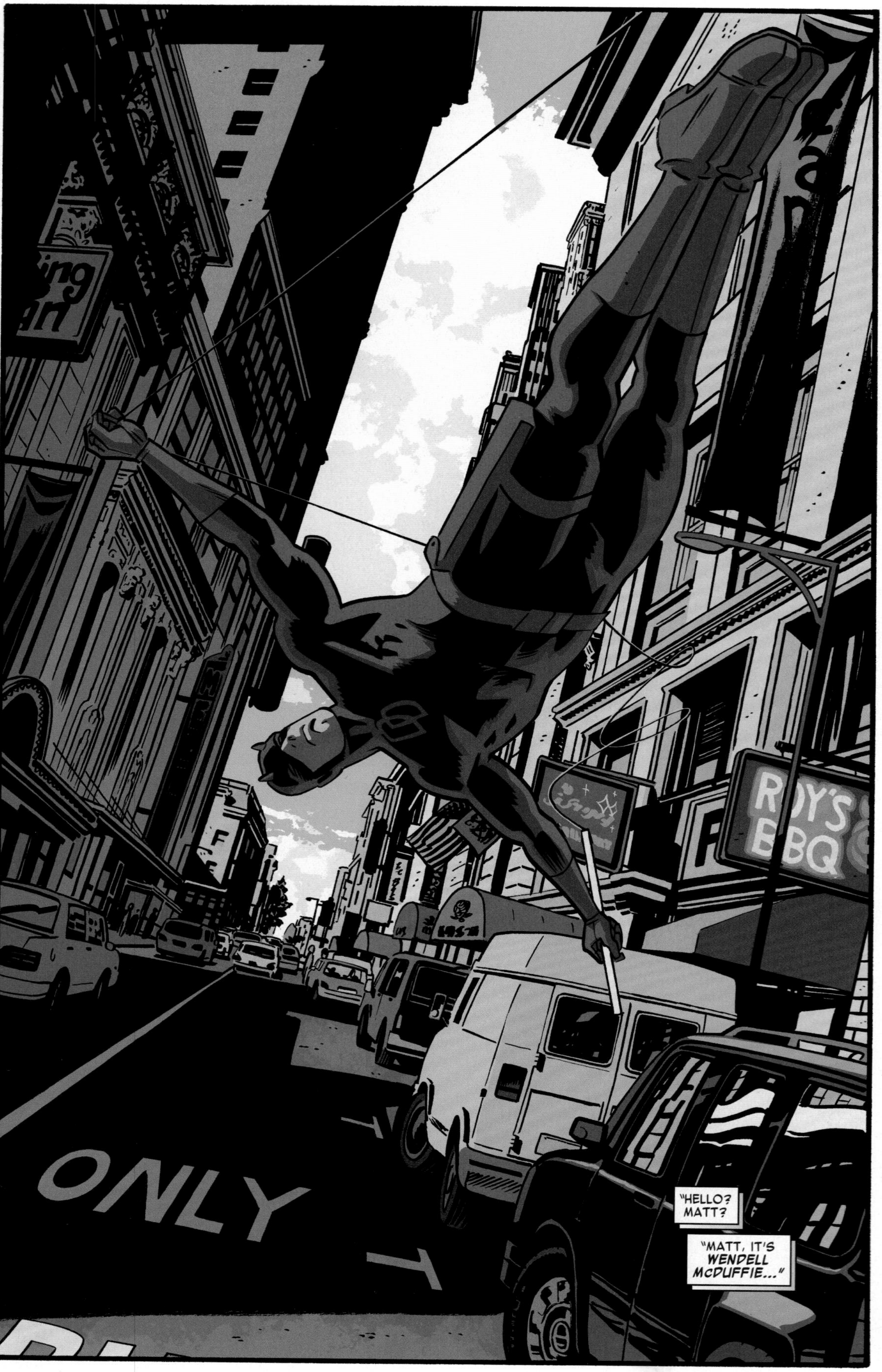

"HELLO? MATT?
"MATT, IT'S WENDELL McDUFFIE..."
ROY'S BBQ
ONLY

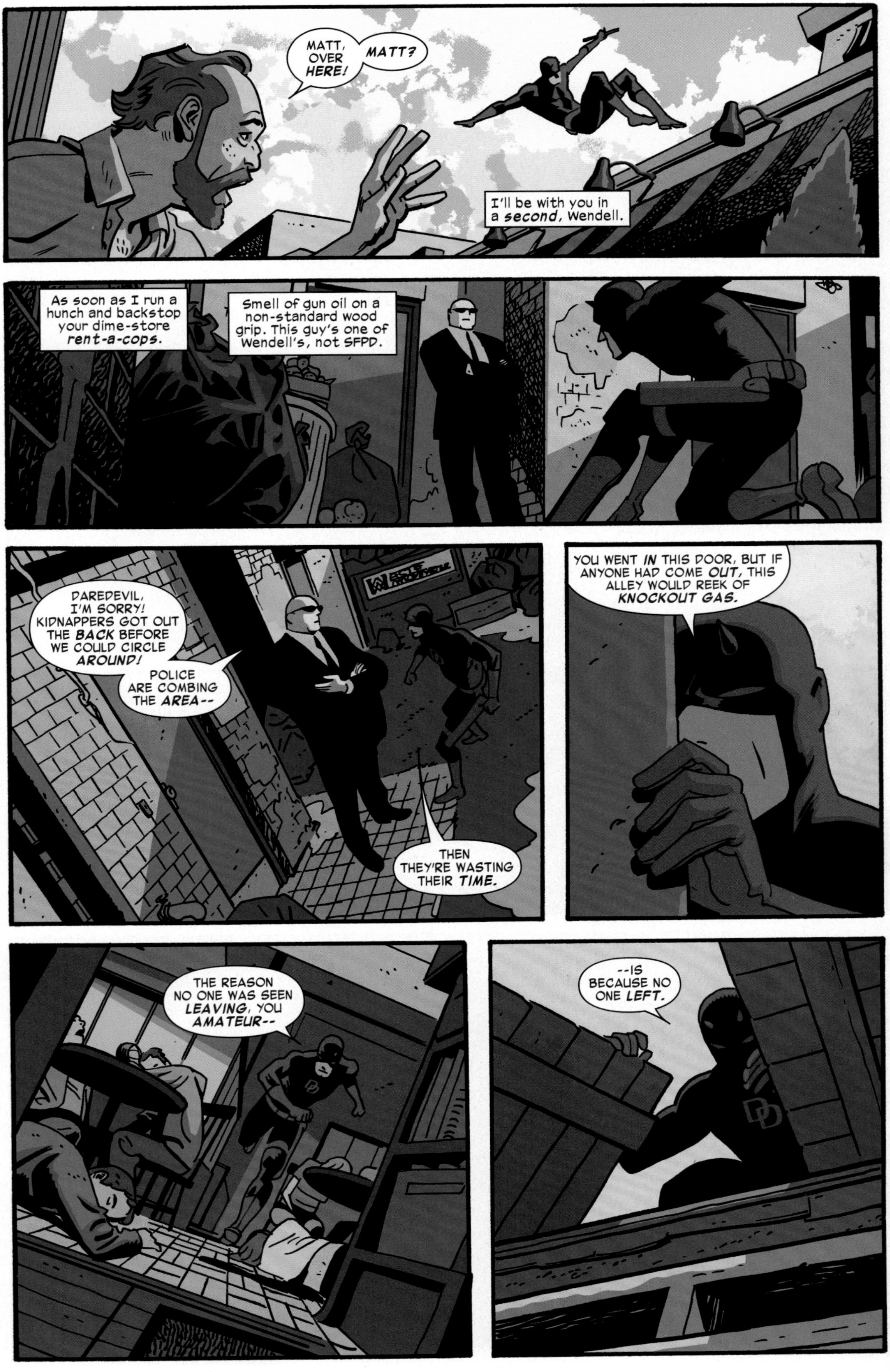
MATT, OVER HERE!
MATT?
I'll be with you in a second, Wendell.
As soon as I run a hunch and backstop your dime-store rent-a-cops.
Smell of gun oil on a non-standard wood grip. This guy's one of Wendell's, not SFPD.
DAREDEVIL, I'M SORRY! KIDNAPPERS GOT OUT THE BACK BEFORE WE COULD CIRCLE AROUND!
POLICE ARE COMBING THE AREA--
THEN THEY'RE WASTING THEIR TIME.
YOU WENT IN THIS DOOR, BUT IF ANYONE HAD COME OUT, THIS ALLEY WOULD REEK OF KNOCKOUT GAS.
THE REASON NO ONE WAS SEEN LEAVING, YOU AMATEUR--
--IS BECAUSE NO ONE LEFT.

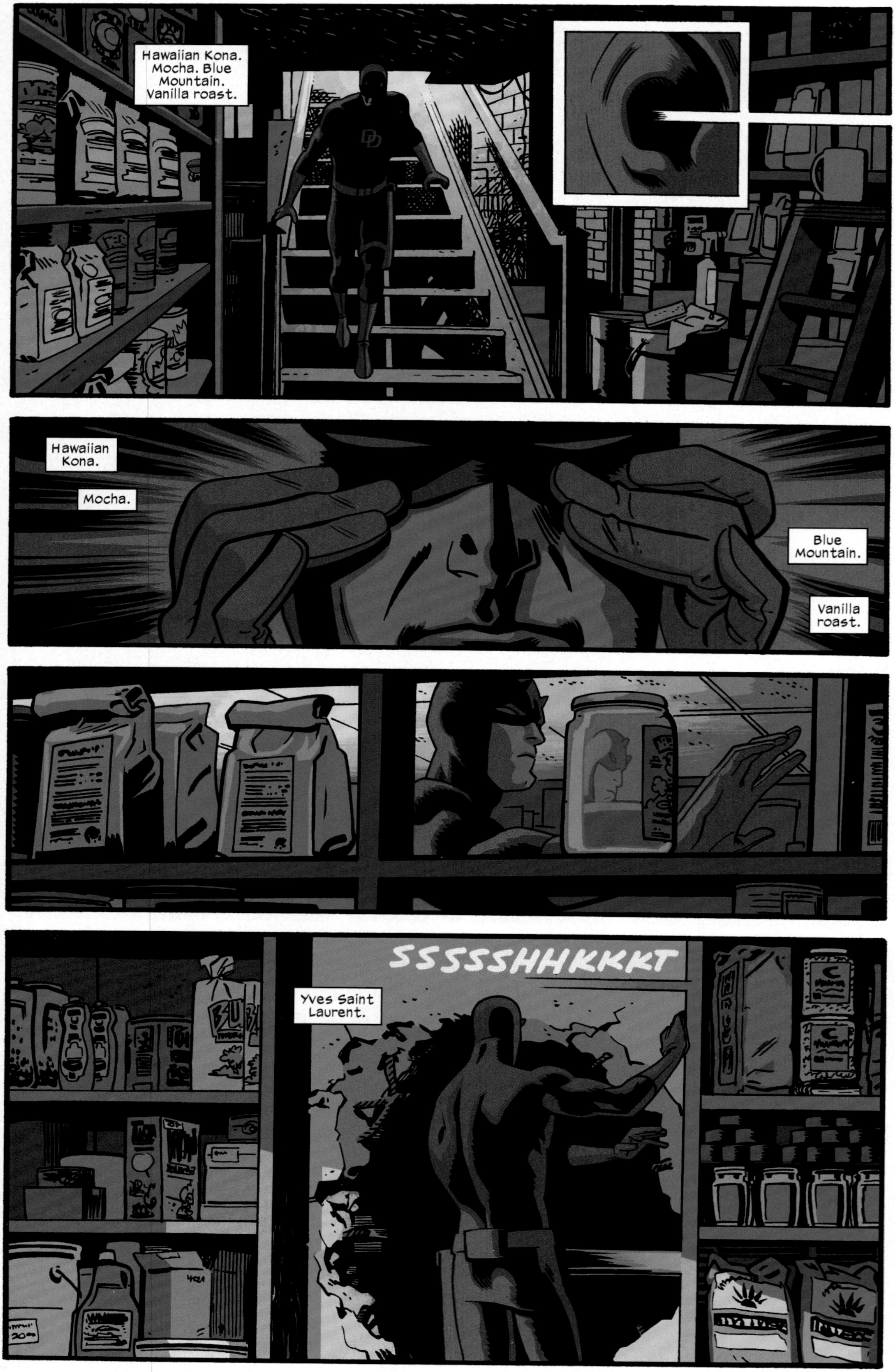
Hawaiian Kona. Mocha. Blue Mountain. Vanilla roast.
Hawaiian Kona.
Mocha.
Blue Mountain.
Vanilla roast.
SSSSSHHKKKT
Yves Saint Laurent.

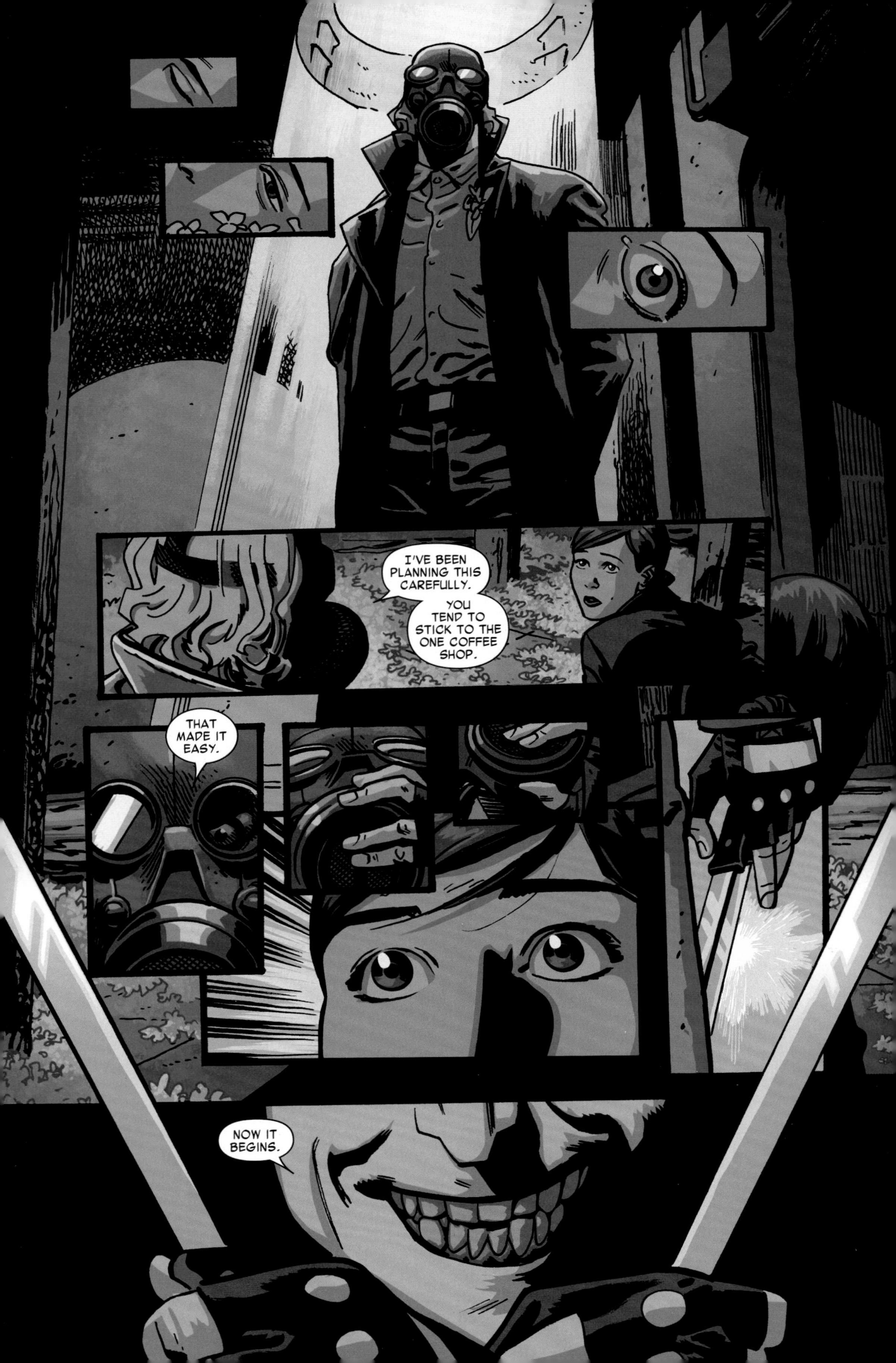
I'VE BEEN PLANNING THIS CAREFULLY.
YOU TEND TO STICK TO THE ONE COFFEE SHOP.
THAT MADE IT EASY.
NOW IT BEGINS.

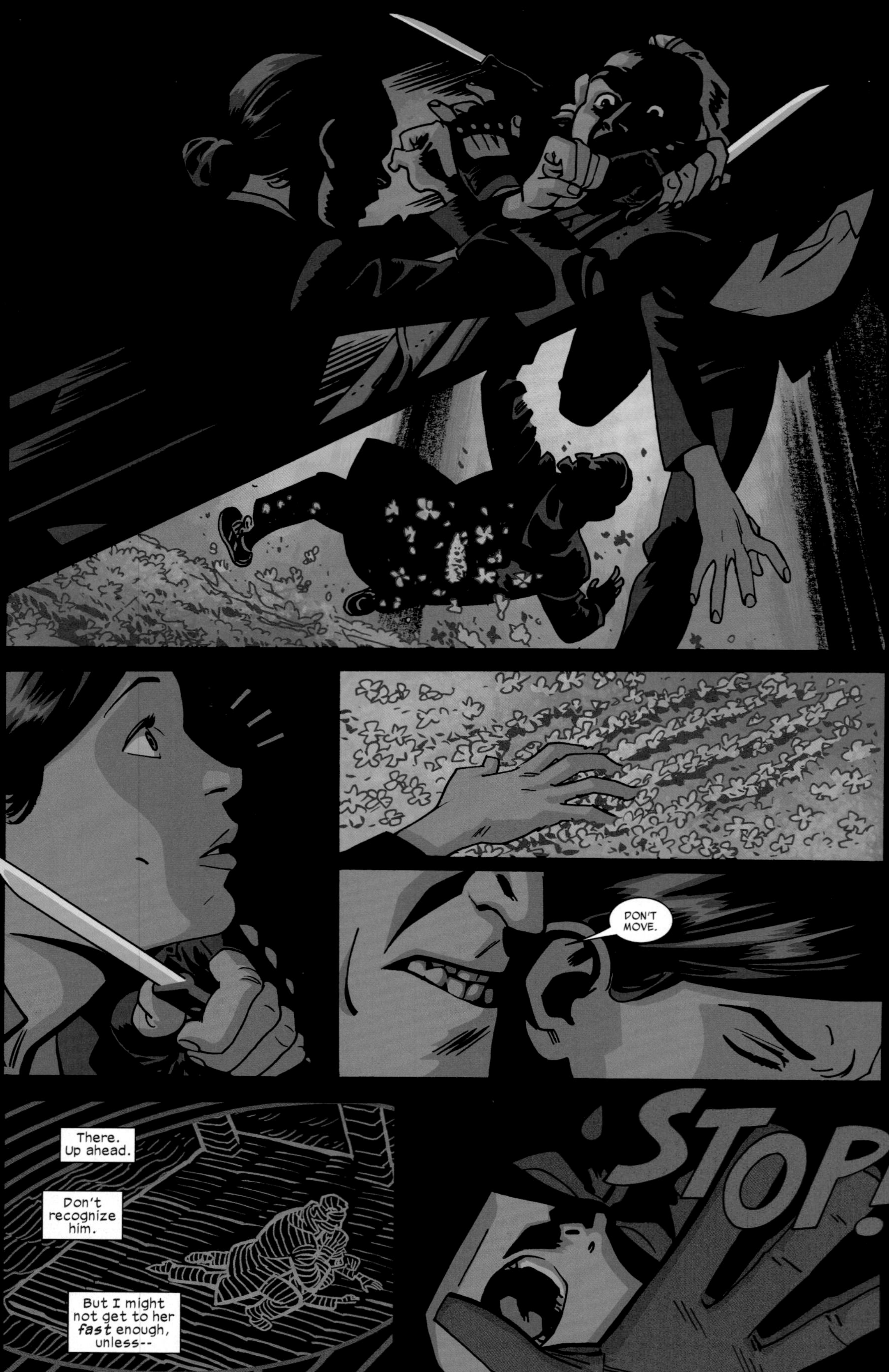
DON'T MOVE.
There. Up ahead.
Don't recognize him.
But I might not get to her *fast* enough, unless--
STOP!

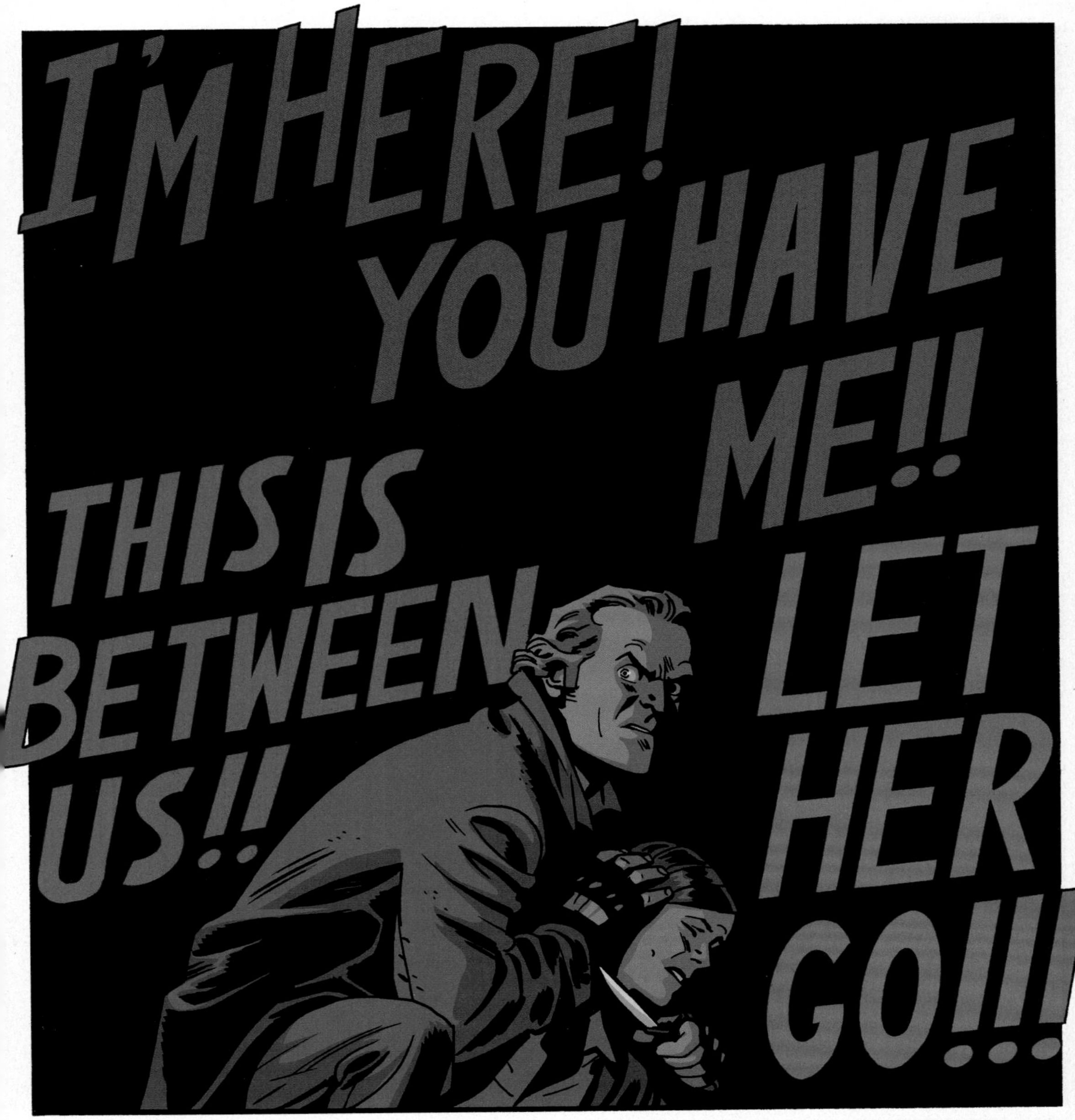
I'M HERE! YOU HAVE ME!!
THIS IS BETWEEN US!!
LET HER GO!!!

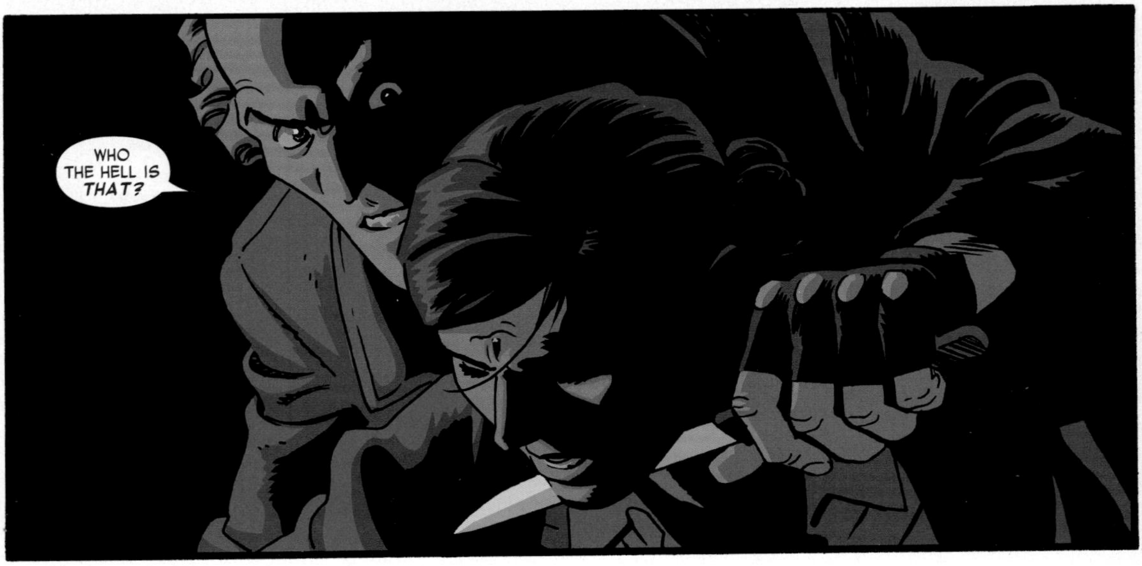
WHO THE HELL IS *THAT?*

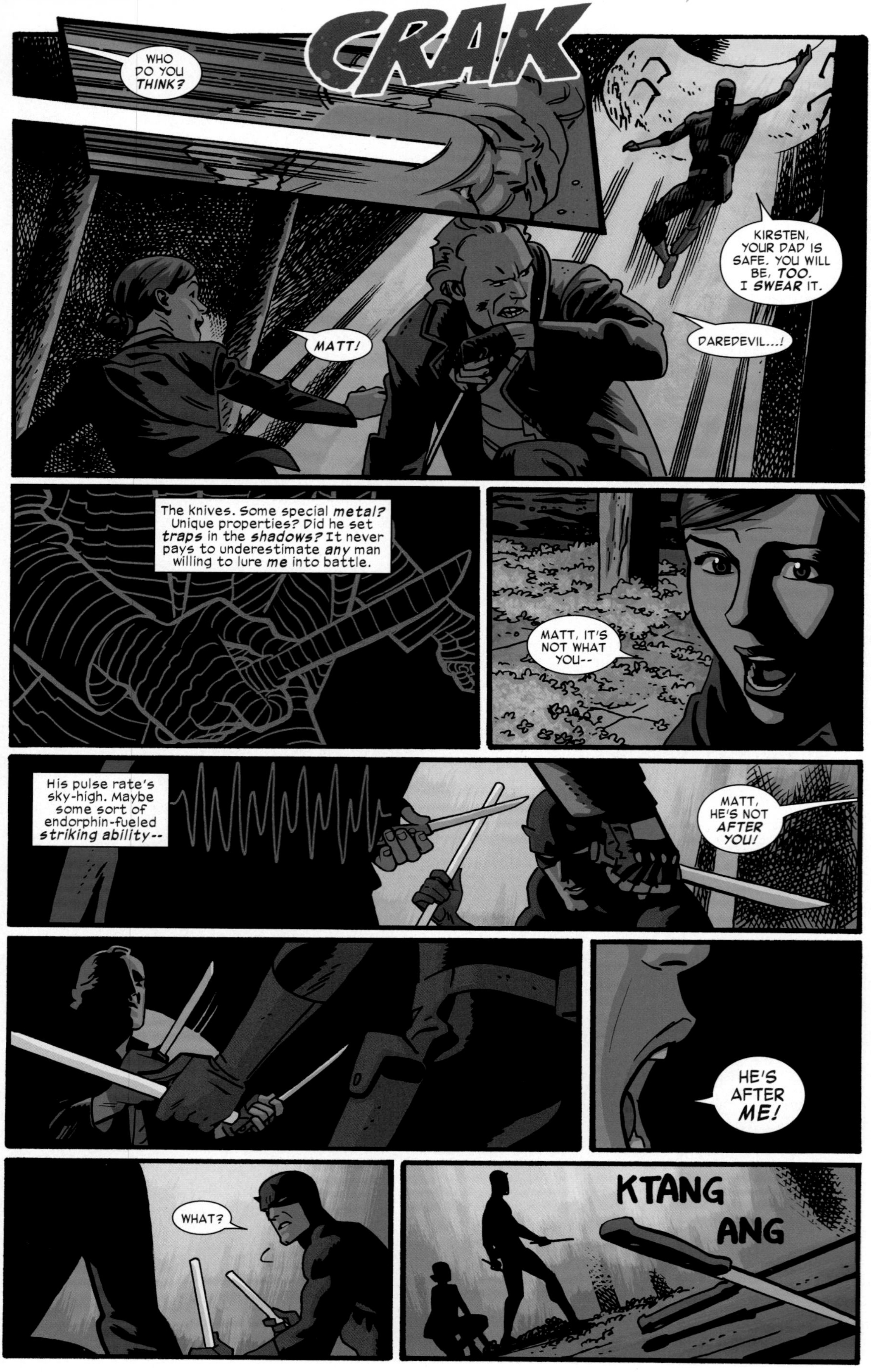

WHO DO YOU THINK?
CRAK
KIRSTEN, YOUR DAD IS SAFE. YOU WILL BE, TOO. I SWEAR IT.
MATT!
DAREDEVIL...!
The knives. Some special metal? Unique properties? Did he set traps in the shadows? It never pays to underestimate any man willing to lure me into battle.
MATT, IT'S NOT WHAT YOU--
His pulse rate's sky-high. Maybe some sort of endorphin-fueled striking ability--
MATT, HE'S NOT AFTER YOU!
HE'S AFTER ME!
WHAT?
KTANG
ANG

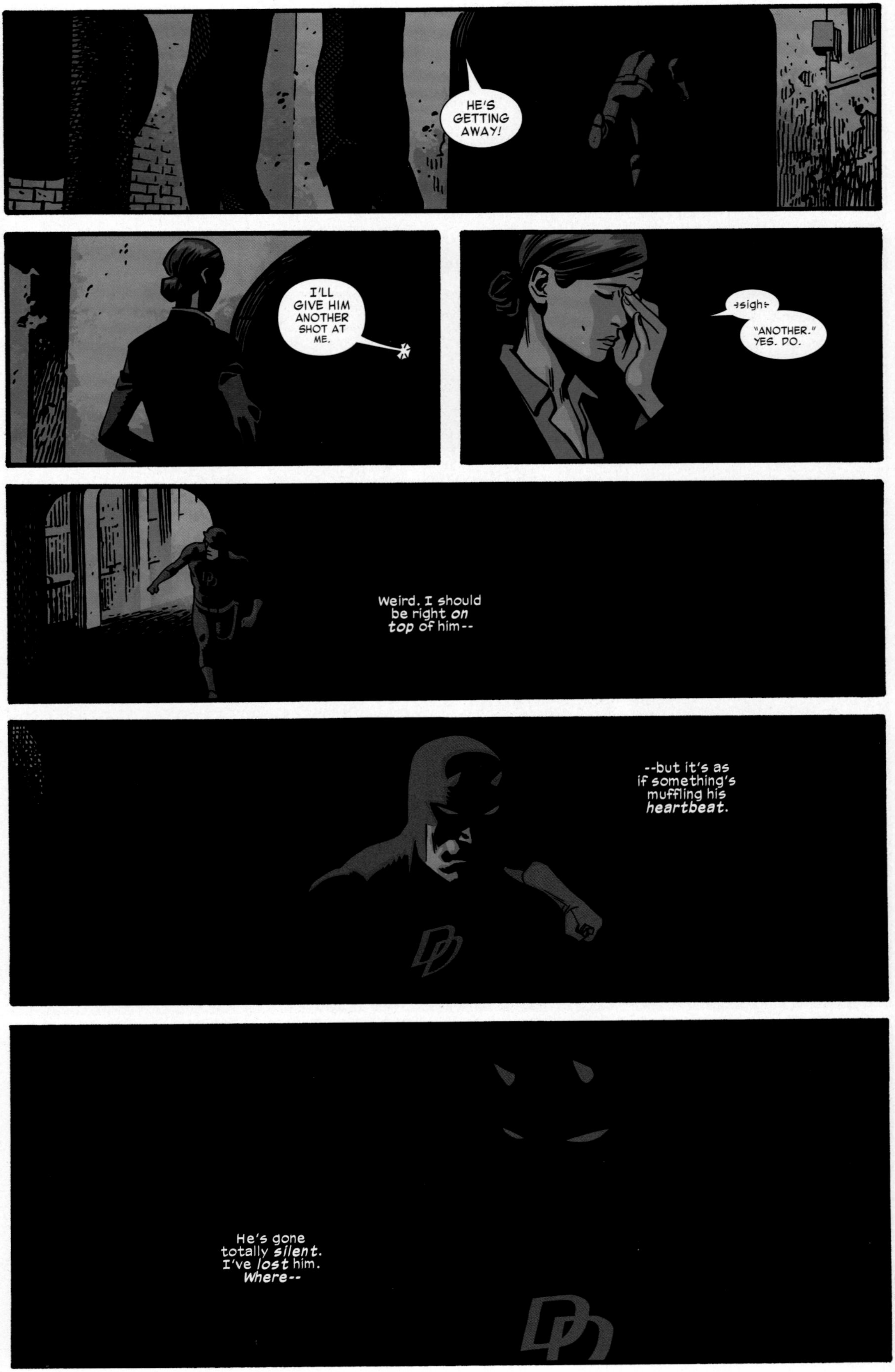
HE'S GETTING AWAY!
I'LL GIVE HIM ANOTHER SHOT AT ME.
+sigh+
"ANOTHER." YES. DO.
Weird. I should be right *on top* of him--
--but it's as if something's muffling his *heartbeat*.
He's gone totally *silent*. I've *lost* him. *Where--*

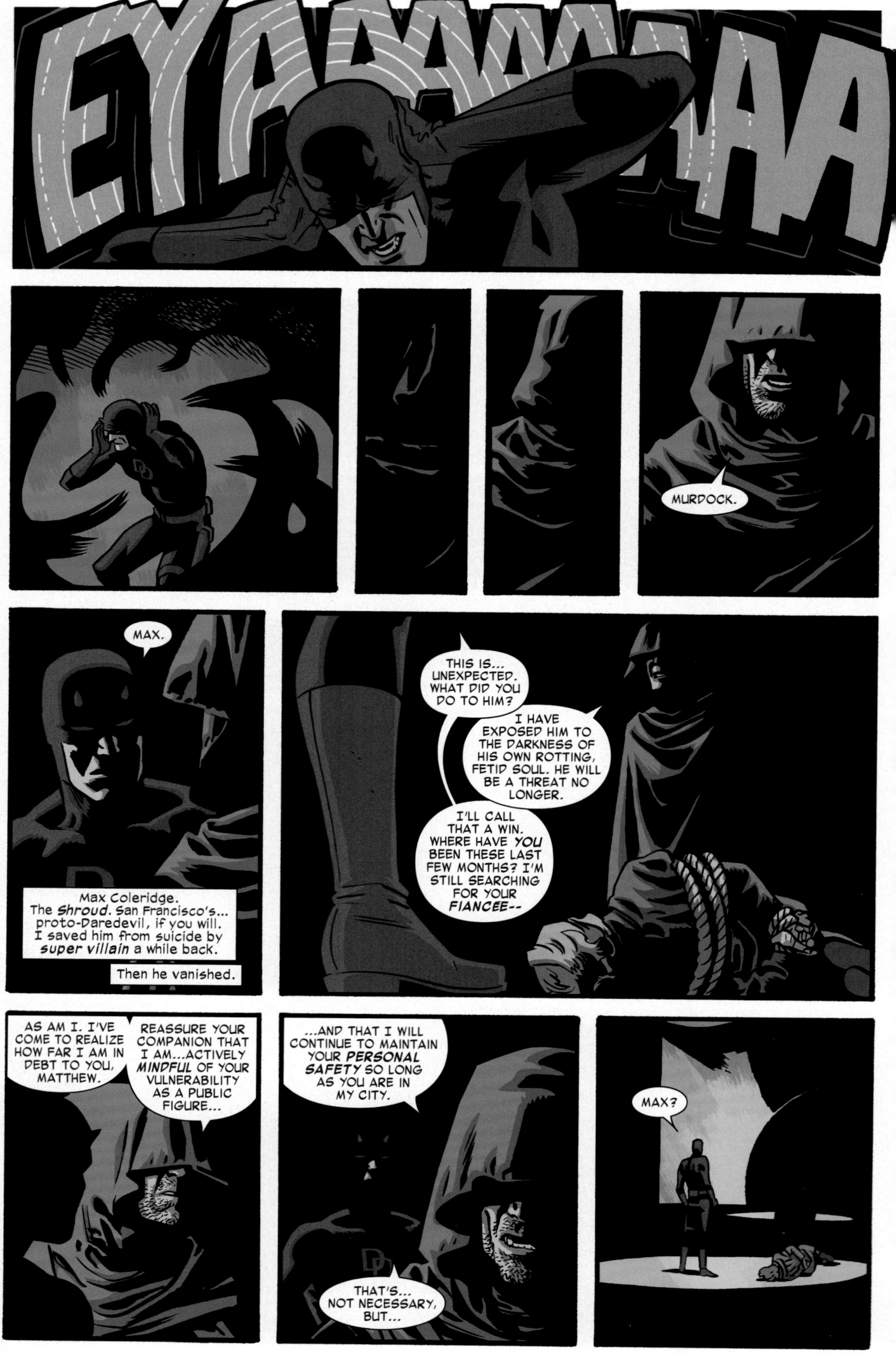
EYAAAAAAA
MURDOCK.
MAX.
Max Coleridge. The Shroud. San Francisco's... proto-Daredevil, if you will. I saved him from suicide by super villain a while back.
Then he vanished.
THIS IS... UNEXPECTED. WHAT DID YOU DO TO HIM?
I HAVE EXPOSED HIM TO THE DARKNESS OF HIS OWN ROTTING, FETID SOUL. HE WILL BE A THREAT NO LONGER.
I'LL CALL THAT A WIN. WHERE HAVE YOU BEEN THESE LAST FEW MONTHS? I'M STILL SEARCHING FOR YOUR FIANCEE--
AS AM I. I'VE COME TO REALIZE HOW FAR I AM IN DEBT TO YOU, MATTHEW.
REASSURE YOUR COMPANION THAT I AM...ACTIVELY MINDFUL OF YOUR VULNERABILITY AS A PUBLIC FIGURE...
...AND THAT I WILL CONTINUE TO MAINTAIN YOUR PERSONAL SAFETY SO LONG AS YOU ARE IN MY CITY.
THAT'S... NOT NECESSARY, BUT...
MAX?

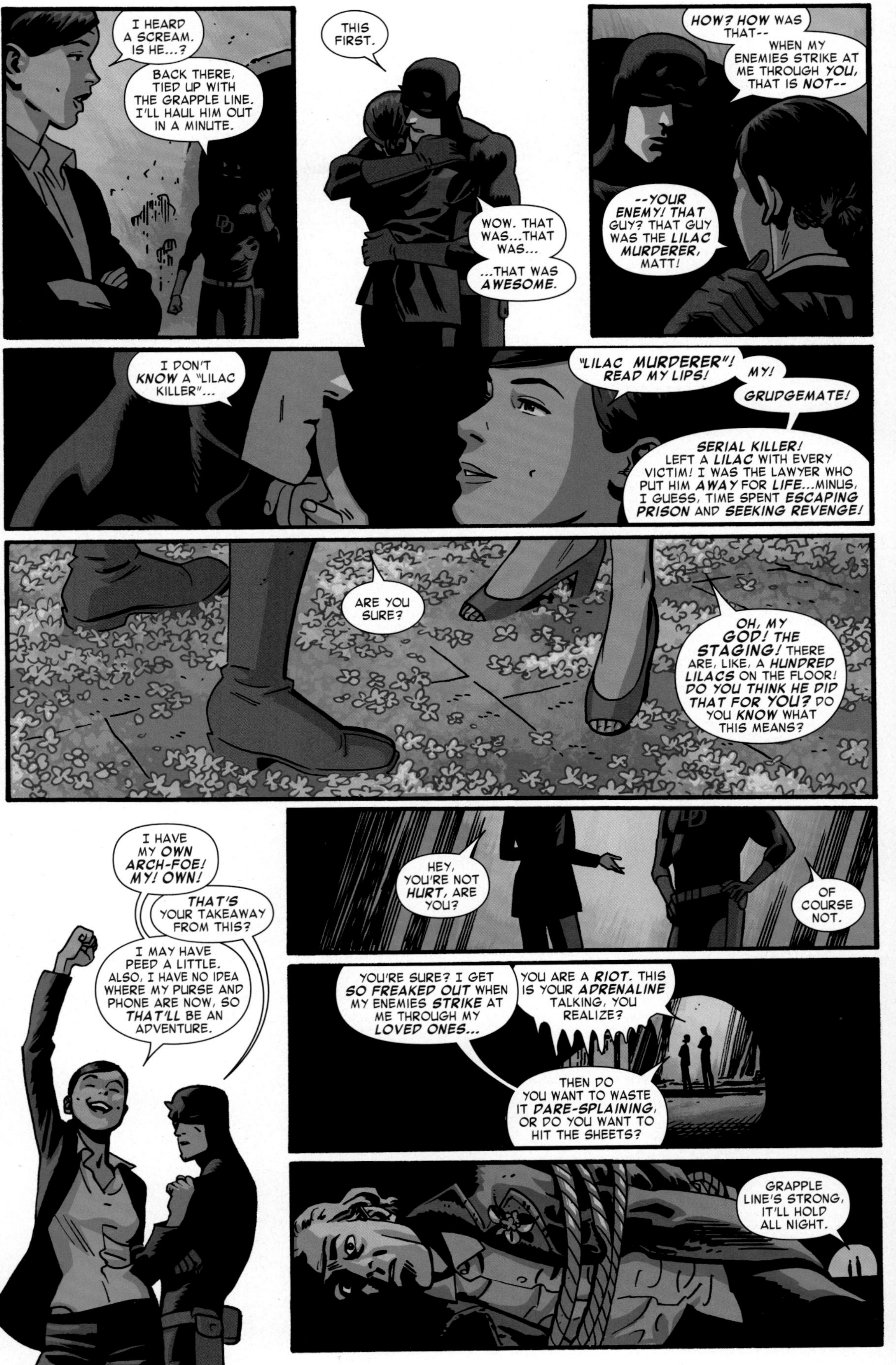

I HEARD A SCREAM. IS HE...?
BACK THERE, TIED UP WITH THE GRAPPLE LINE. I'LL HAUL HIM OUT IN A MINUTE.
THIS FIRST.
WOW. THAT WAS...THAT WAS...
...THAT WAS AWESOME.
HOW? HOW WAS THAT--
WHEN MY ENEMIES STRIKE AT ME THROUGH YOU, THAT IS NOT--
--YOUR ENEMY! THAT GUY? THAT GUY WAS THE LILAC MURDERER, MATT!
I DON'T KNOW A "LILAC KILLER"...
"LILAC MURDERER"! READ MY LIPS!
MY!
GRUDGEMATE!
SERIAL KILLER! LEFT A LILAC WITH EVERY VICTIM! I WAS THE LAWYER WHO PUT HIM AWAY FOR LIFE...MINUS, I GUESS, TIME SPENT ESCAPING PRISON AND SEEKING REVENGE!
ARE YOU SURE?
OH, MY GOD! THE STAGING! THERE ARE, LIKE, A HUNDRED LILACS ON THE FLOOR! DO YOU THINK HE DID THAT FOR YOU? DO YOU KNOW WHAT THIS MEANS?
I HAVE MY OWN ARCH-FOE! MY! OWN!
THAT'S YOUR TAKEAWAY FROM THIS?
I MAY HAVE PEED A LITTLE. ALSO, I HAVE NO IDEA WHERE MY PURSE AND PHONE ARE NOW, SO THAT'LL BE AN ADVENTURE.
HEY, YOU'RE NOT HURT, ARE YOU?
OF COURSE NOT.
YOU'RE SURE? I GET SO FREAKED OUT WHEN MY ENEMIES STRIKE AT ME THROUGH MY LOVED ONES...
YOU ARE A RIOT. THIS IS YOUR ADRENALINE TALKING, YOU REALIZE?
THEN DO YOU WANT TO WASTE IT DARE-SPLAINING, OR DO YOU WANT TO HIT THE SHEETS?
GRAPPLE LINE'S STRONG, IT'LL HOLD ALL NIGHT.

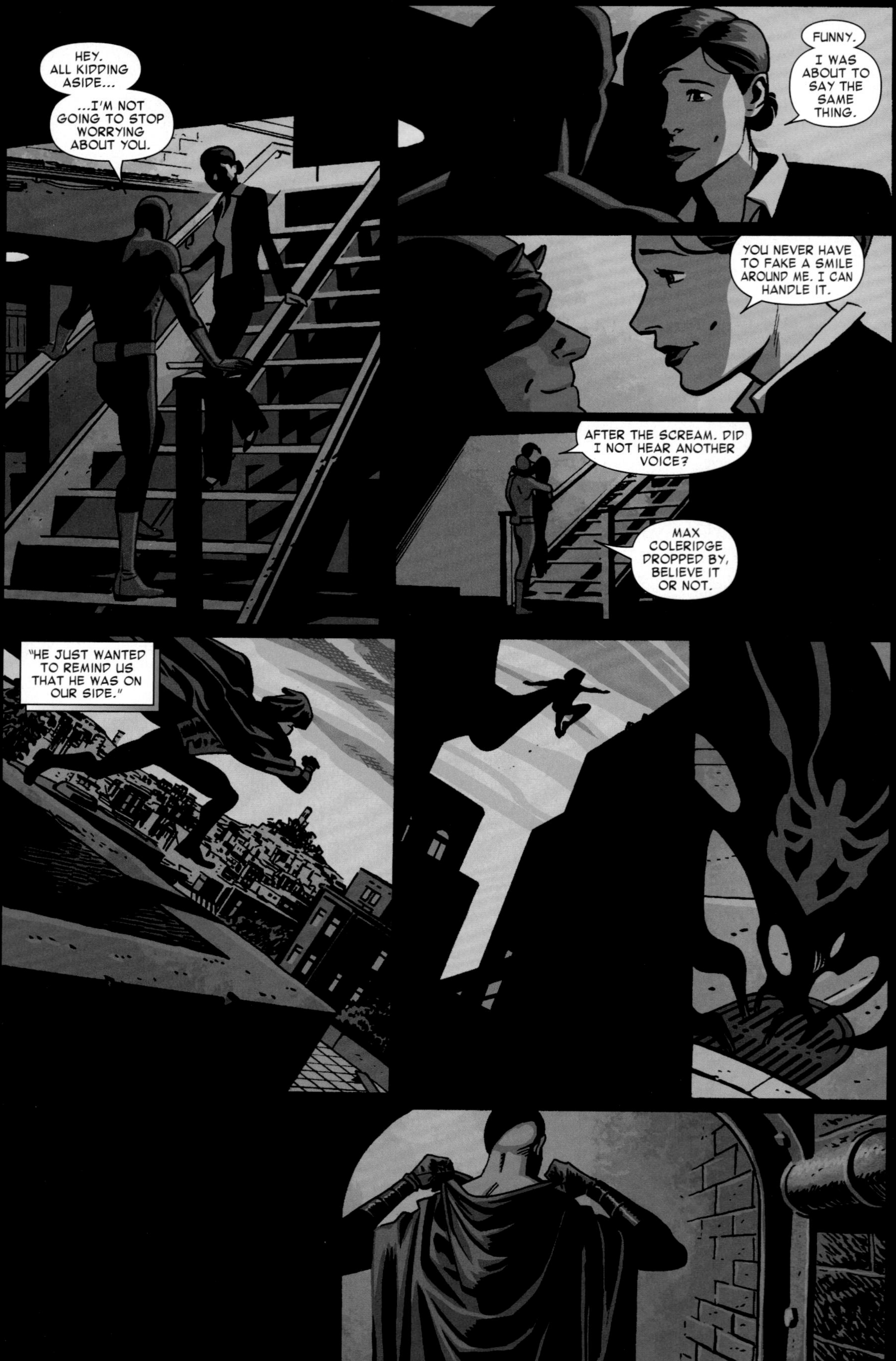
HEY. ALL KIDDING ASIDE...
...I'M NOT GOING TO STOP WORRYING ABOUT YOU.
FUNNY.
I WAS ABOUT TO SAY THE SAME THING.
YOU NEVER HAVE TO FAKE A SMILE AROUND ME. I CAN HANDLE IT.
AFTER THE SCREAM. DID I NOT HEAR ANOTHER VOICE?
MAX COLERIDGE DROPPED BY, BELIEVE IT OR NOT.
"HE JUST WANTED TO REMIND US THAT HE WAS ON OUR SIDE."

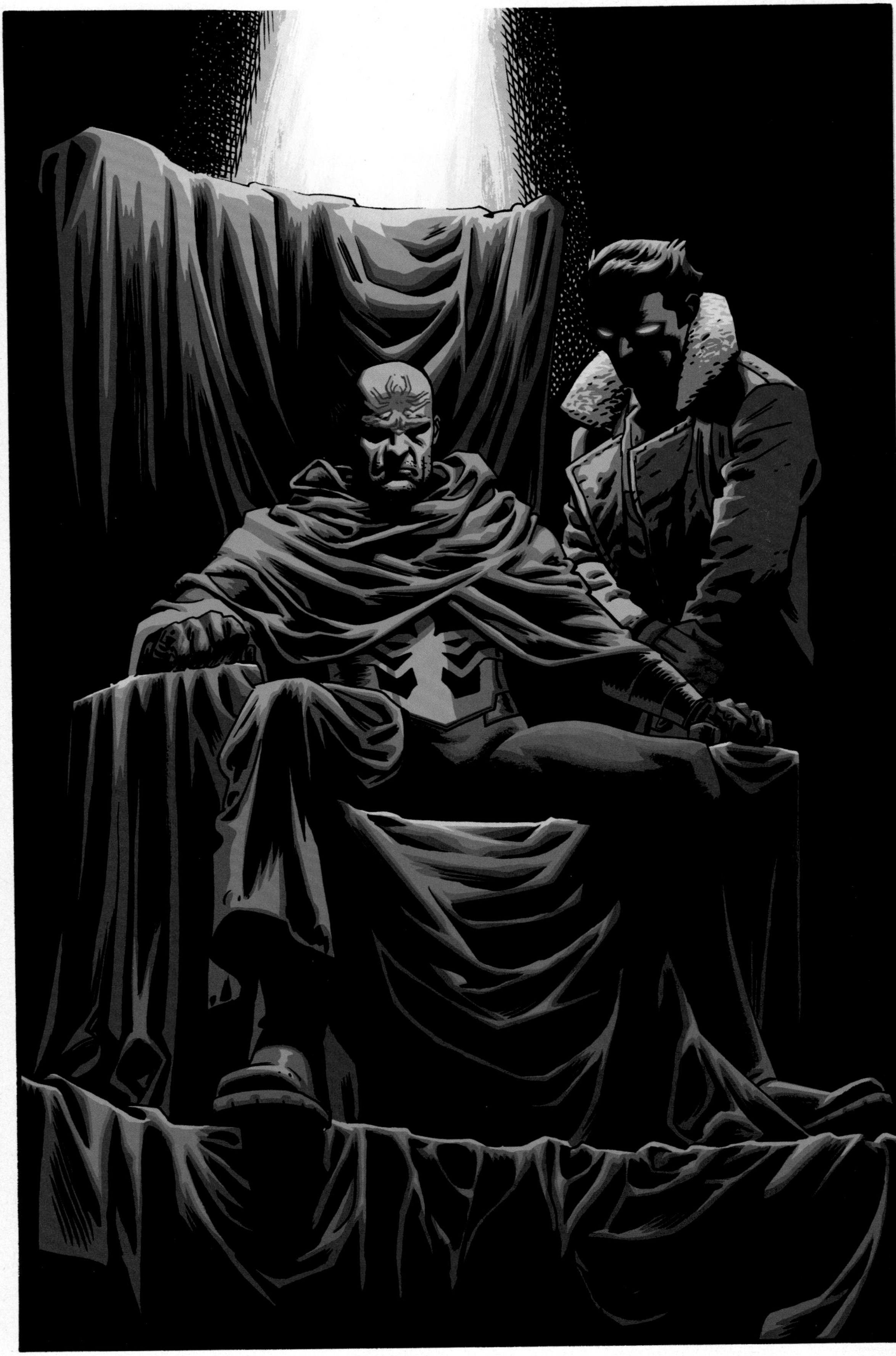

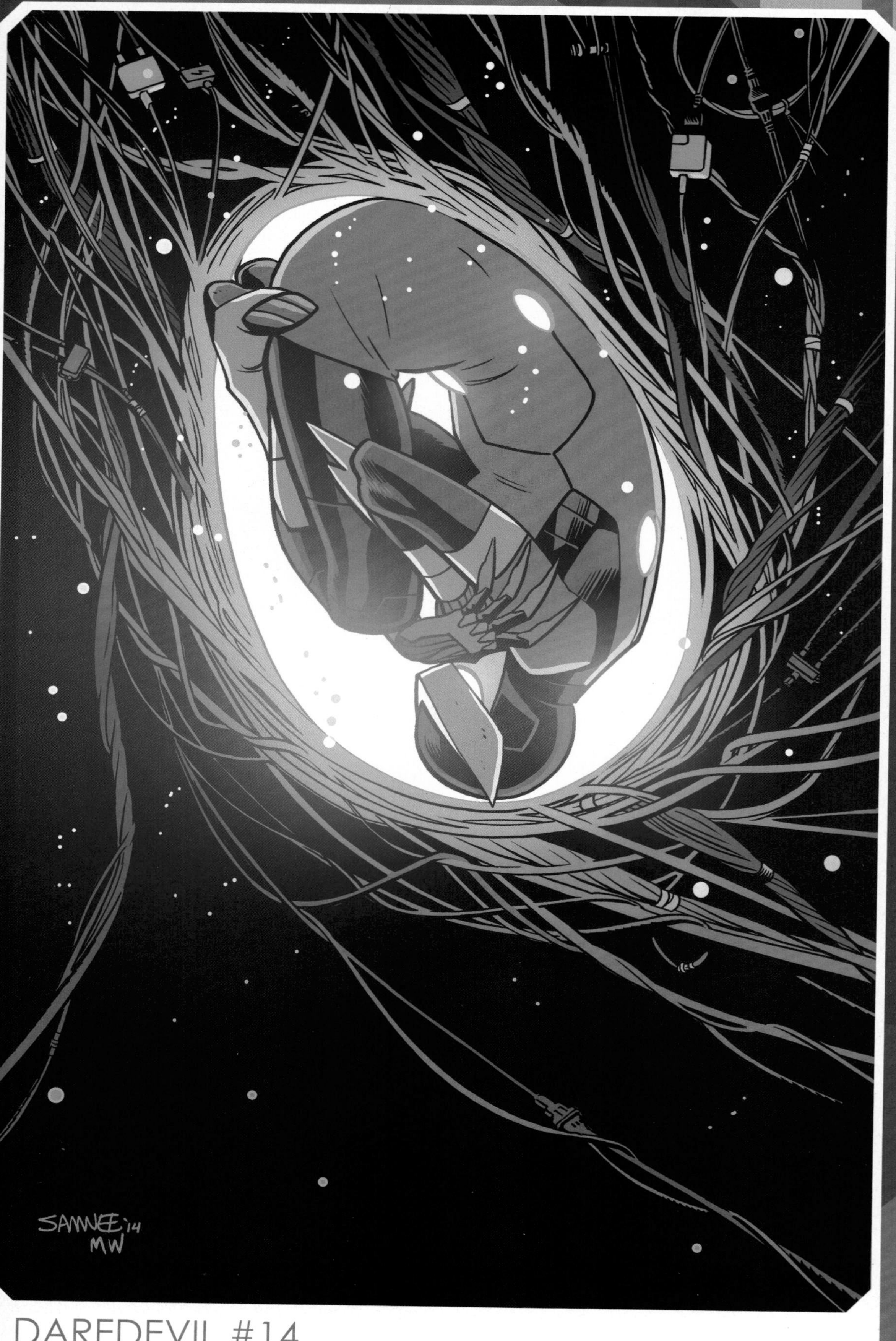
SAMNEE '14
MW

DAREDEVIL #14

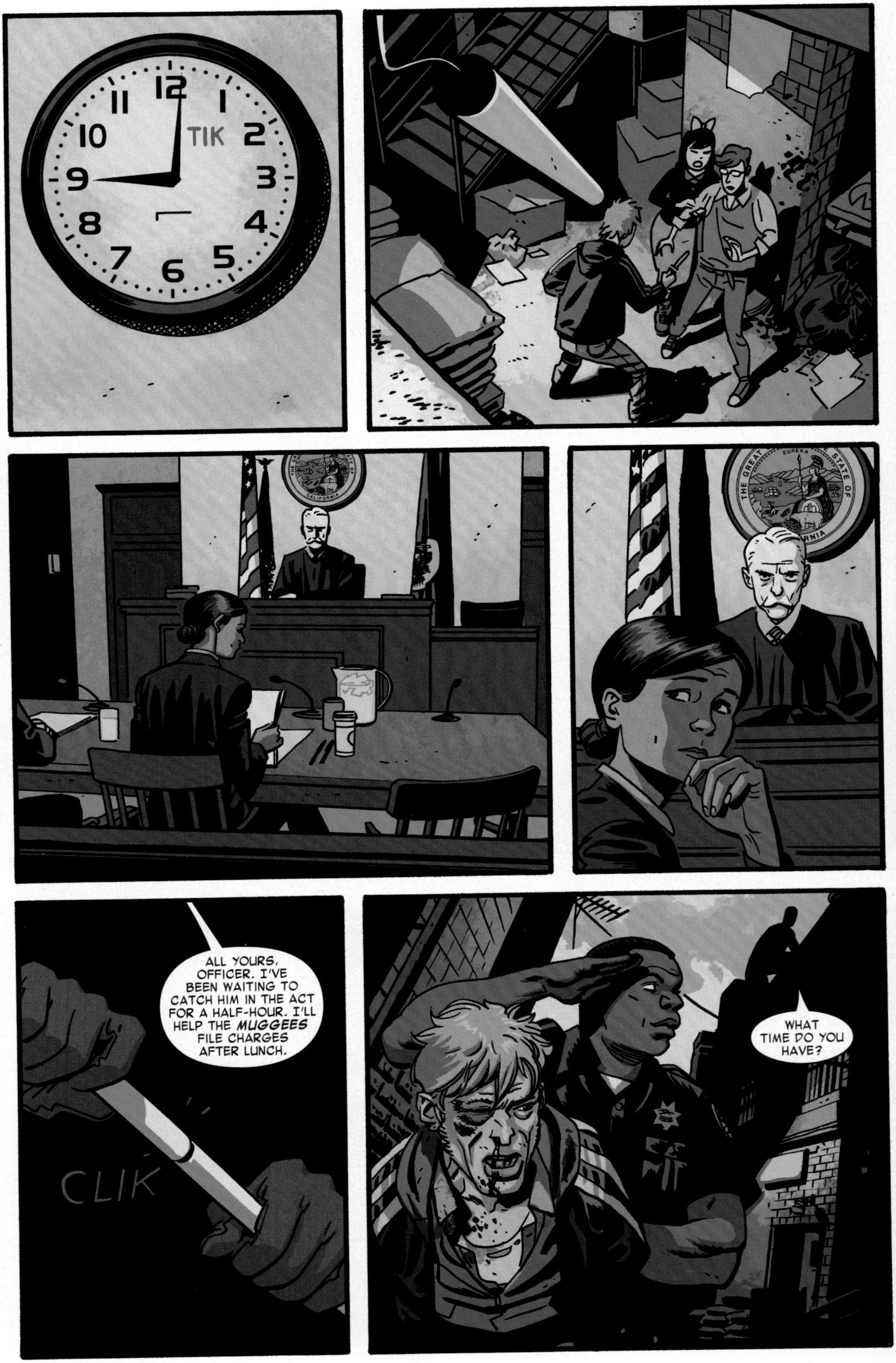
TIK
ALL YOURS, OFFICER. I'VE BEEN WAITING TO CATCH HIM IN THE ACT FOR A HALF-HOUR. I'LL HELP THE MUGGEES FILE CHARGES AFTER LUNCH.
CLIK
WHAT TIME DO YOU HAVE?

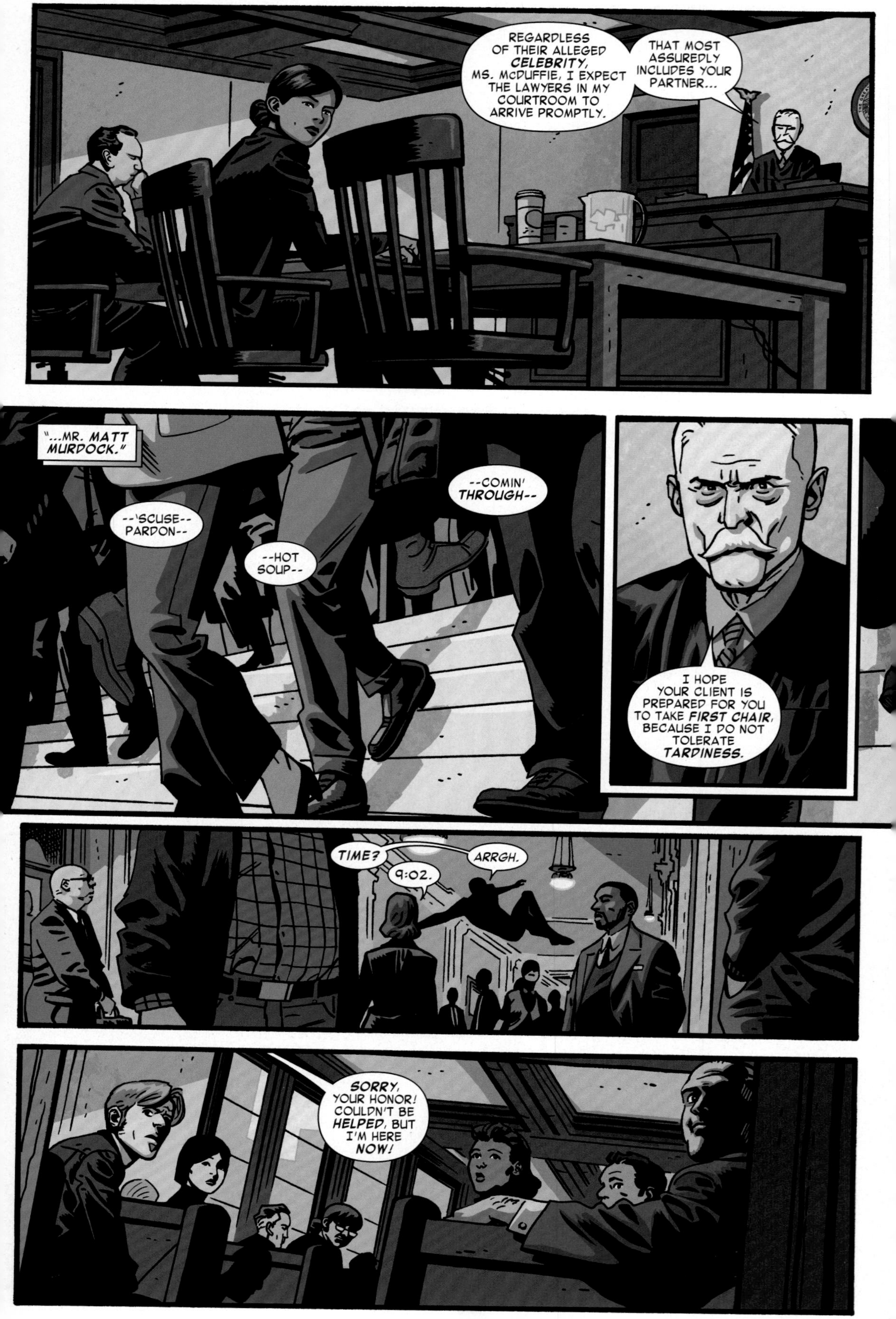
REGARDLESS OF THEIR ALLEGED CELEBRITY, MS. McDUFFIE, I EXPECT THE LAWYERS IN MY COURTROOM TO ARRIVE PROMPTLY.
THAT MOST ASSUREDLY INCLUDES YOUR PARTNER...
"...MR. MATT MURDOCK."
--'SCUSE-- PARDON--
--HOT SOUP--
--COMIN' THROUGH--
I HOPE YOUR CLIENT IS PREPARED FOR YOU TO TAKE FIRST CHAIR, BECAUSE I DO NOT TOLERATE TARDINESS.
TIME?
9:02.
ARRGH.
SORRY, YOUR HONOR! COULDN'T BE HELPED, BUT I'M HERE NOW!

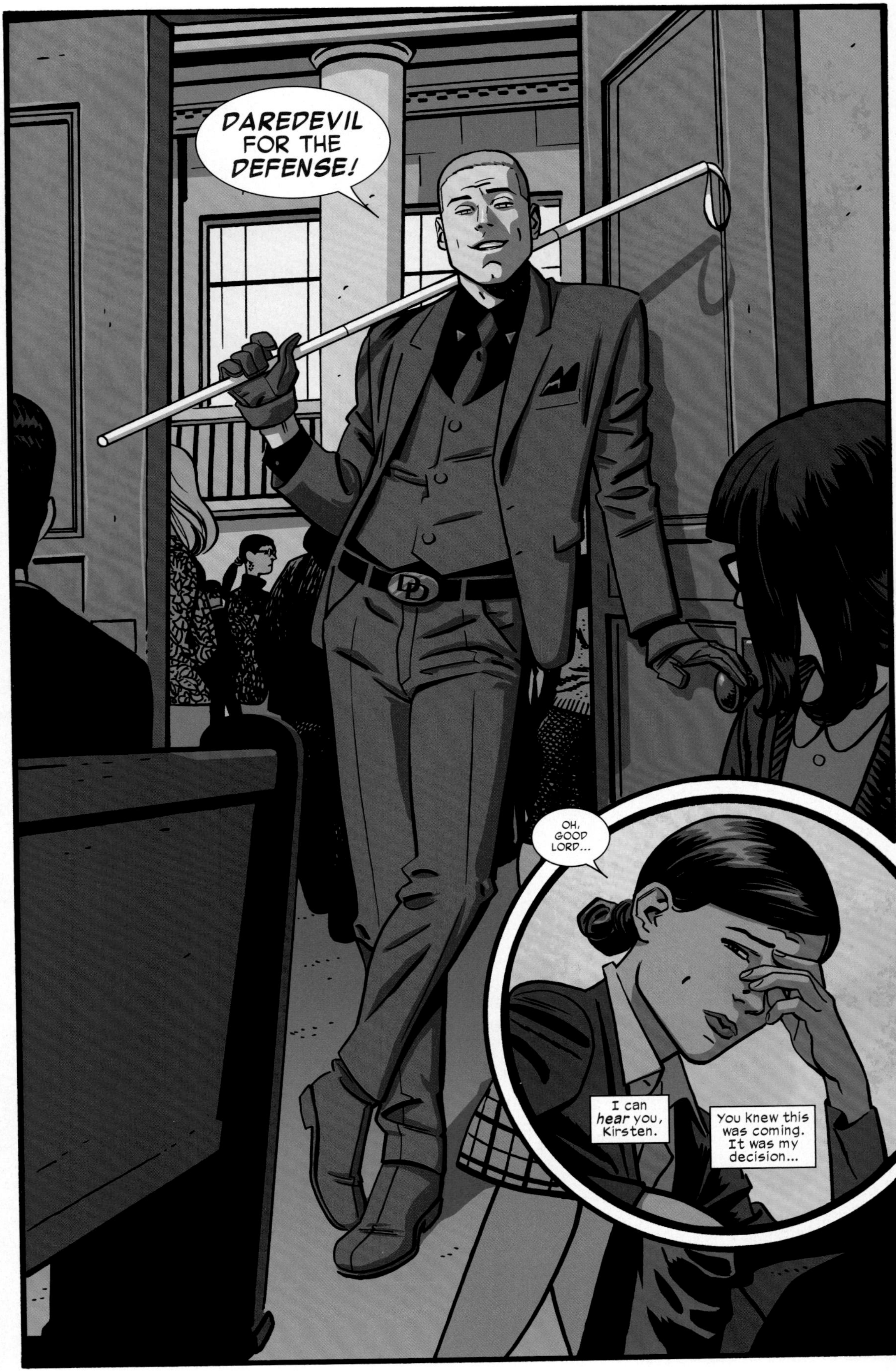
DAREDEVIL FOR THE DEFENSE!
OH, GOOD LORD...
I can hear you, Kirsten.
You knew this was coming. It was my decision...

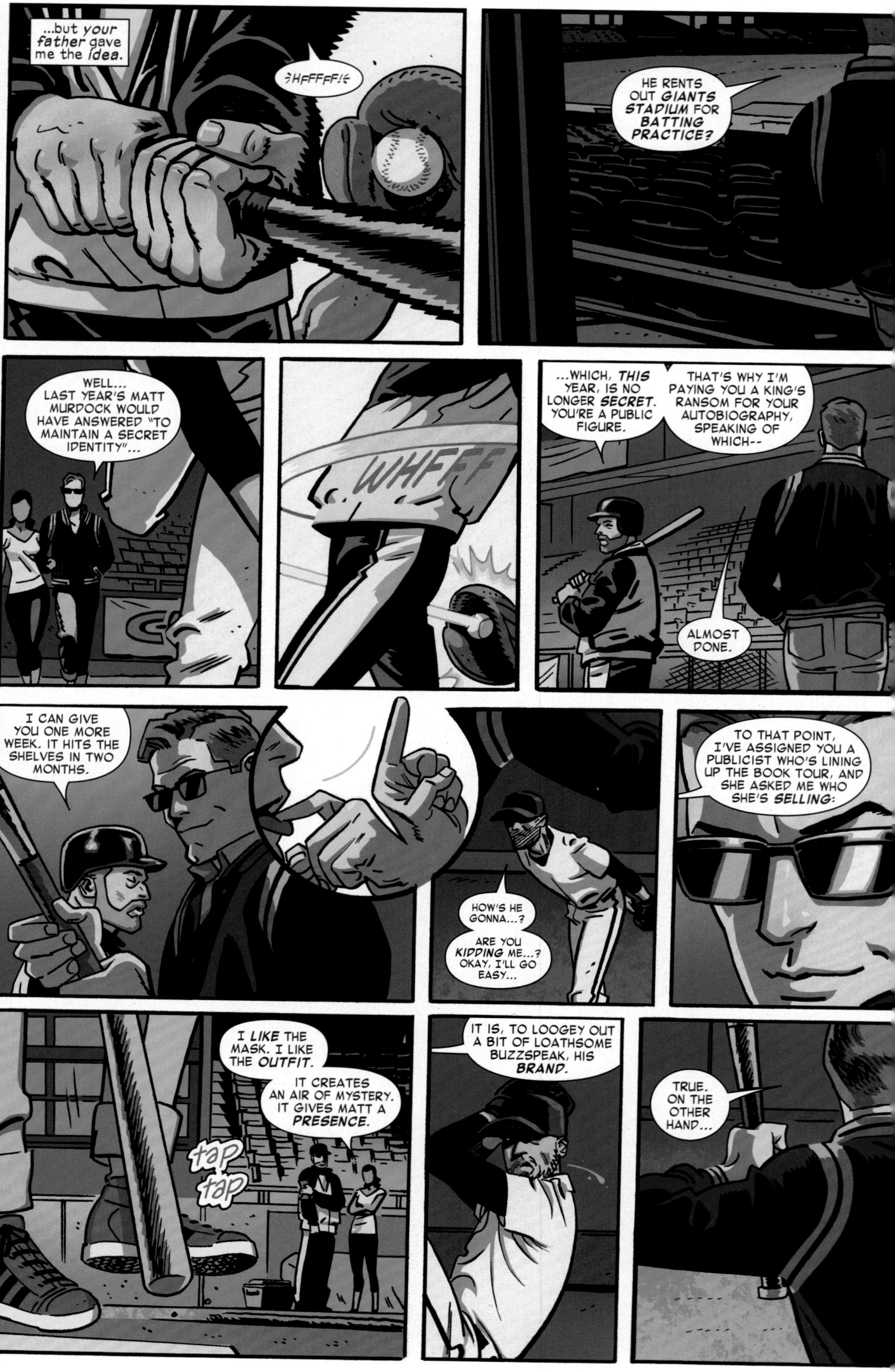
...but your father gave me the idea.
HFFFFF!
HE RENTS OUT GIANTS STADIUM FOR BATTING PRACTICE?
WELL... LAST YEAR'S MATT MURDOCK WOULD HAVE ANSWERED "TO MAINTAIN A SECRET IDENTITY"...
WHFFF
...WHICH, THIS YEAR, IS NO LONGER SECRET. YOU'RE A PUBLIC FIGURE.
THAT'S WHY I'M PAYING YOU A KING'S RANSOM FOR YOUR AUTOBIOGRAPHY, SPEAKING OF WHICH--
ALMOST DONE.
I CAN GIVE YOU ONE MORE WEEK. IT HITS THE SHELVES IN TWO MONTHS.
HOW'S HE GONNA...?
ARE YOU KIDDING ME...? OKAY, I'LL GO EASY...
TO THAT POINT, I'VE ASSIGNED YOU A PUBLICIST WHO'S LINING UP THE BOOK TOUR, AND SHE ASKED ME WHO SHE'S SELLING:
I LIKE THE MASK. I LIKE THE OUTFIT.
IT CREATES AN AIR OF MYSTERY. IT GIVES MATT A PRESENCE.
tap tap
IT IS, TO LOOGEY OUT A BIT OF LOATHSOME BUZZSPEAK, HIS BRAND.
TRUE. ON THE OTHER HAND...

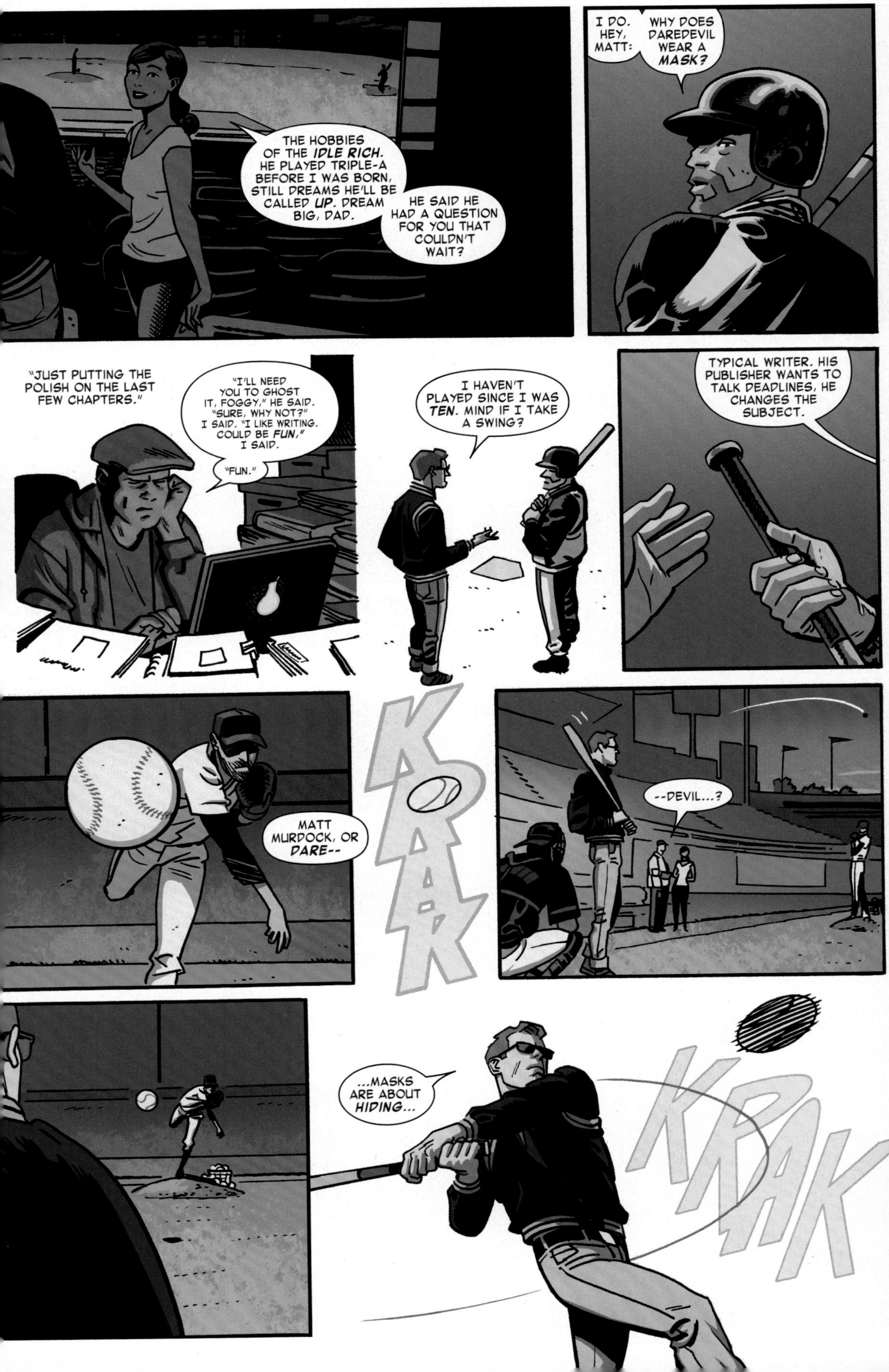
THE HOBBIES OF THE IDLE RICH. HE PLAYED TRIPLE-A BEFORE I WAS BORN, STILL DREAMS HE'LL BE CALLED UP. DREAM BIG, DAD.
HE SAID HE HAD A QUESTION FOR YOU THAT COULDN'T WAIT?
I DO. HEY, MATT:
WHY DOES DAREDEVIL WEAR A MASK?
"JUST PUTTING THE POLISH ON THE LAST FEW CHAPTERS."
"I'LL NEED YOU TO GHOST IT, FOGGY," HE SAID. "SURE, WHY NOT?" I SAID. "I LIKE WRITING. COULD BE FUN," I SAID.
"FUN."
I HAVEN'T PLAYED SINCE I WAS TEN. MIND IF I TAKE A SWING?
TYPICAL WRITER. HIS PUBLISHER WANTS TO TALK DEADLINES, HE CHANGES THE SUBJECT.
MATT MURDOCK, OR DARE--
KRAK
--DEVIL...?
...MASKS ARE ABOUT HIDING...
KRAK

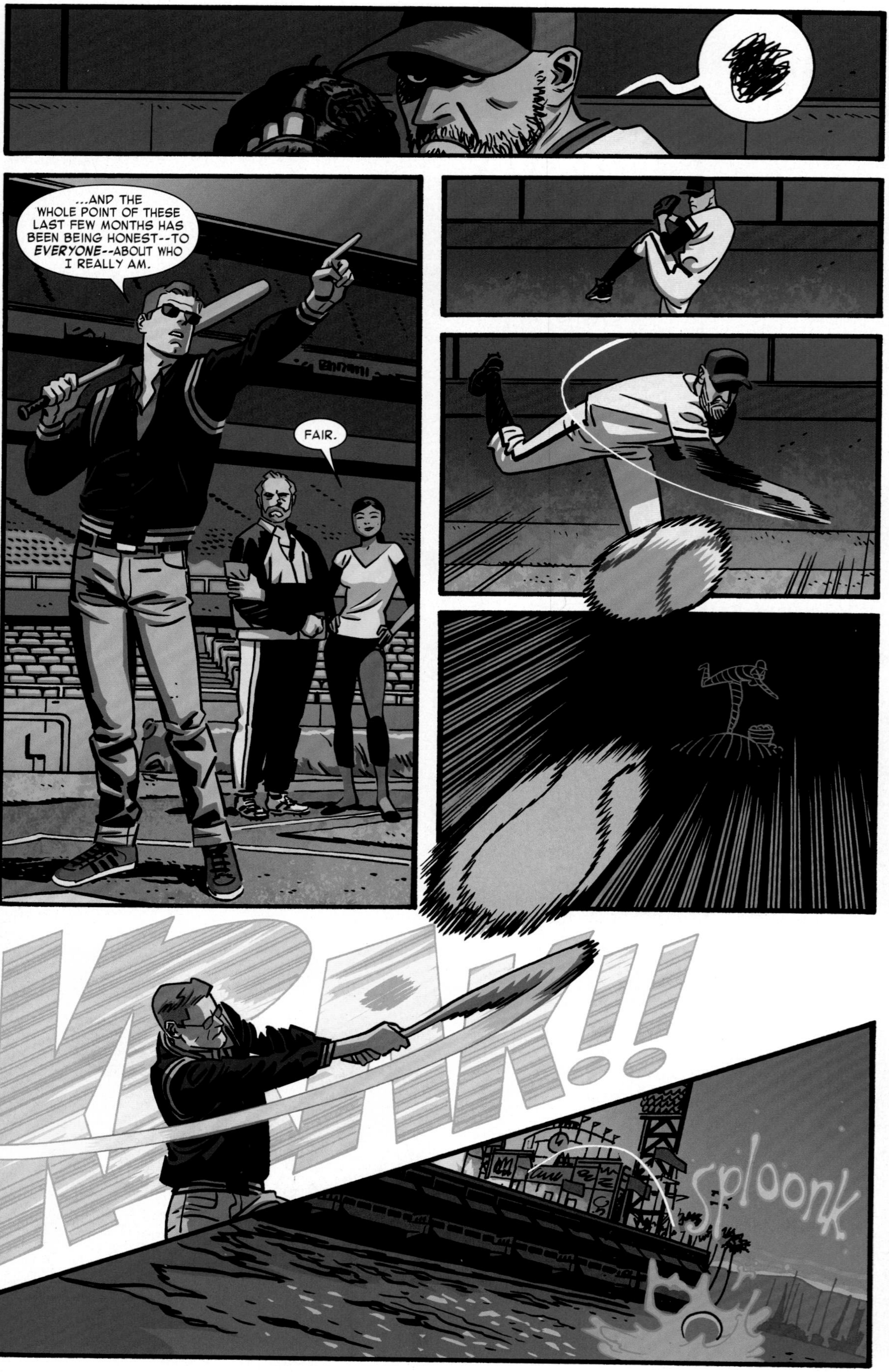
...AND THE WHOLE POINT OF THESE LAST FEW MONTHS HAS BEEN BEING HONEST--TO *EVERYONE*--ABOUT WHO I REALLY AM.
FAIR.
sploonk

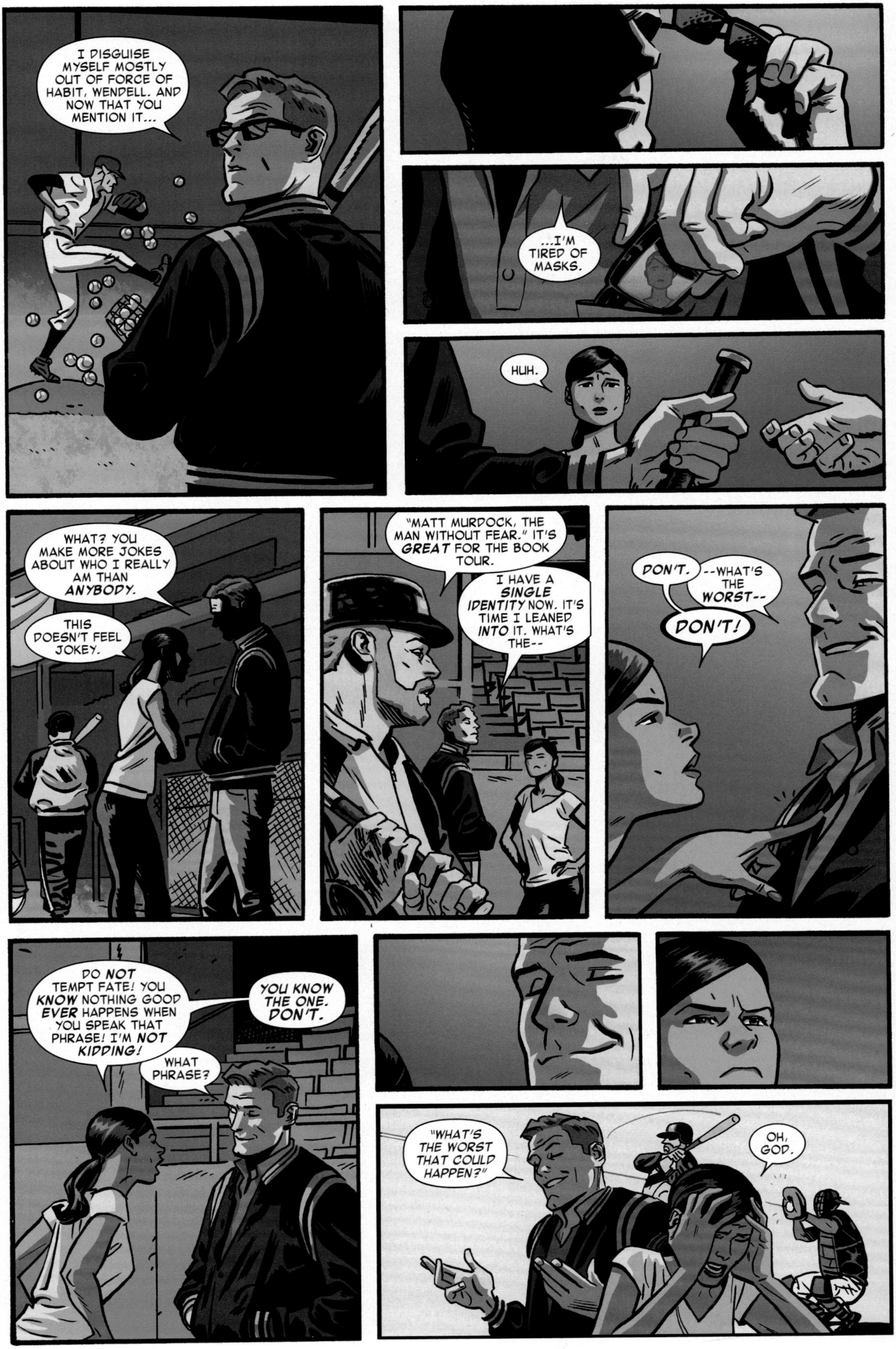
I DISGUISE MYSELF MOSTLY OUT OF FORCE OF HABIT, WENDELL. AND NOW THAT YOU MENTION IT...
...I'M TIRED OF MASKS.
HUH.
WHAT? YOU MAKE MORE JOKES ABOUT WHO I REALLY AM THAN ANYBODY.
THIS DOESN'T FEEL JOKEY.
"MATT MURDOCK, THE MAN WITHOUT FEAR." IT'S GREAT FOR THE BOOK TOUR.
I HAVE A SINGLE IDENTITY NOW. IT'S TIME I LEANED INTO IT. WHAT'S THE--
DON'T.
--WHAT'S THE WORST--
DON'T!
DO NOT TEMPT FATE! YOU KNOW NOTHING GOOD EVER HAPPENS WHEN YOU SPEAK THAT PHRASE! I'M NOT KIDDING!
WHAT PHRASE?
YOU KNOW THE ONE. DON'T.
"WHAT'S THE WORST THAT COULD HAPPEN?"
OH, GOD.

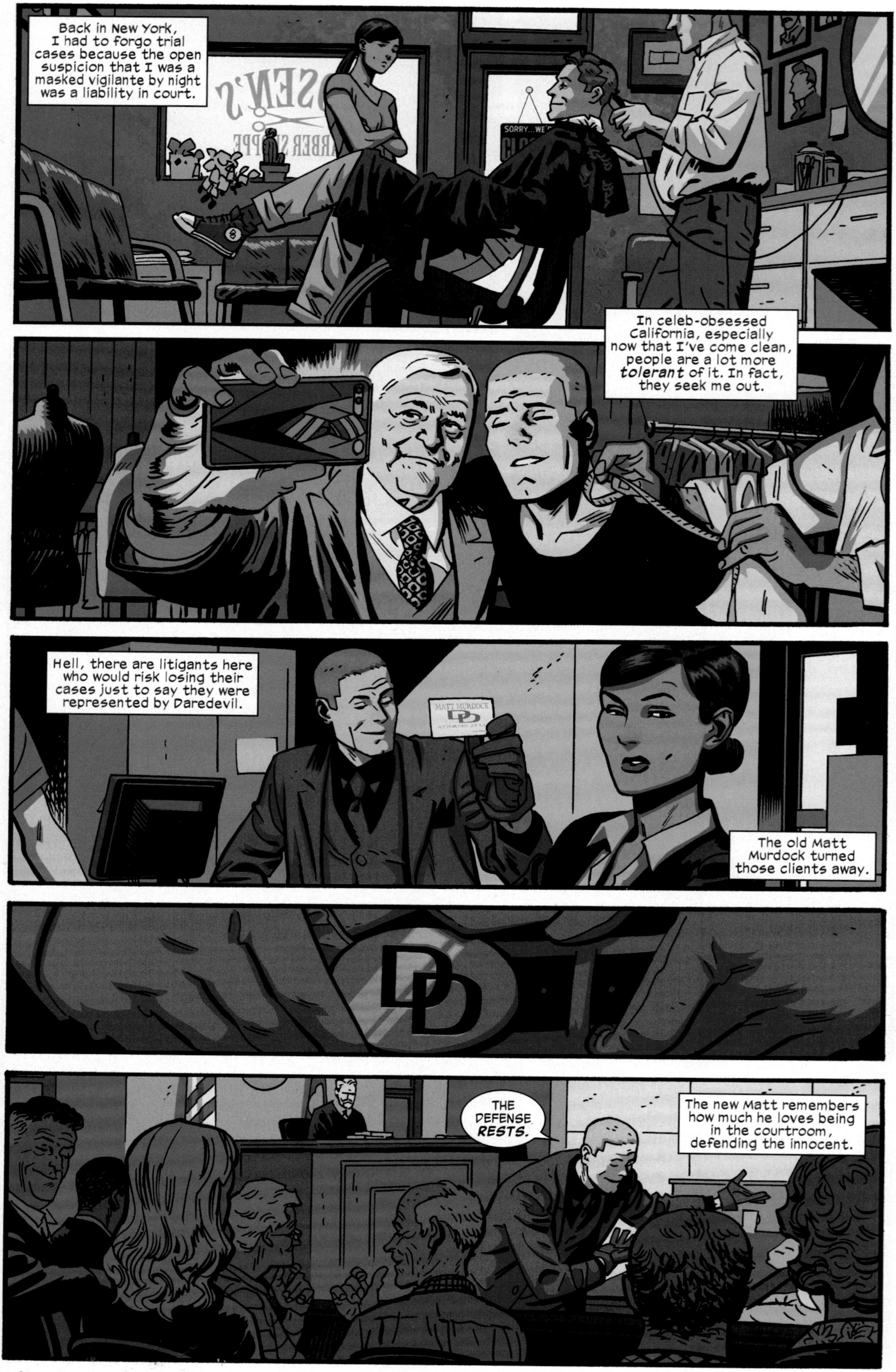
Back in New York, I had to forgo trial cases because the open suspicion that I was a masked vigilante by night was a liability in court.
In celeb-obsessed California, especially now that I've come clean, people are a lot more tolerant of it. In fact, they seek me out.
Hell, there are litigants here who would risk losing their cases just to say they were represented by Daredevil.
MATT MURDOCK
DD
The old Matt Murdock turned those clients away.
DD
THE DEFENSE RESTS.
The new Matt remembers how much he loves being in the courtroom, defending the innocent.

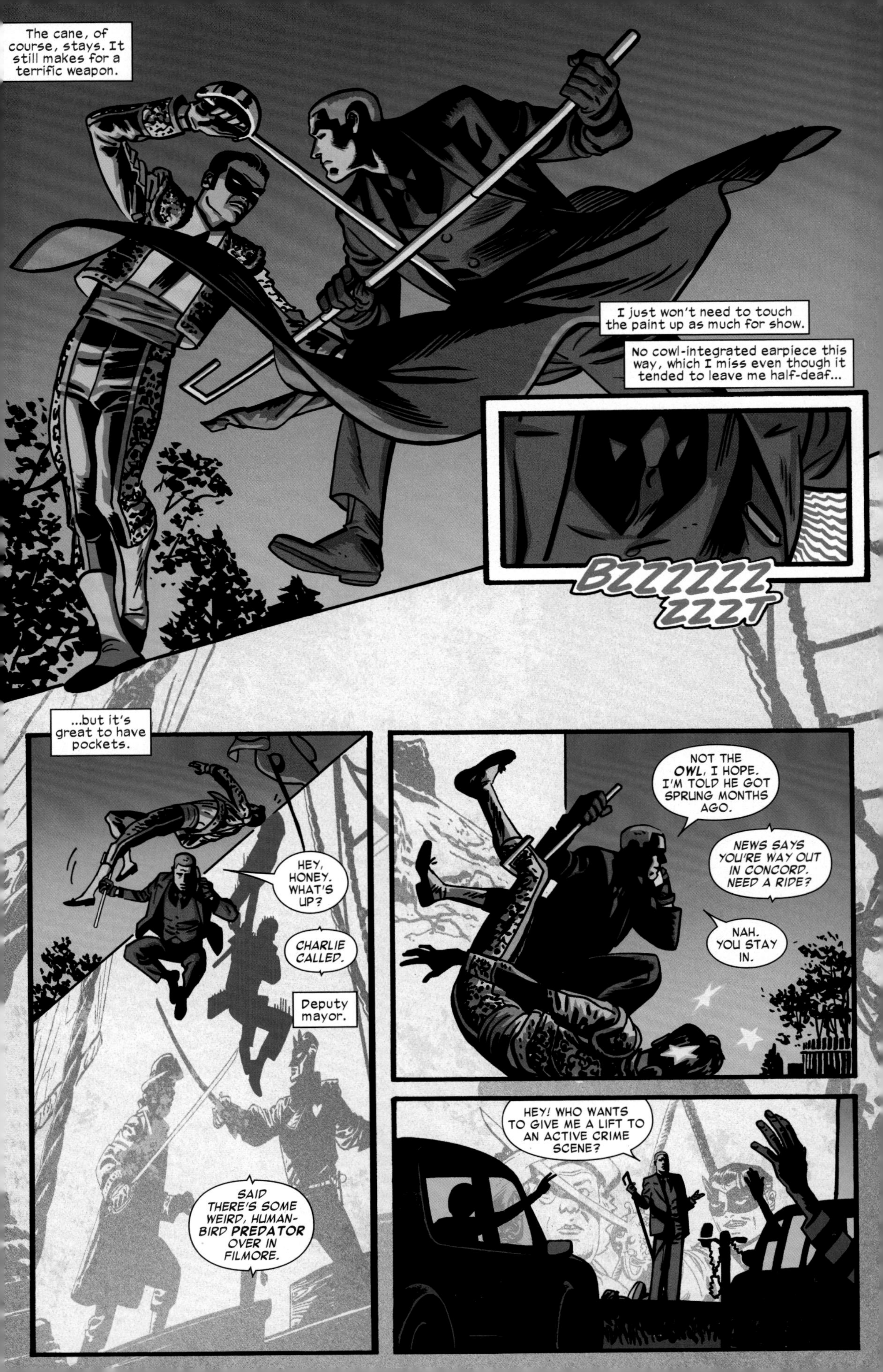

The cane, of course, stays. It still makes for a terrific weapon.
I just won't need to touch the paint up as much for show.
No cowl-integrated earpiece this way, which I miss even though it tended to leave me half-deaf...
BZZZZZZ ZZZT
...but it's great to have pockets.
HEY, HONEY. WHAT'S UP?
CHARLIE CALLED.
Deputy mayor.
SAID THERE'S SOME WEIRD, HUMAN-BIRD PREDATOR OVER IN FILMORE.
NOT THE OWL, I HOPE. I'M TOLD HE GOT SPRUNG MONTHS AGO.
NEWS SAYS YOU'RE WAY OUT IN CONCORD. NEED A RIDE?
NAH. YOU STAY IN.
HEY! WHO WANTS TO GIVE ME A LIFT TO AN ACTIVE CRIME SCENE?

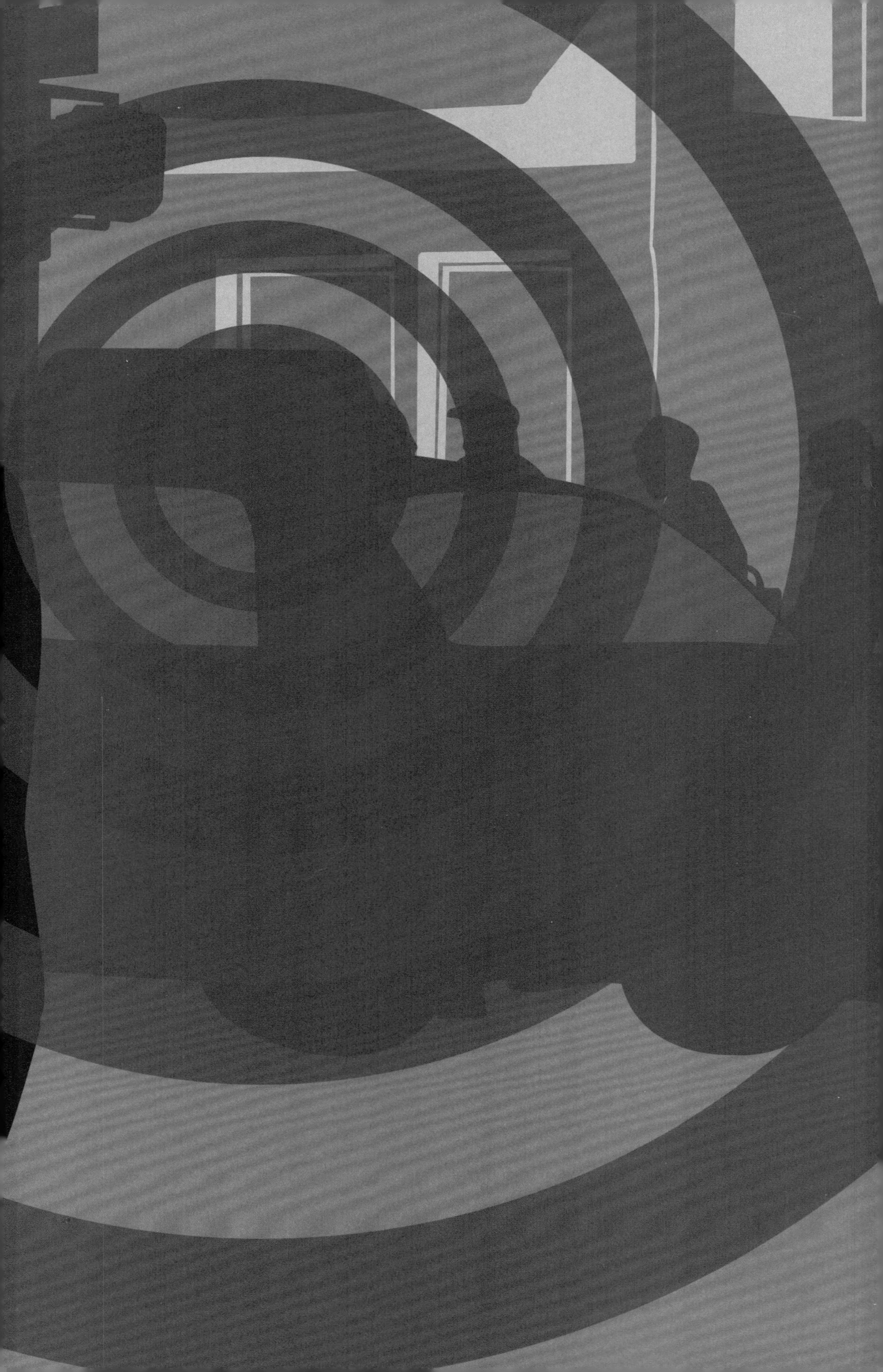

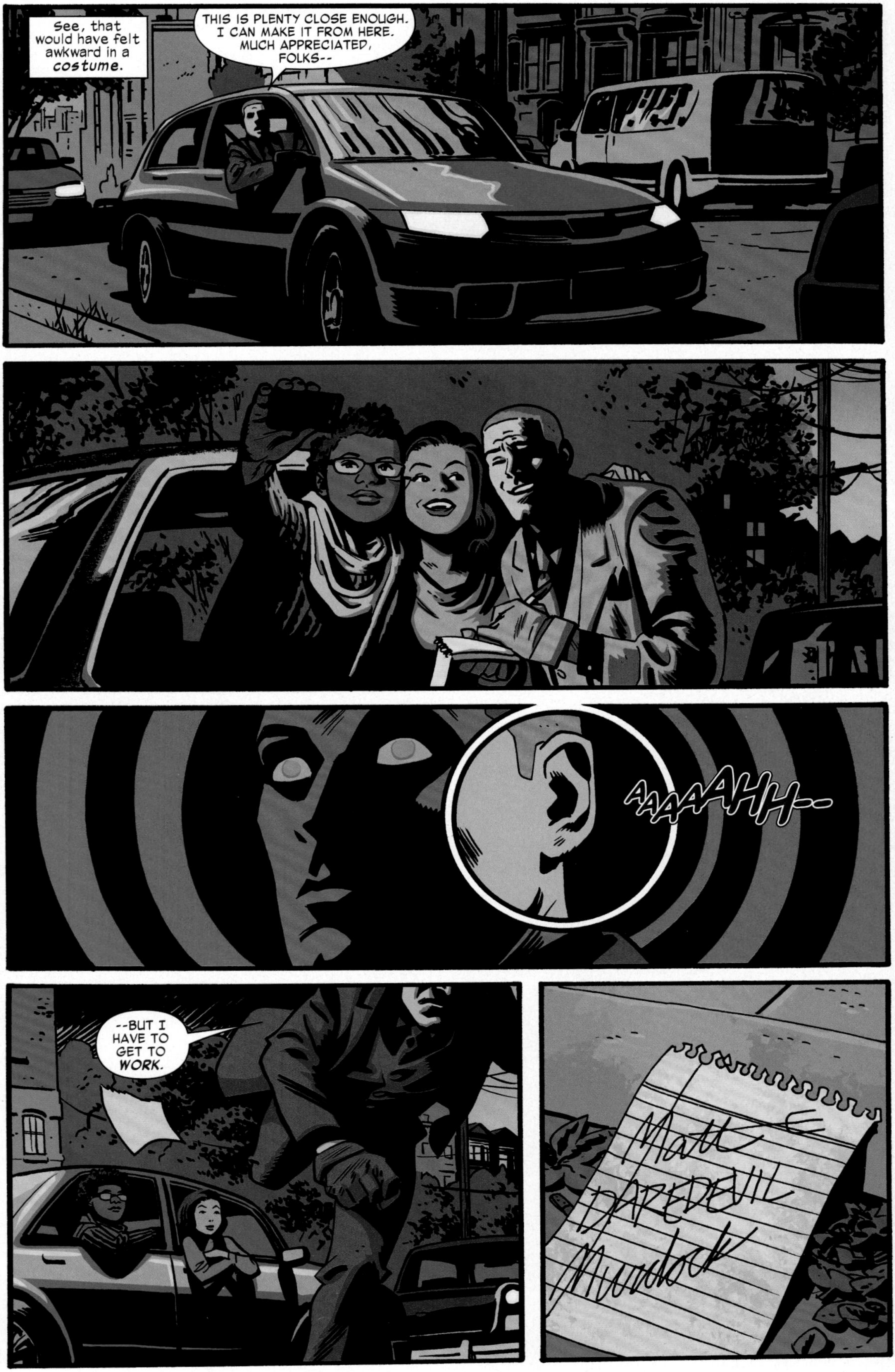

See, that would have felt awkward in a *costume*.
THIS IS PLENTY CLOSE ENOUGH. I CAN MAKE IT FROM HERE. MUCH APPRECIATED, FOLKS--
AAAAAHH--
--BUT I HAVE TO GET TO *WORK*.
Matt
DAREDEVIL
Murdock

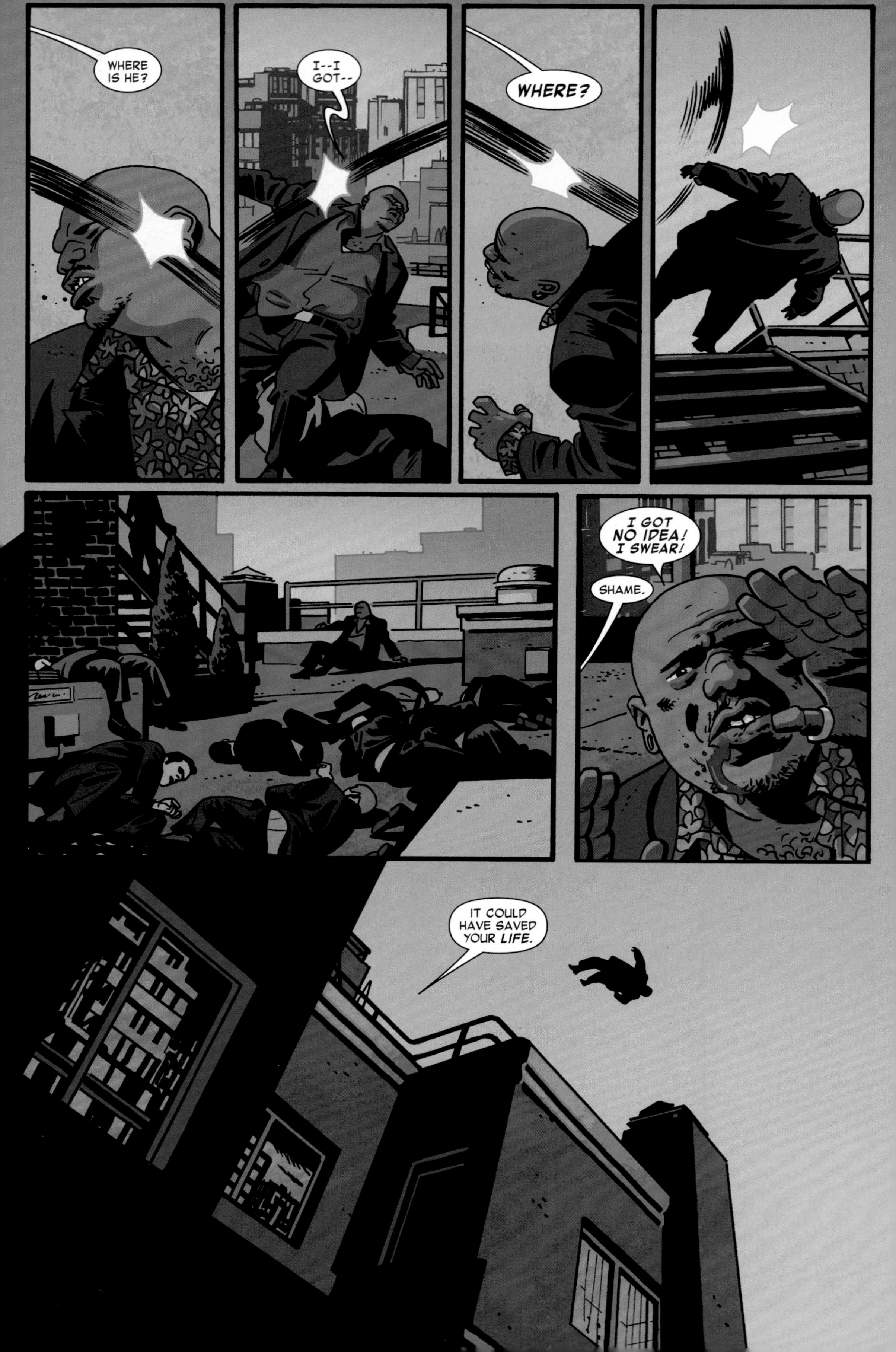
WHERE IS HE?
I--I GOT--
WHERE?
I GOT NO IDEA! I SWEAR!
SHAME.
IT COULD HAVE SAVED YOUR LIFE.

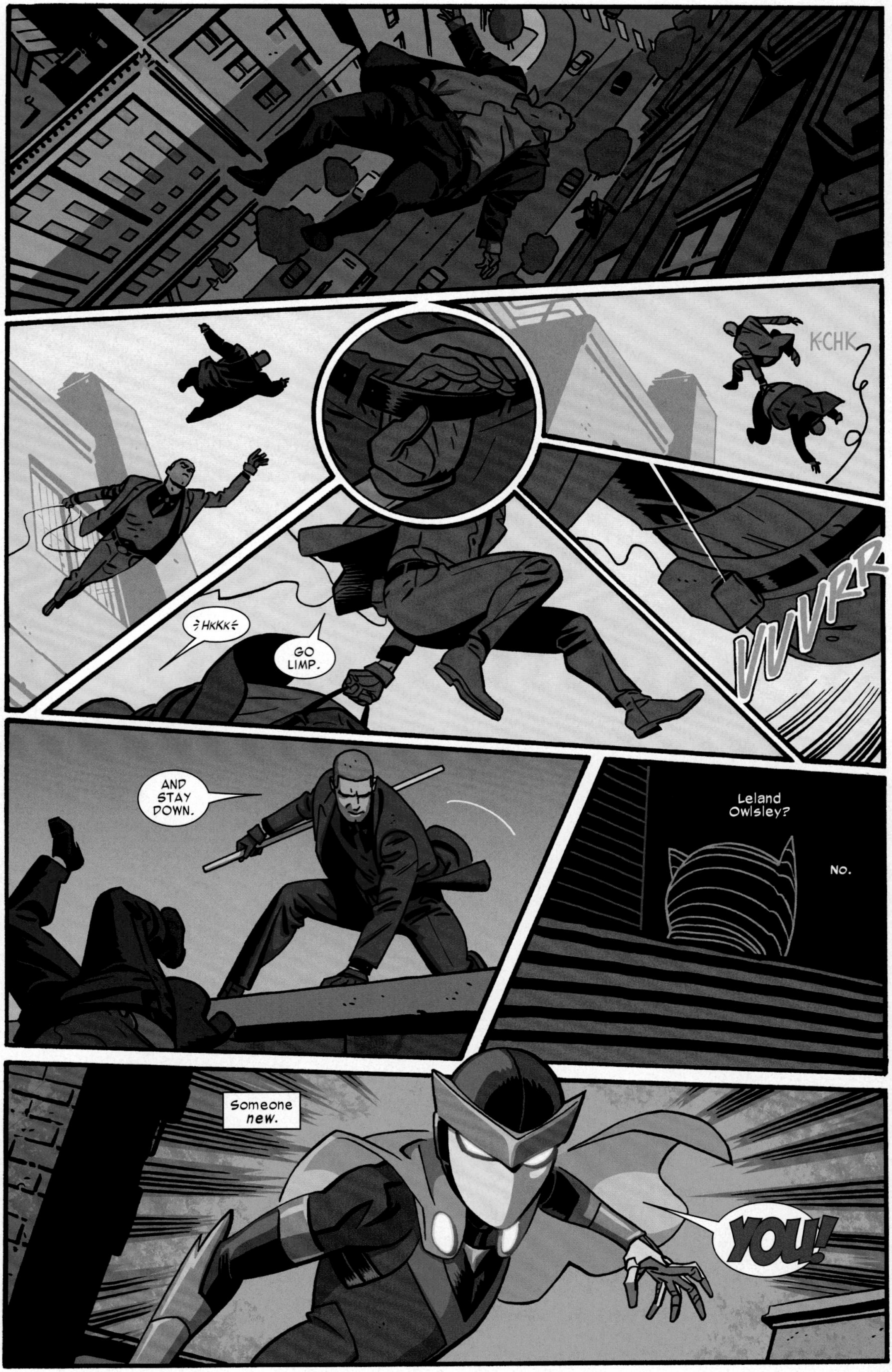
K-CHK
HKKK
GO LIMP.
VVVRR
AND STAY DOWN.
Leland Owlsley?
NO.
Someone new.
YOU!

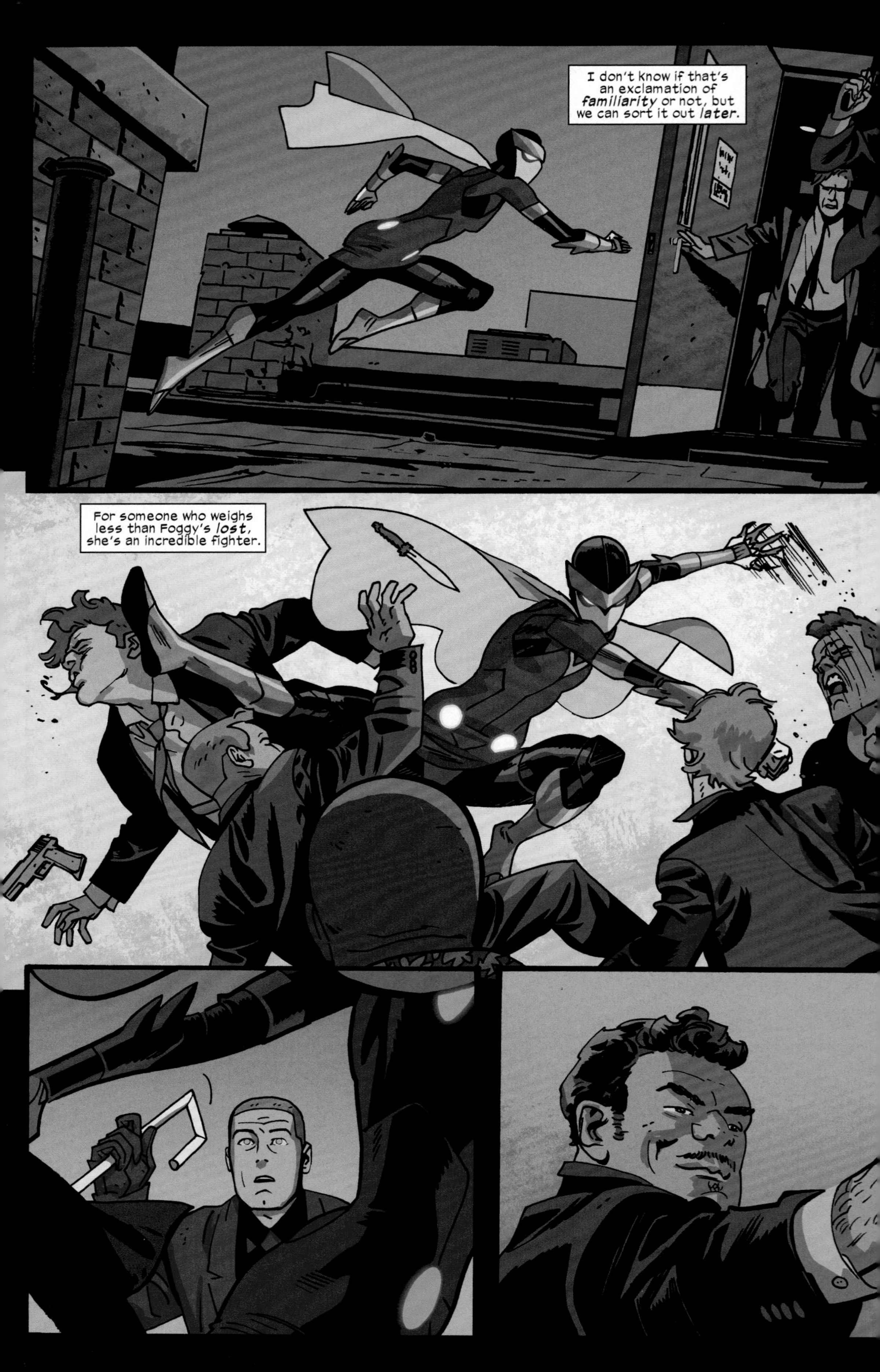
I don't know if that's an exclamation of familiarity or not, but we can sort it out later.
For someone who weighs less than Foggy's lost, she's an incredible fighter.

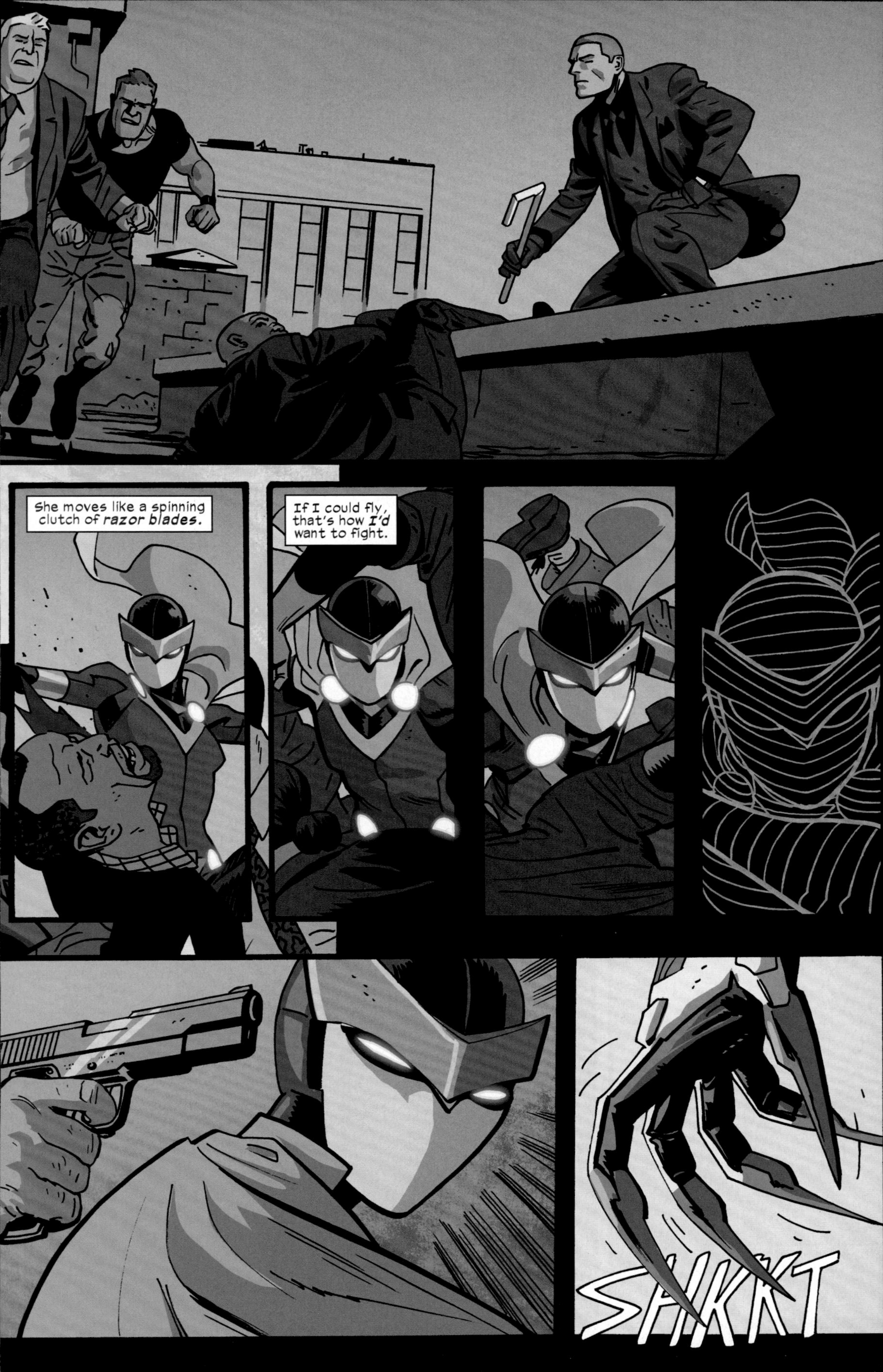
She moves like a spinning clutch of *razor blades*.
If I could fly, that's how *I'd* want to fight.
SHKKT

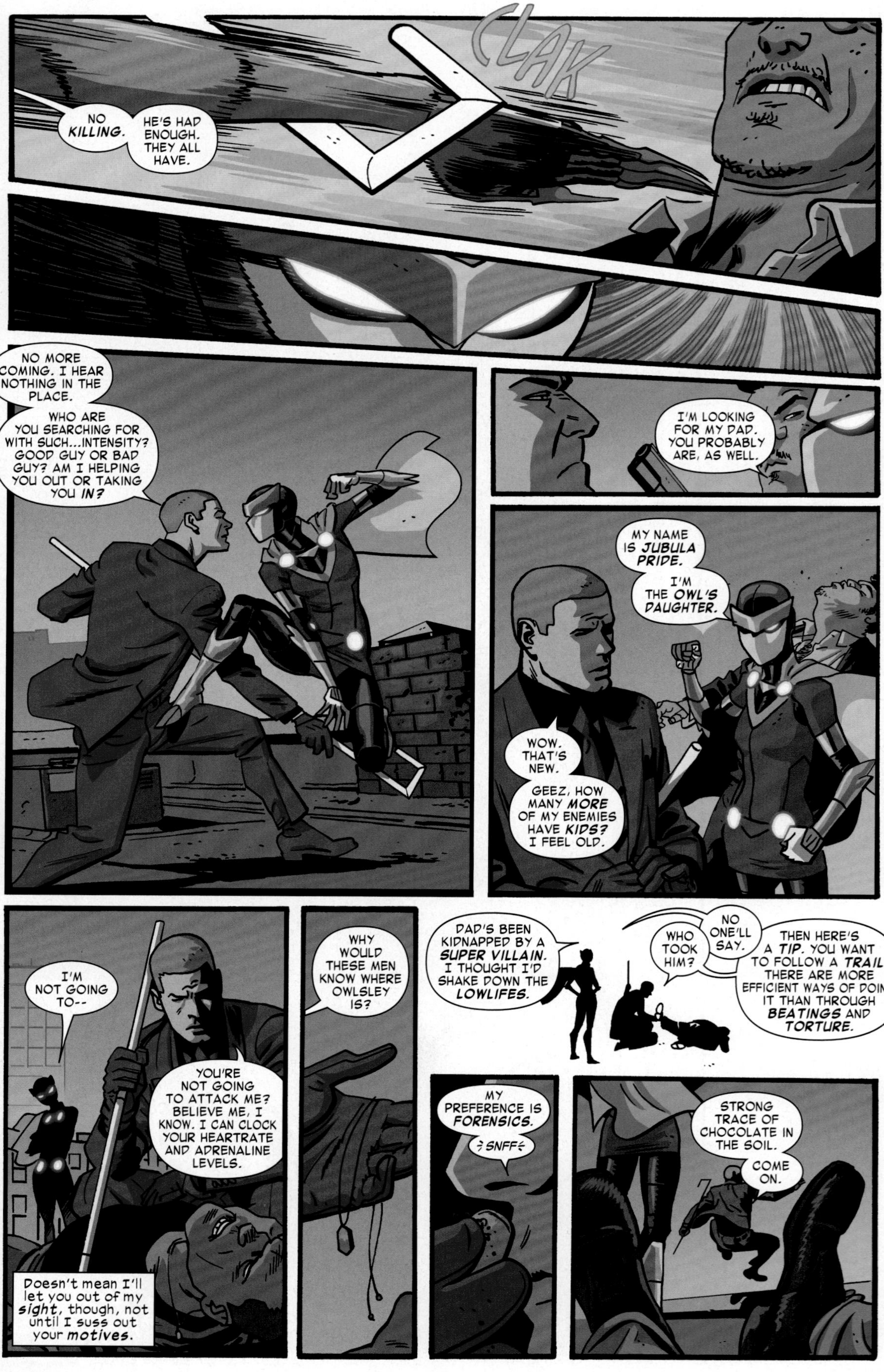
CLAK
NO KILLING.
HE'S HAD ENOUGH. THEY ALL HAVE.
NO MORE COMING. I HEAR NOTHING IN THE PLACE.
WHO ARE YOU SEARCHING FOR WITH SUCH...INTENSITY? GOOD GUY OR BAD GUY? AM I HELPING YOU OUT OR TAKING YOU IN?
I'M LOOKING FOR MY DAD. YOU PROBABLY ARE, AS WELL.
MY NAME IS JUBULA PRIDE.
I'M THE OWL'S DAUGHTER.
WOW. THAT'S NEW.
GEEZ, HOW MANY MORE OF MY ENEMIES HAVE KIDS? I FEEL OLD.
I'M NOT GOING TO--
YOU'RE NOT GOING TO ATTACK ME? BELIEVE ME, I KNOW. I CAN CLOCK YOUR HEARTRATE AND ADRENALINE LEVELS.
Doesn't mean I'll let you out of my sight, though, not until I suss out your motives.
WHY WOULD THESE MEN KNOW WHERE OWLSLEY IS?
DAD'S BEEN KIDNAPPED BY A SUPER VILLAIN. I THOUGHT I'D SHAKE DOWN THE LOWLIFES.
WHO TOOK HIM?
NO ONE'LL SAY.
THEN HERE'S A TIP. YOU WANT TO FOLLOW A TRAIL, THERE ARE MORE EFFICIENT WAYS OF DOING IT THAN THROUGH BEATINGS AND TORTURE.
MY PREFERENCE IS FORENSICS.
SNFF
STRONG TRACE OF CHOCOLATE IN THE SOIL.
COME ON.

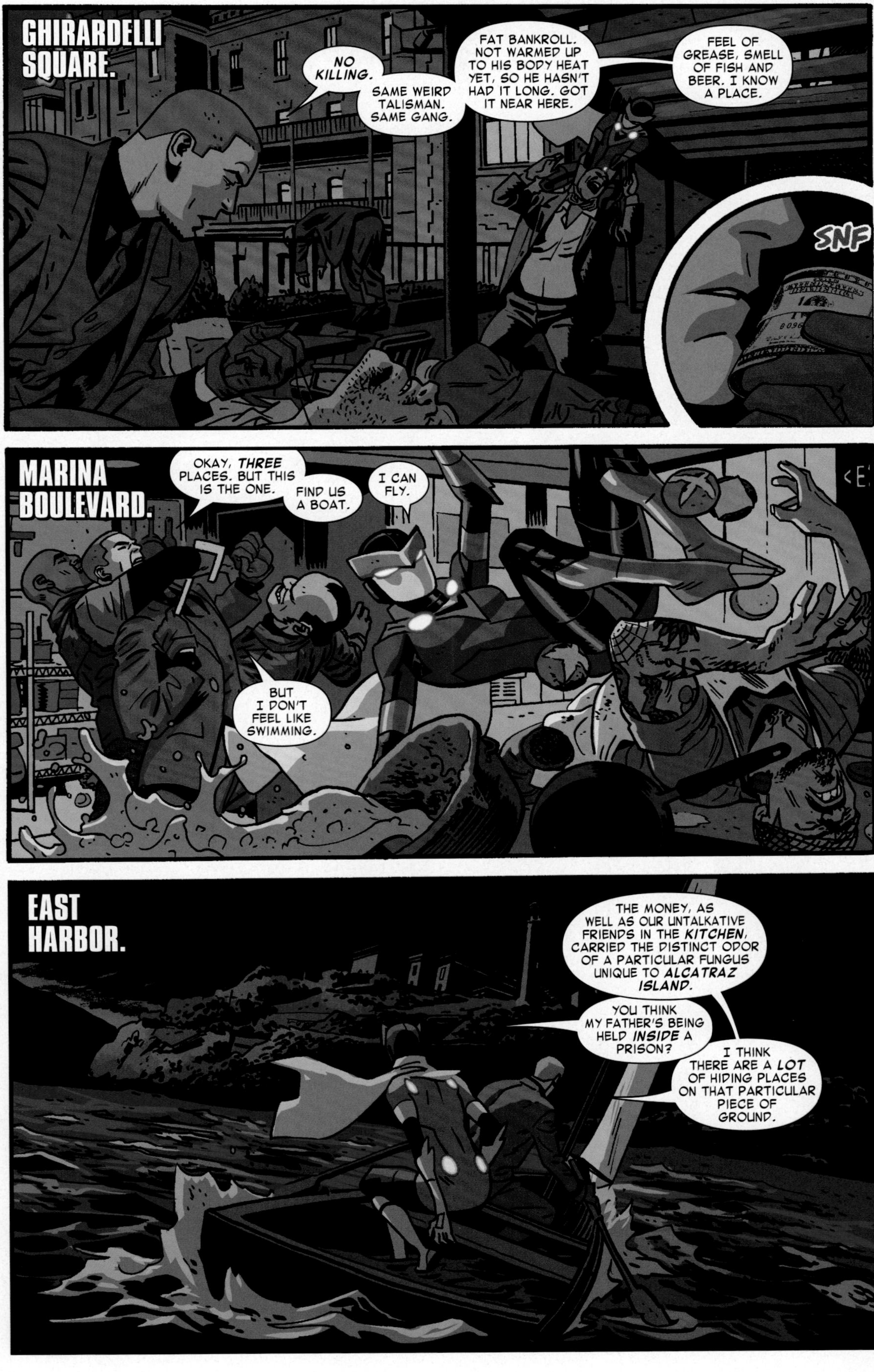
GHIRARDELLI SQUARE.
NO KILLING.
SAME WEIRD TALISMAN. SAME GANG.
FAT BANKROLL. NOT WARMED UP TO HIS BODY HEAT YET, SO HE HASN'T HAD IT LONG. GOT IT NEAR HERE.
FEEL OF GREASE, SMELL OF FISH AND BEER. I KNOW A PLACE.
SNF
MARINA BOULEVARD.
OKAY, THREE PLACES. BUT THIS IS THE ONE.
FIND US A BOAT.
I CAN FLY.
BUT I DON'T FEEL LIKE SWIMMING.
EAST HARBOR.
THE MONEY, AS WELL AS OUR UNTALKATIVE FRIENDS IN THE KITCHEN, CARRIED THE DISTINCT ODOR OF A PARTICULAR FUNGUS UNIQUE TO ALCATRAZ ISLAND.
YOU THINK MY FATHER'S BEING HELD INSIDE A PRISON?
I THINK THERE ARE A LOT OF HIDING PLACES ON THAT PARTICULAR PIECE OF GROUND.

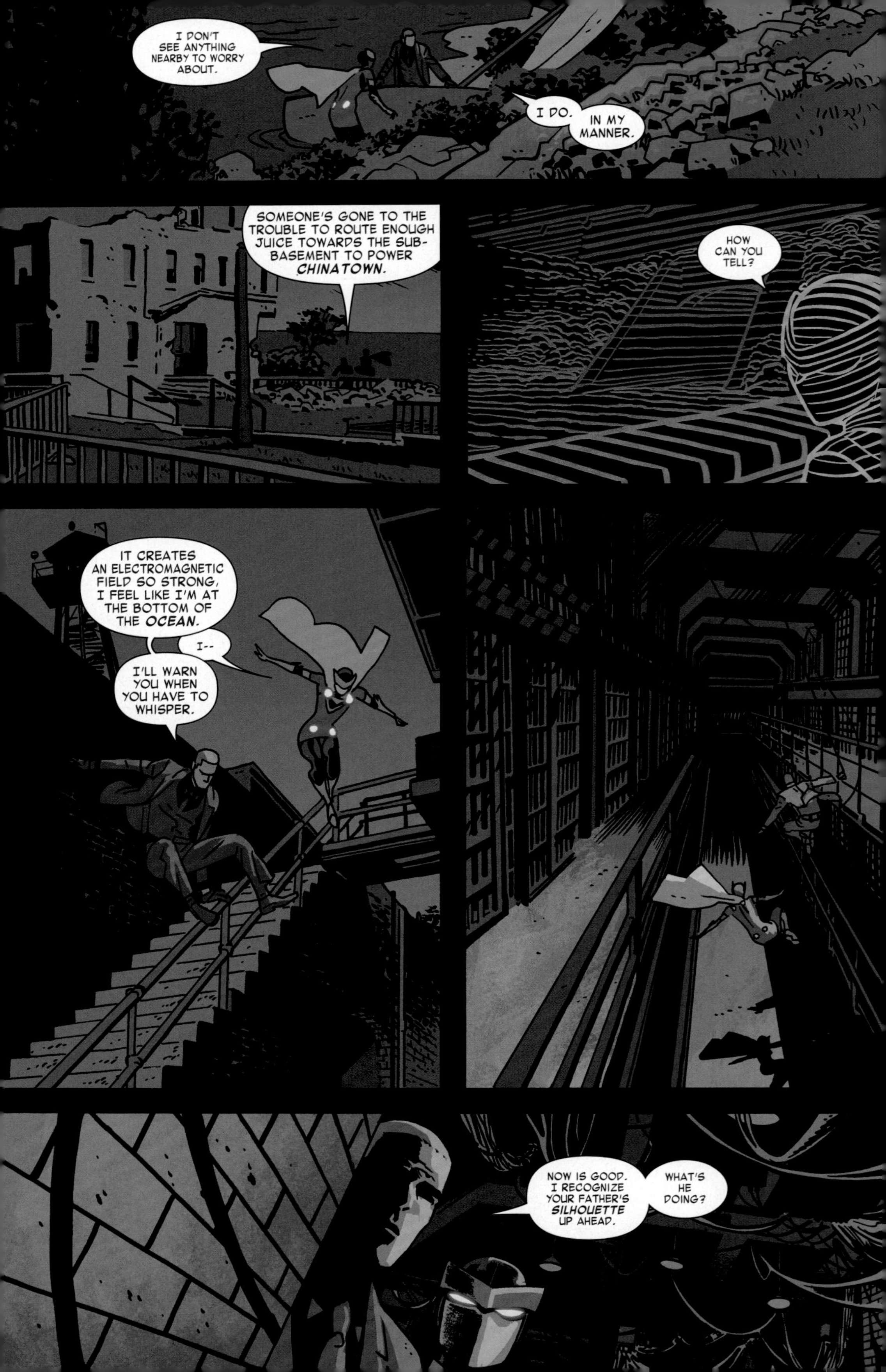
I DON'T SEE ANYTHING NEARBY TO WORRY ABOUT.
I DO.
IN MY MANNER.
SOMEONE'S GONE TO THE TROUBLE TO ROUTE ENOUGH JUICE TOWARDS THE SUB-BASEMENT TO POWER CHINATOWN.
HOW CAN YOU TELL?
IT CREATES AN ELECTROMAGNETIC FIELD SO STRONG, I FEEL LIKE I'M AT THE BOTTOM OF THE OCEAN.
I--
I'LL WARN YOU WHEN YOU HAVE TO WHISPER.
NOW IS GOOD. I RECOGNIZE YOUR FATHER'S SILHOUETTE UP AHEAD.
WHAT'S HE DOING?

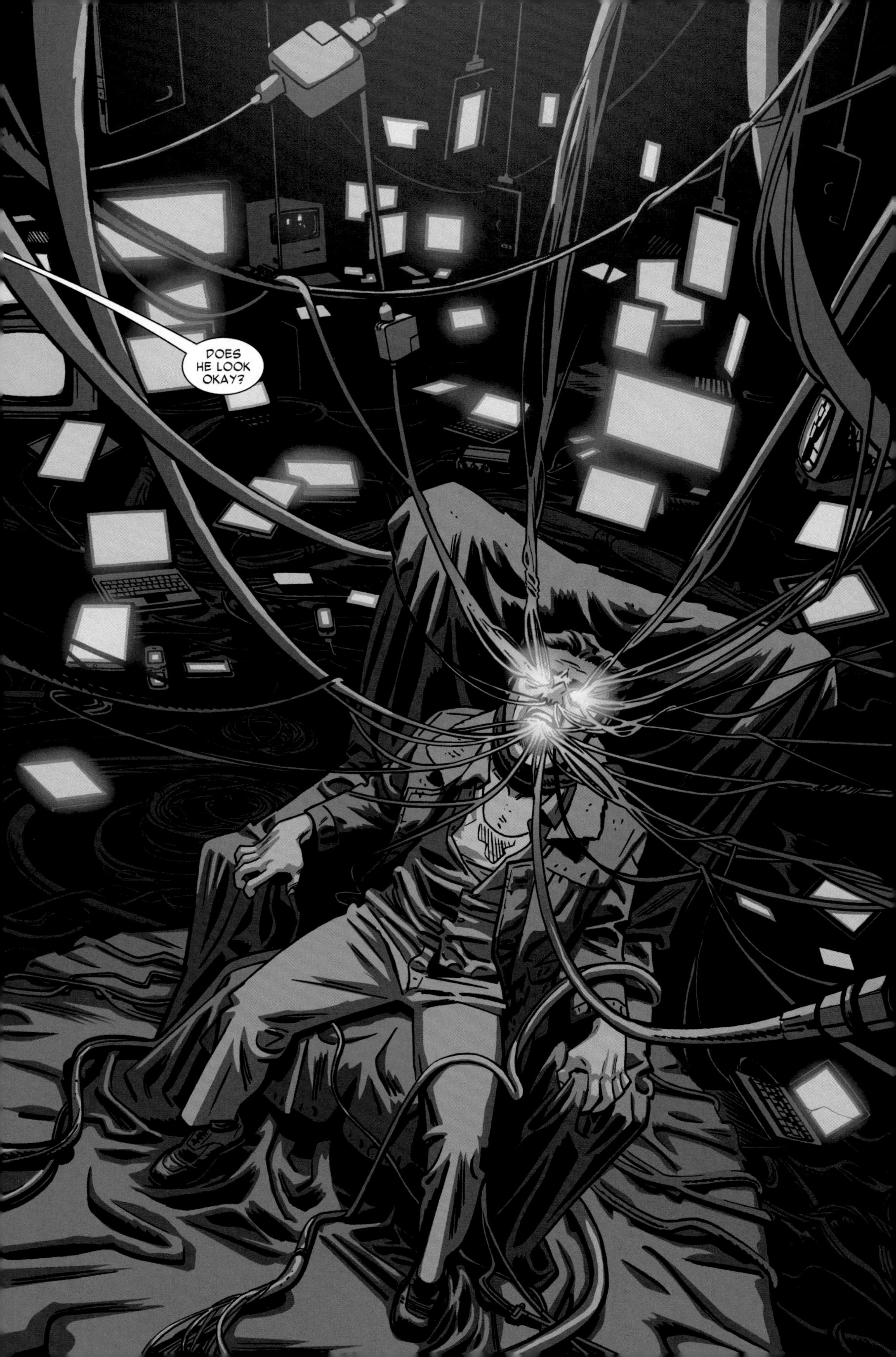
DOES HE LOOK OKAY?

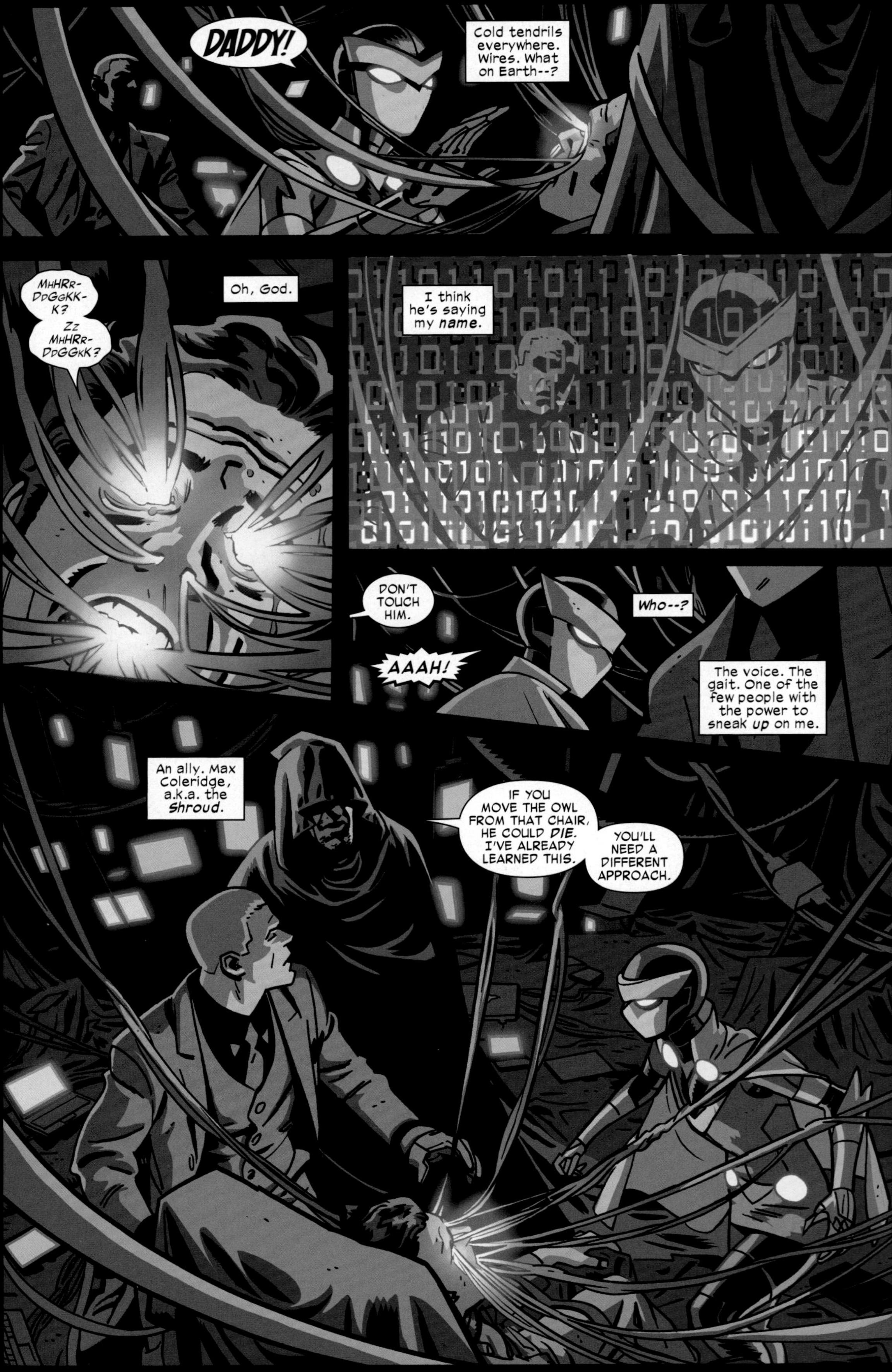
DADDY!
Cold tendrils everywhere. Wires. What on Earth--?
MHHRR-DDGGKK-K?
ZZ MHHRR-DDGGKK?
Oh, God.
I think he's saying my name.
DON'T TOUCH HIM.
AAAH!
Who--?
The voice. The gait. One of the few people with the power to sneak up on me.
An ally. Max Coleridge, a.k.a. the Shroud.
IF YOU MOVE THE OWL FROM THAT CHAIR, HE COULD DIE. I'VE ALREADY LEARNED THIS.
YOU'LL NEED A DIFFERENT APPROACH.

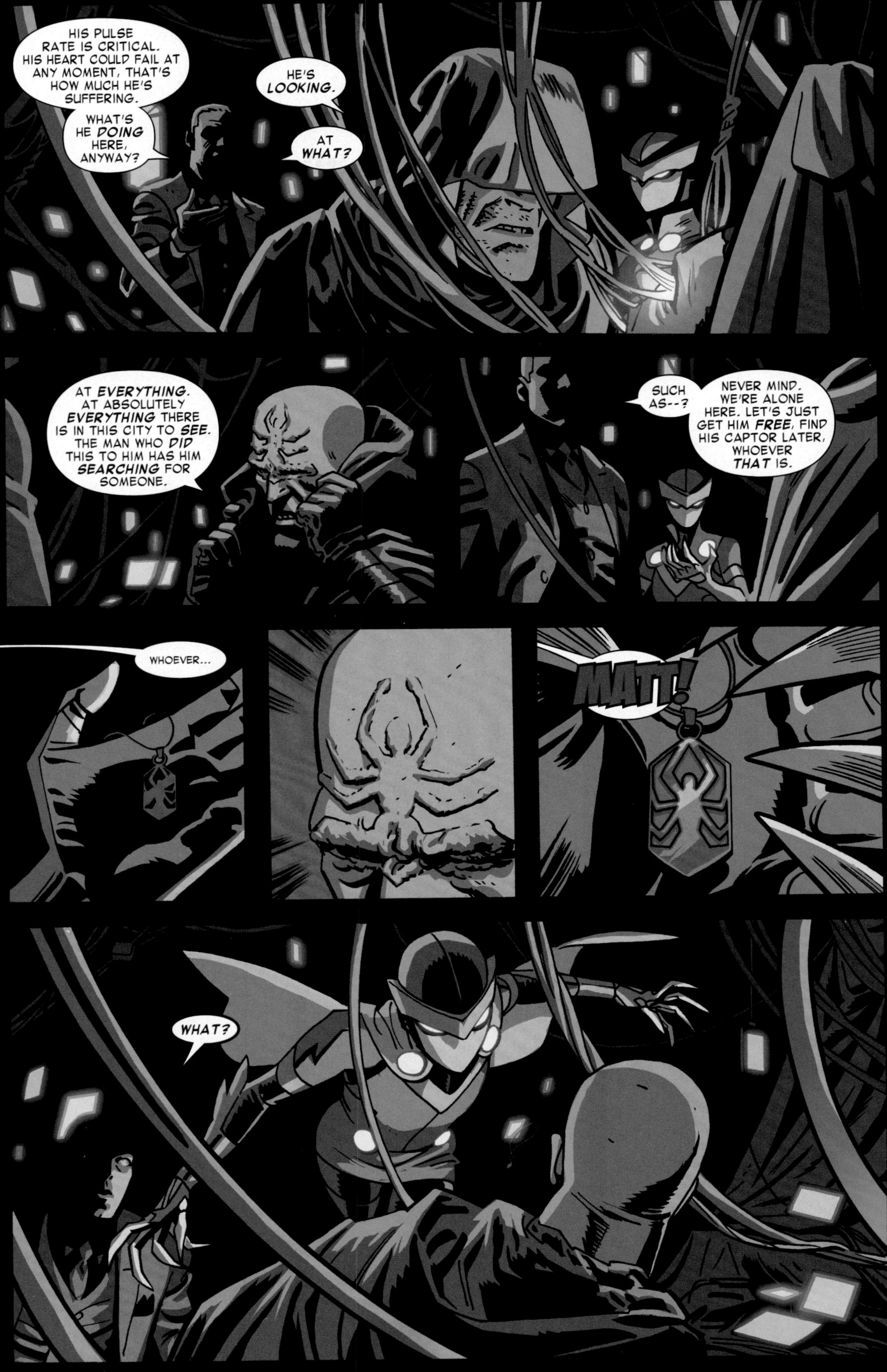
HIS PULSE RATE IS CRITICAL. HIS HEART COULD FAIL AT ANY MOMENT, THAT'S HOW MUCH HE'S SUFFERING.
WHAT'S HE *DOING* HERE, ANYWAY?
HE'S *LOOKING.*
AT *WHAT?*
AT *EVERYTHING.* AT ABSOLUTELY *EVERYTHING* THERE IS IN THIS CITY TO *SEE.* THE MAN WHO *DID* THIS TO HIM HAS HIM *SEARCHING* FOR SOMEONE.
SUCH AS--?
NEVER MIND. WE'RE ALONE HERE. LET'S JUST GET HIM *FREE*, FIND HIS CAPTOR LATER, WHOEVER *THAT* IS.
WHOEVER...
MATT!
WHAT?

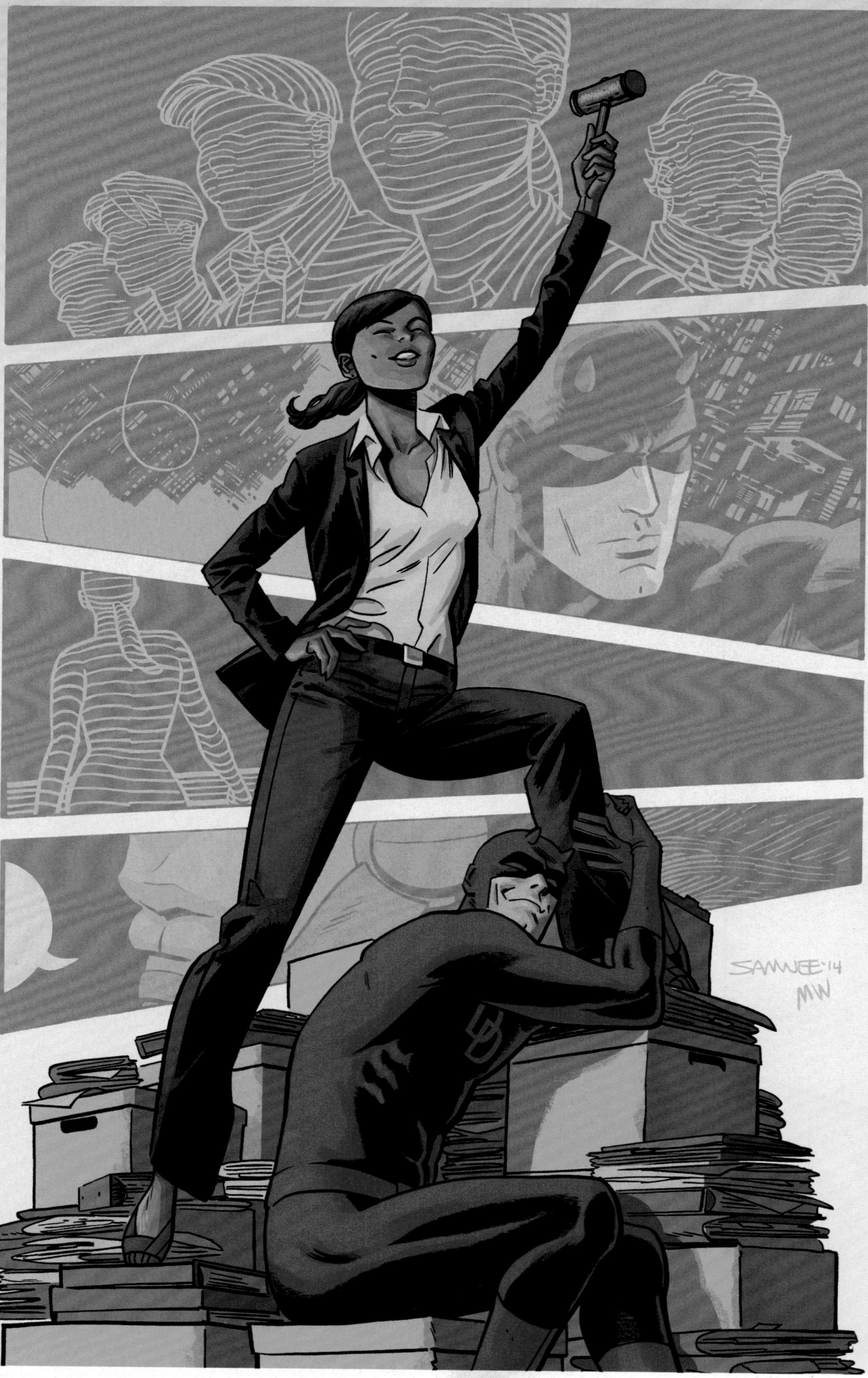
SAMNEE '14
MW

DAREDEVIL #15

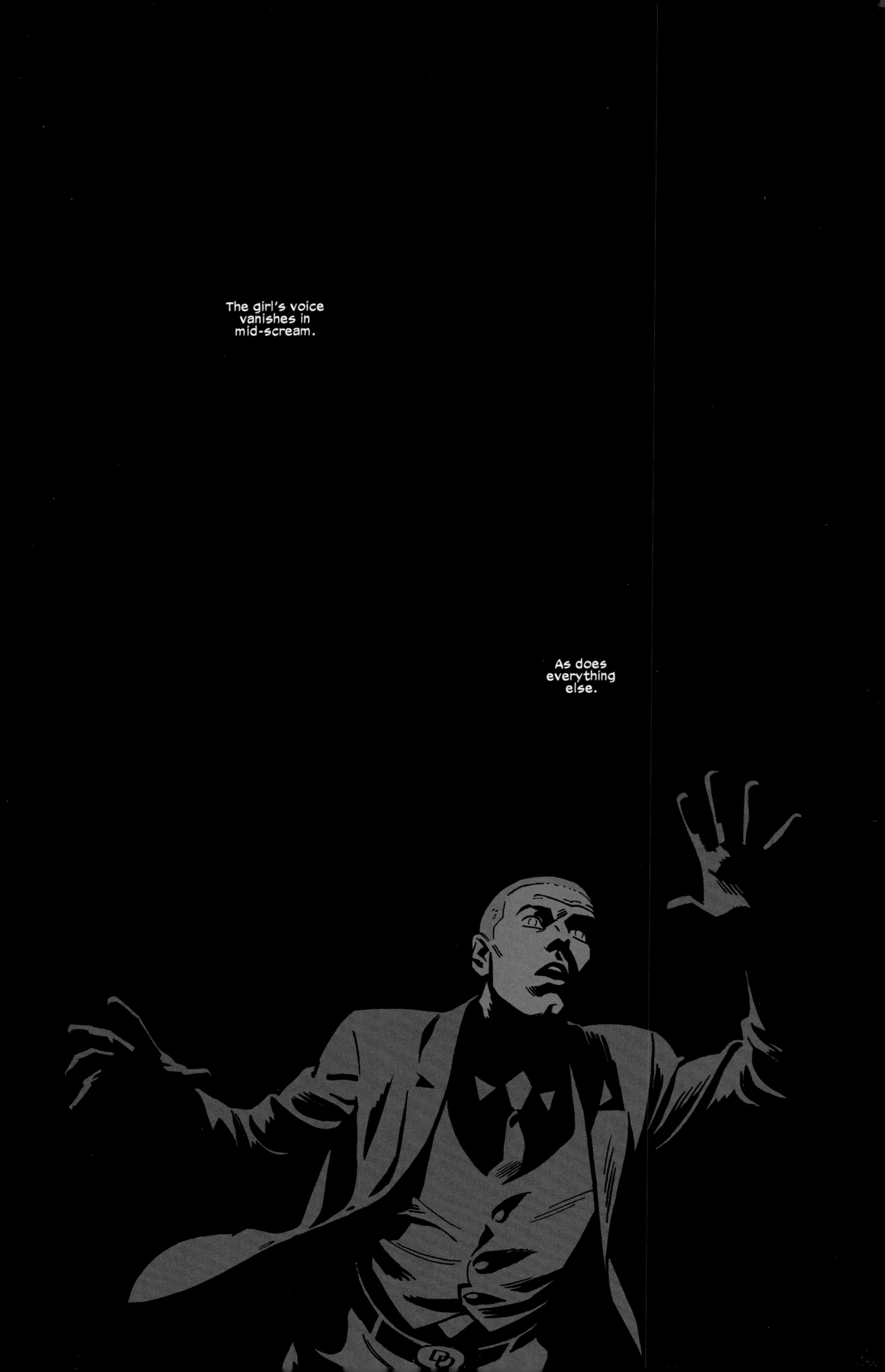
The girl's voice vanishes in mid-scream.
As does everything else.

Weightless.

Literally senseless.

And familiar.

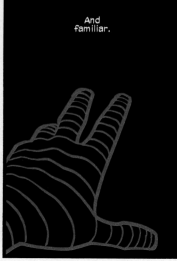

Captured by the *living shadows* of the *Shroud,* someone I thought was on *my* side.

I walked right into his trap.

Luckily for *me*--

GET M ATHER G--

--I didn't come in *alone.*

If Shroud was lying in wait for *Matt Murdock,* using the captive *Leland Owlsley* as *bait*--

--he hadn't counted on my bringing Owlsley's *daughter with* me.

--HAVE OU DONE TO HIM?

For all his mystic abilities, Shroud's not much of a *multitasker.*

As Jubula Pride rips *into* Shroud, she shatters his *focus*--

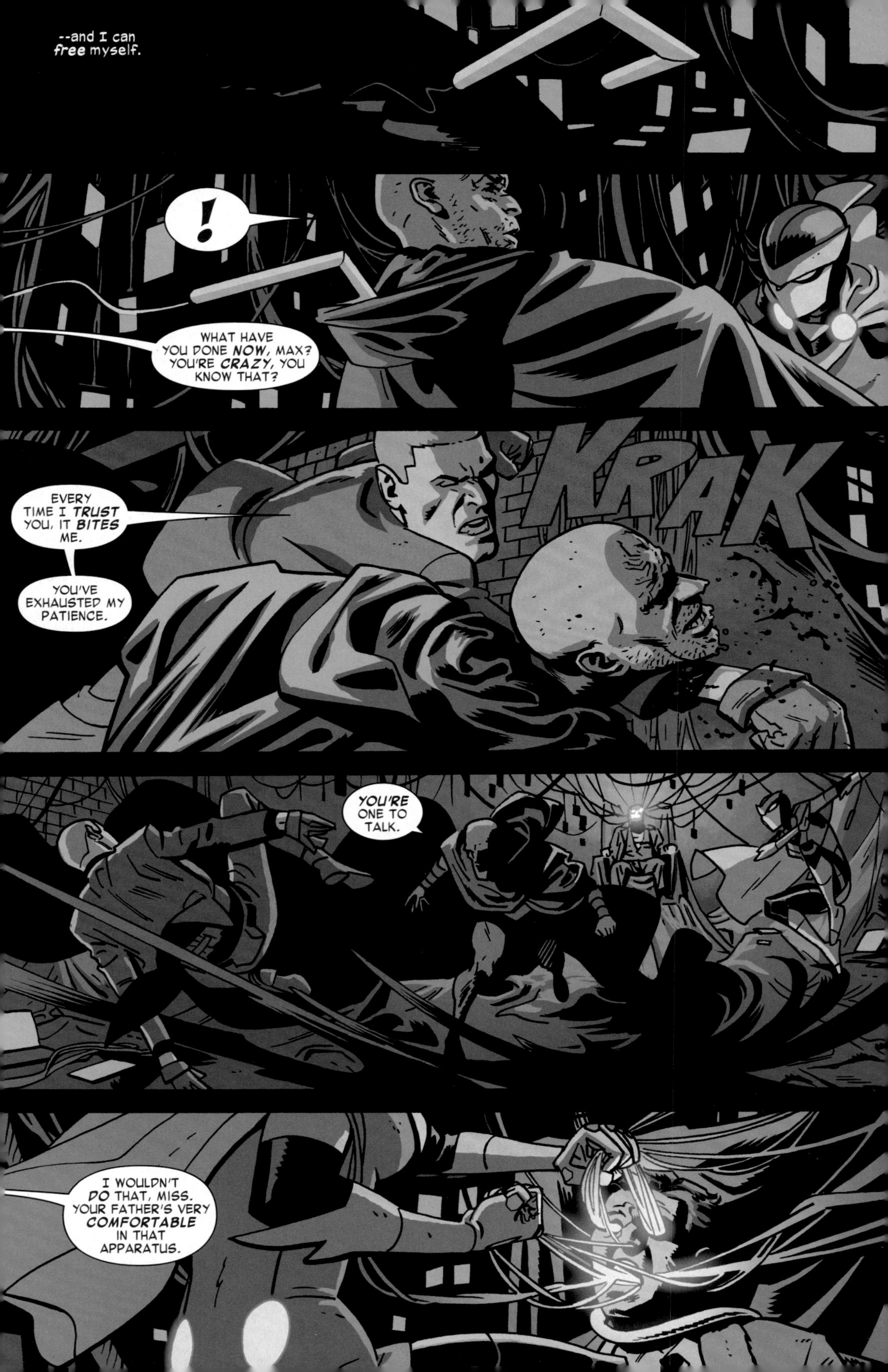
--and I can free myself.
!
WHAT HAVE YOU DONE NOW, MAX? YOU'RE CRAZY, YOU KNOW THAT?
KRAK
EVERY TIME I TRUST YOU, IT BITES ME.
YOU'VE EXHAUSTED MY PATIENCE.
YOU'RE ONE TO TALK.
I WOULDN'T DO THAT, MISS. YOUR FATHER'S VERY COMFORTABLE IN THAT APPARATUS.

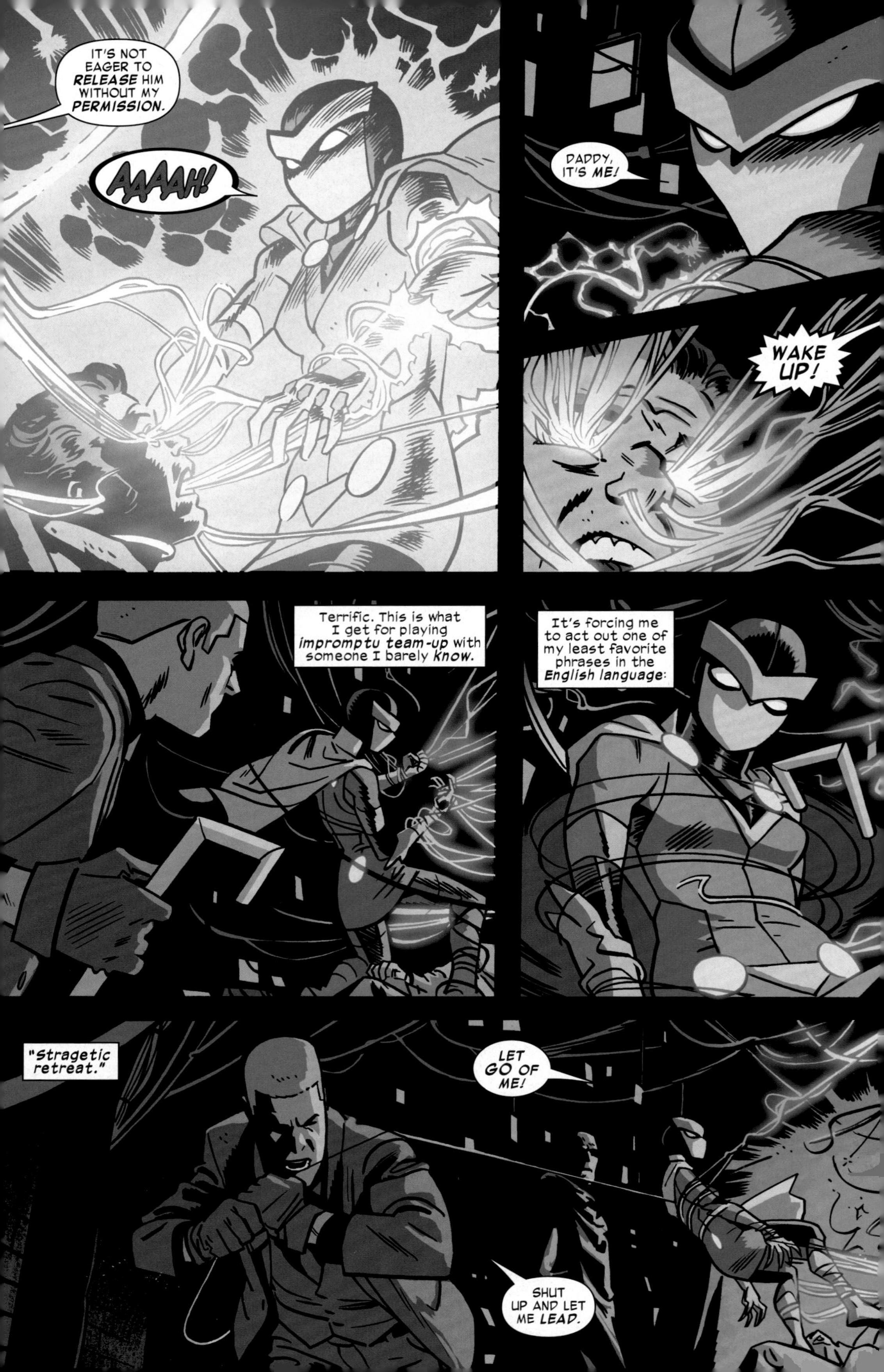
IT'S NOT EAGER TO RELEASE HIM WITHOUT MY PERMISSION.
AAAAH!
DADDY, IT'S ME!
WAKE UP!
Terrific. This is what I get for playing impromptu team-up with someone I barely know.
It's forcing me to act out one of my least favorite phrases in the English language:
"Stragetic retreat."
LET GO OF ME!
SHUT UP AND LET ME LEAD.

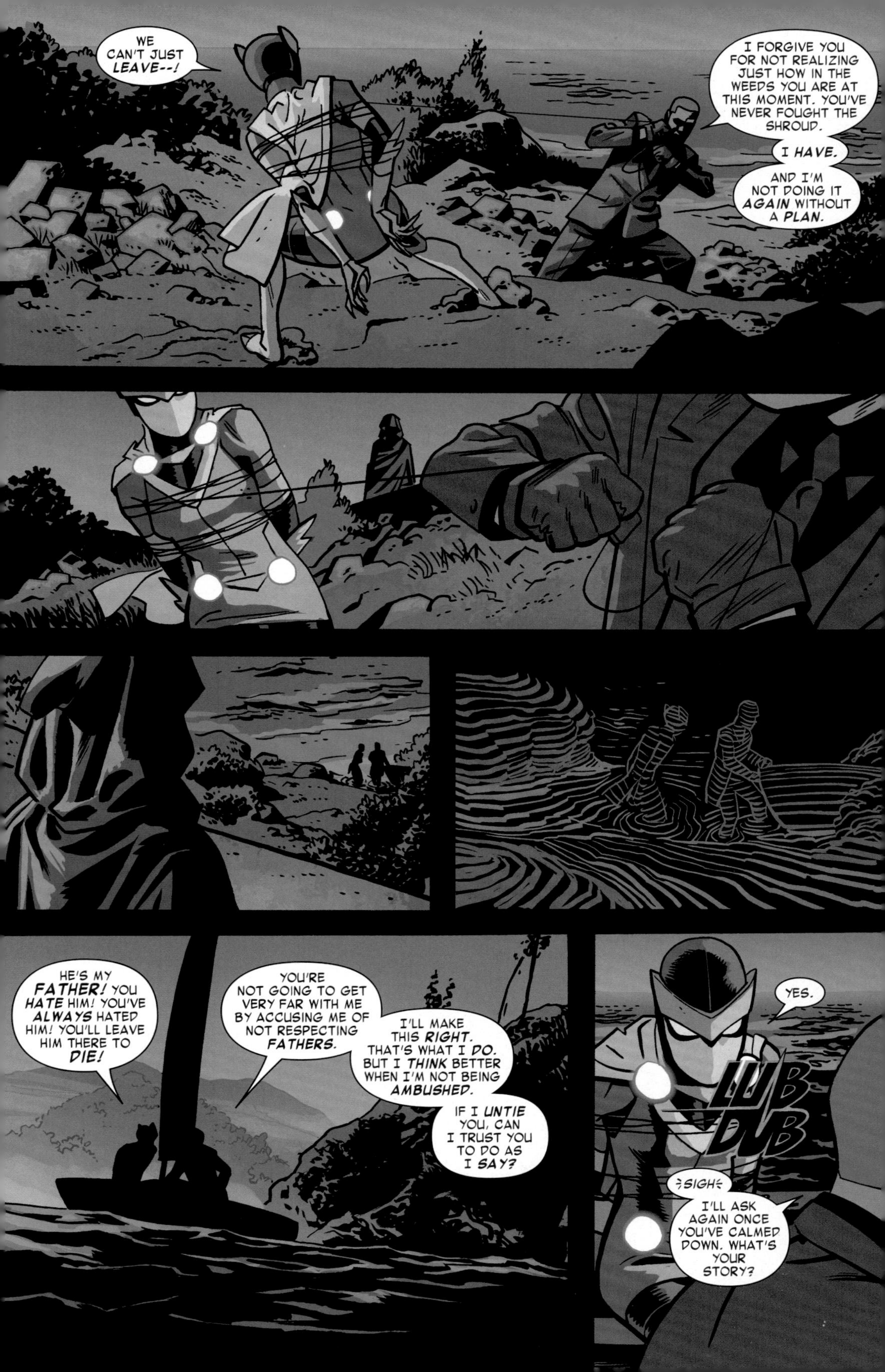
WE CAN'T JUST LEAVE--!
I FORGIVE YOU FOR NOT REALIZING JUST HOW IN THE WEEDS YOU ARE AT THIS MOMENT. YOU'VE NEVER FOUGHT THE SHROUD.
I HAVE.
AND I'M NOT DOING IT AGAIN WITHOUT A PLAN.
HE'S MY FATHER! YOU HATE HIM! YOU'VE ALWAYS HATED HIM! YOU'LL LEAVE HIM THERE TO DIE!
YOU'RE NOT GOING TO GET VERY FAR WITH ME BY ACCUSING ME OF NOT RESPECTING FATHERS.
I'LL MAKE THIS RIGHT. THAT'S WHAT I DO. BUT I THINK BETTER WHEN I'M NOT BEING AMBUSHED.
IF I UNTIE YOU, CAN I TRUST YOU TO DO AS I SAY?
YES.
LUB DUB
SIGH
I'LL ASK AGAIN ONCE YOU'VE CALMED DOWN. WHAT'S YOUR STORY?

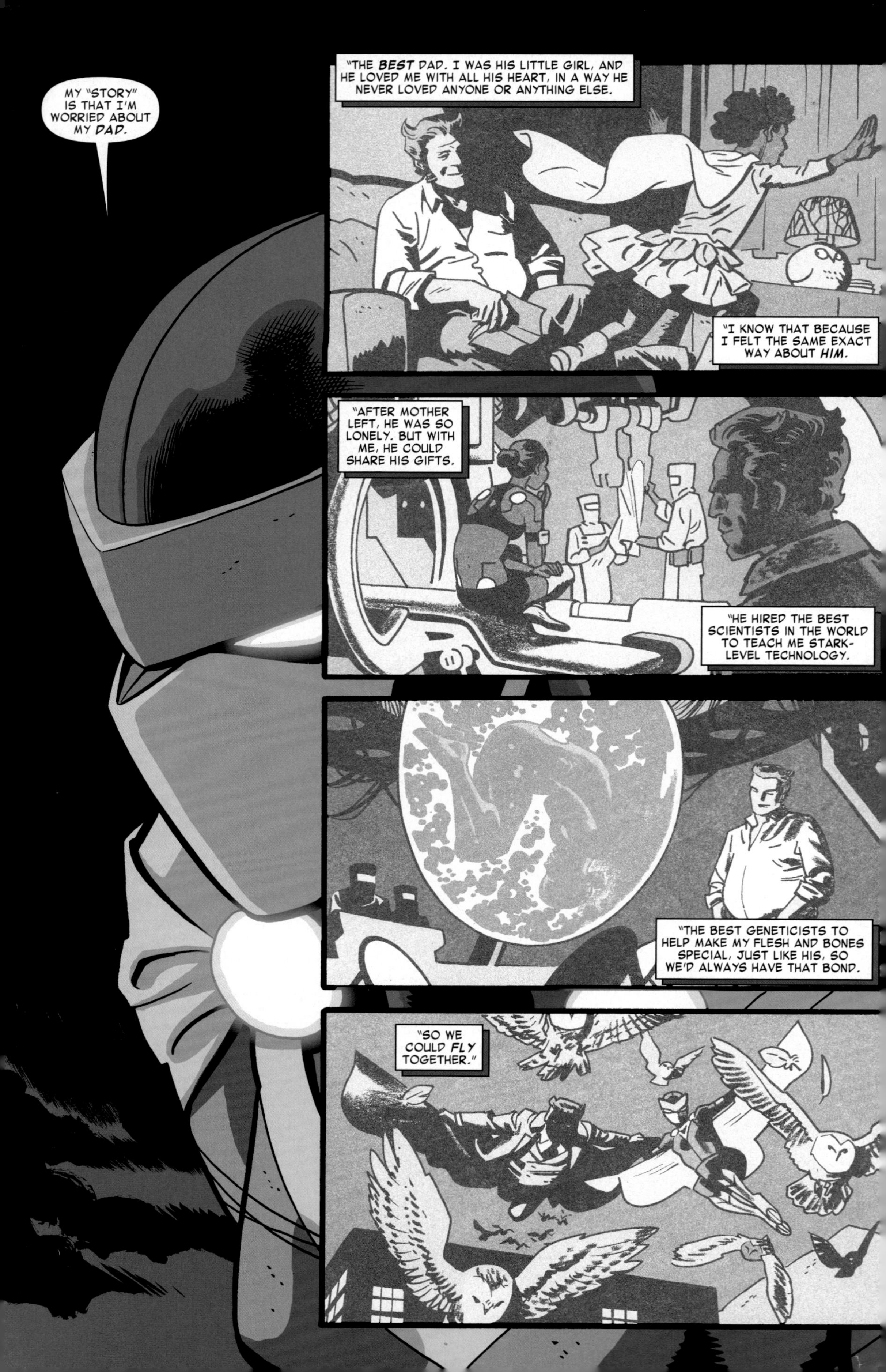
MY "STORY" IS THAT I'M WORRIED ABOUT MY DAD.
"THE BEST DAD. I WAS HIS LITTLE GIRL, AND HE LOVED ME WITH ALL HIS HEART, IN A WAY HE NEVER LOVED ANYONE OR ANYTHING ELSE.
"I KNOW THAT BECAUSE I FELT THE SAME EXACT WAY ABOUT HIM.
"AFTER MOTHER LEFT, HE WAS SO LONELY. BUT WITH ME, HE COULD SHARE HIS GIFTS.
"HE HIRED THE BEST SCIENTISTS IN THE WORLD TO TEACH ME STARK-LEVEL TECHNOLOGY.
"THE BEST GENETICISTS TO HELP MAKE MY FLESH AND BONES SPECIAL, JUST LIKE HIS, SO WE'D ALWAYS HAVE THAT BOND.
"SO WE COULD FLY TOGETHER."

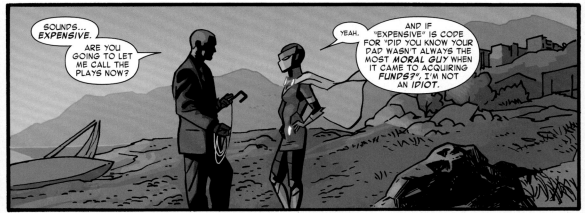

SOUNDS... *EXPENSIVE.* ARE YOU GOING TO LET ME CALL THE PLAYS NOW?

YEAH. AND IF *"EXPENSIVE"* IS CODE FOR *"DID YOU KNOW YOUR DAD WASN'T ALWAYS THE MOST MORAL GUY WHEN IT CAME TO ACQUIRING FUNDS?"*, I'M NOT AN *IDIOT.*

IT'S NO SECRET WHERE--

FIND A *CAB.* WE'LL GO TO MY *OFFICE.*

--IT'S NO SECRET WHERE MY DAD FALLS ON THE *F.B.I.* LISTS. ALL THAT MATTERS TO ME IS THAT HE WAS *GOOD* TO ME. *PROUD* OF ME.

chk

IF HE WAS SO *PROUD,* HOW COME I'VE NEVER HEARD OF YOU BEFORE TONIGHT?

WHY WOULD HE WANT *ANYONE* TO KNOW EVERY DETAIL OF HIS *PERSONAL LIFE?* WHAT KIND OF MORON WOULD GIVE THAT KIND OF LEVERAGE TO HIS *ENEMIES?*

NO OFFENSE.

MUCH TAKEN.

HE CERTAINLY WASN'T STINGY WITH THE *CONFIDENCE* HE GAVE YOU. WAS YOUR DAD THE ONE WHO TAUGHT YOU HOW TO FIGHT?

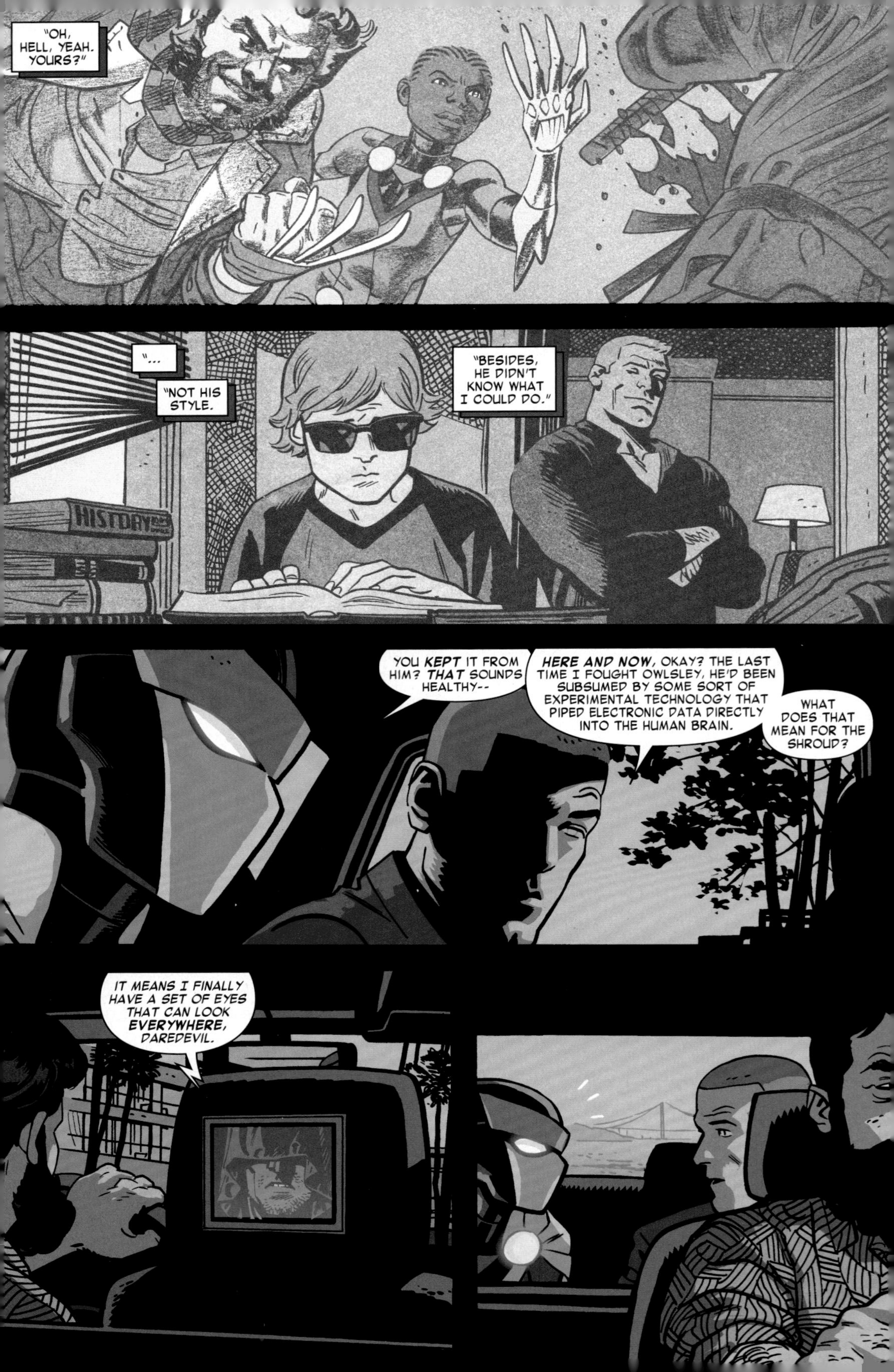
"OH, HELL, YEAH. YOURS?"
"...
"NOT HIS STYLE.
"BESIDES, HE DIDN'T KNOW WHAT I COULD DO."
HISTORY
YOU KEPT IT FROM HIM? THAT SOUNDS HEALTHY--
HERE AND NOW, OKAY? THE LAST TIME I FOUGHT OWLSLEY, HE'D BEEN SUBSUMED BY SOME SORT OF EXPERIMENTAL TECHNOLOGY THAT PIPED ELECTRONIC DATA DIRECTLY INTO THE HUMAN BRAIN.
WHAT DOES THAT MEAN FOR THE SHROUD?
IT MEANS I FINALLY HAVE A SET OF EYES THAT CAN LOOK EVERYWHERE, DAREDEVIL.

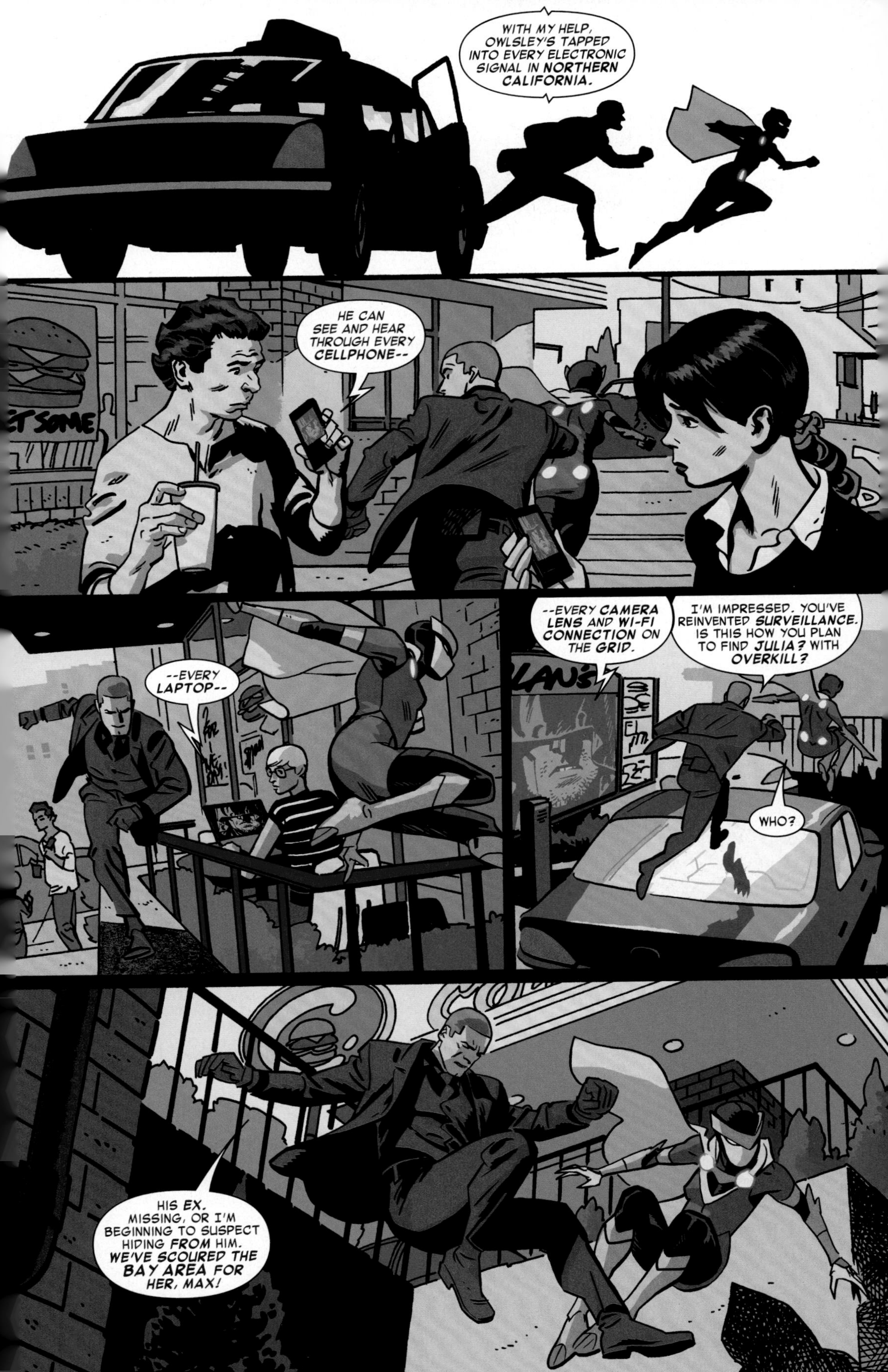
WITH MY HELP, OWLSLEY'S TAPPED INTO EVERY ELECTRONIC SIGNAL IN NORTHERN CALIFORNIA.
HE CAN SEE AND HEAR THROUGH EVERY CELLPHONE--
--EVERY LAPTOP--
--EVERY CAMERA LENS AND WI-FI CONNECTION ON THE GRID.
I'M IMPRESSED. YOU'VE REINVENTED SURVEILLANCE. IS THIS HOW YOU PLAN TO FIND JULIA? WITH OVERKILL?
WHO?
HIS EX. MISSING, OR I'M BEGINNING TO SUSPECT HIDING FROM HIM. WE'VE SCOURED THE BAY AREA FOR HER, MAX!

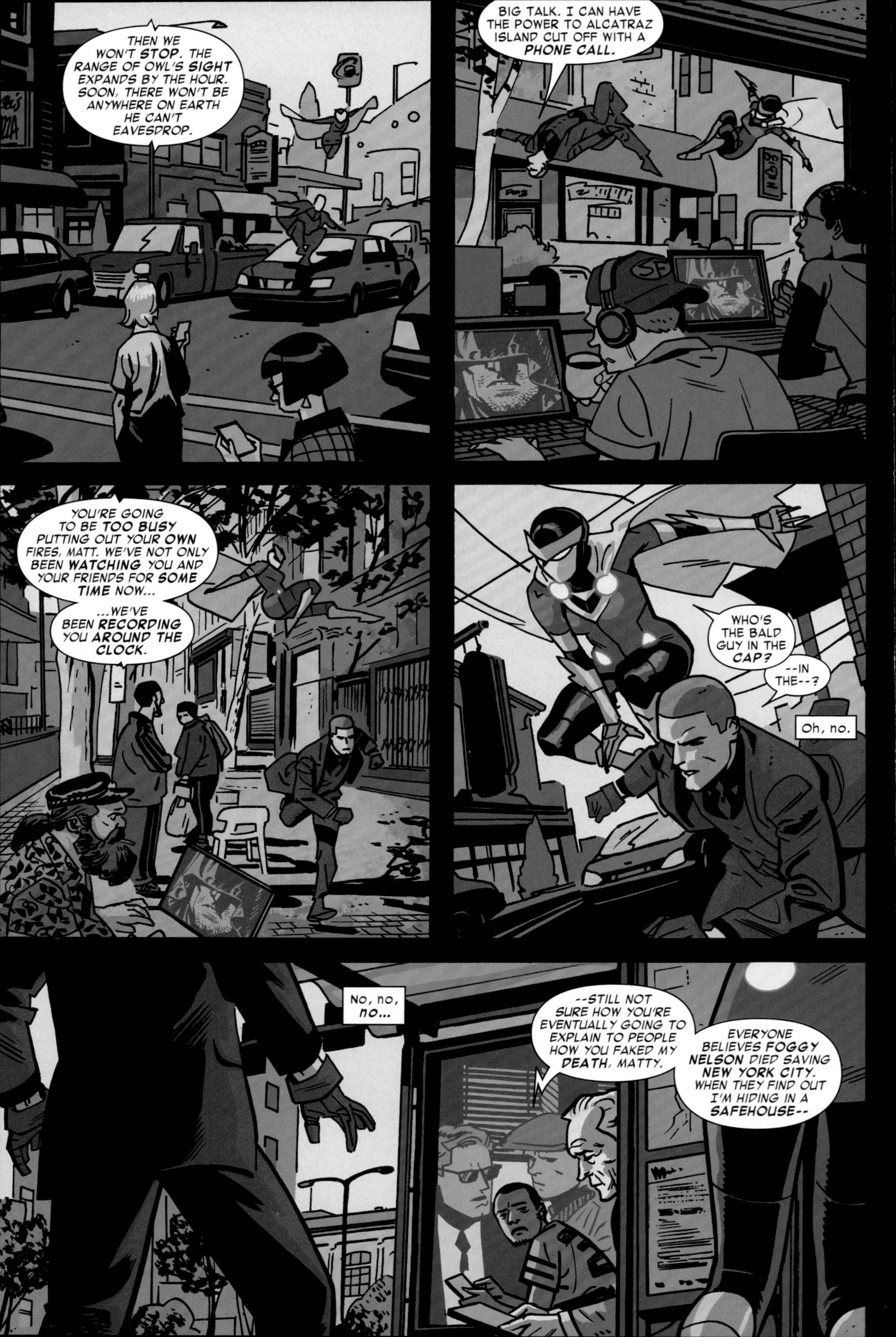
THEN WE WON'T STOP. THE RANGE OF OWL'S SIGHT EXPANDS BY THE HOUR. SOON, THERE WON'T BE ANYWHERE ON EARTH HE CAN'T EAVESDROP.
BIG TALK. I CAN HAVE THE POWER TO ALCATRAZ ISLAND CUT OFF WITH A PHONE CALL.
YOU'RE GOING TO BE TOO BUSY PUTTING OUT YOUR OWN FIRES, MATT. WE'VE NOT ONLY BEEN WATCHING YOU AND YOUR FRIENDS FOR SOME TIME NOW...
...WE'VE BEEN RECORDING YOU AROUND THE CLOCK.
WHO'S THE BALD GUY IN THE CAP?
--IN THE--?
Oh, no.
No, no, no...
--STILL NOT SURE HOW YOU'RE EVENTUALLY GOING TO EXPLAIN TO PEOPLE HOW YOU FAKED MY DEATH, MATTY.
EVERYONE BELIEVES FOGGY NELSON DIED SAVING NEW YORK CITY. WHEN THEY FIND OUT I'M HIDING IN A SAFEHOUSE--

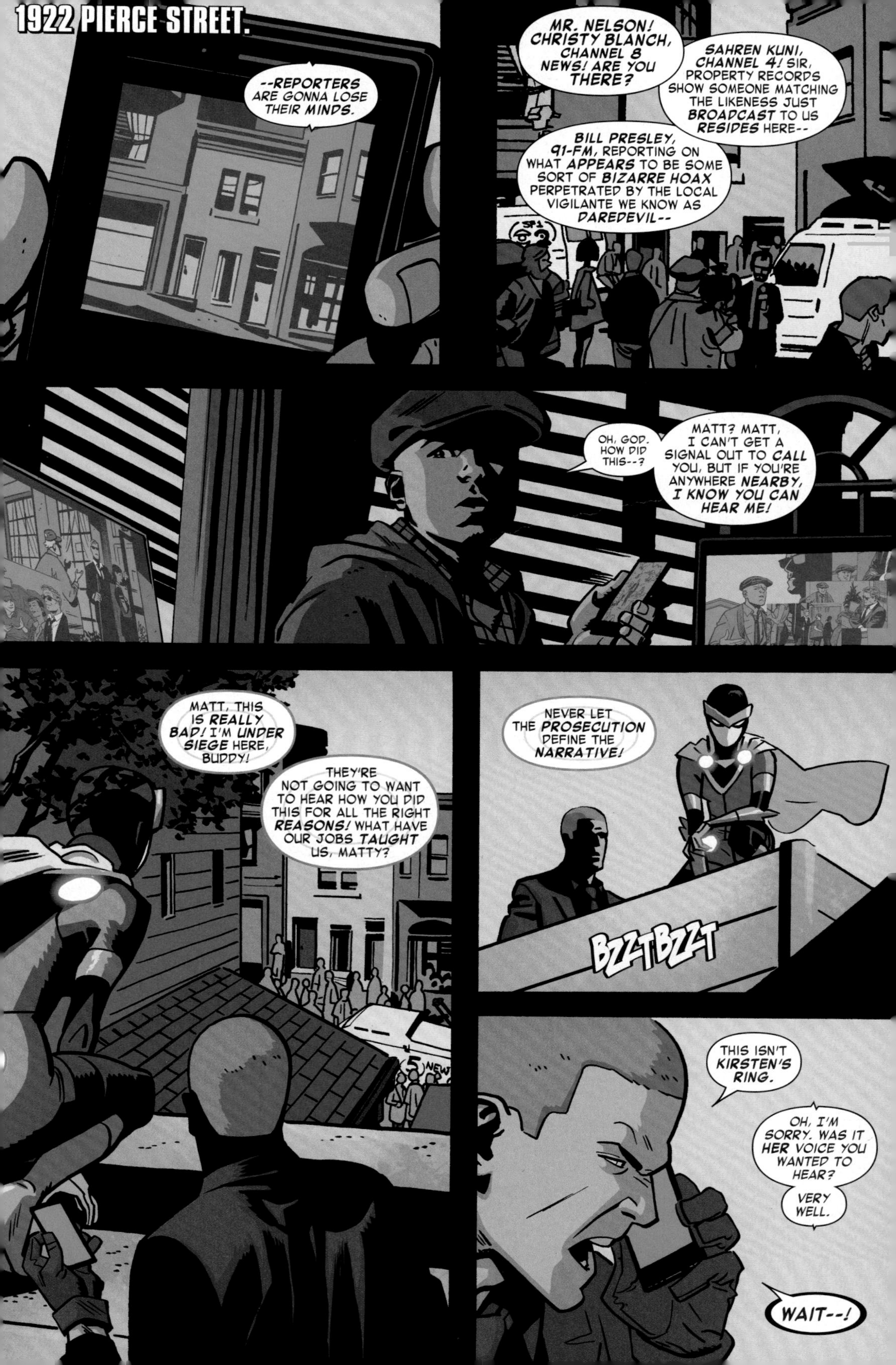
1922 PIERCE STREET.
--REPORTERS ARE GONNA LOSE THEIR MINDS.
MR. NELSON! CHRISTY BLANCH, CHANNEL 8 NEWS! ARE YOU THERE?
SAHREN KUNI, CHANNEL 4! SIR, PROPERTY RECORDS SHOW SOMEONE MATCHING THE LIKENESS JUST BROADCAST TO US RESIDES HERE--
BILL PRESLEY, 91-FM, REPORTING ON WHAT APPEARS TO BE SOME SORT OF BIZARRE HOAX PERPETRATED BY THE LOCAL VIGILANTE WE KNOW AS DAREDEVIL--
OH, GOD. HOW DID THIS--?
MATT? MATT, I CAN'T GET A SIGNAL OUT TO CALL YOU, BUT IF YOU'RE ANYWHERE NEARBY, I KNOW YOU CAN HEAR ME!
MATT, THIS IS REALLY BAD! I'M UNDER SIEGE HERE, BUDDY!
THEY'RE NOT GOING TO WANT TO HEAR HOW YOU DID THIS FOR ALL THE RIGHT REASONS! WHAT HAVE OUR JOBS TAUGHT US, MATTY?
NEVER LET THE PROSECUTION DEFINE THE NARRATIVE!
BZZTBZZT
THIS ISN'T KIRSTEN'S RING.
OH, I'M SORRY. WAS IT HER VOICE YOU WANTED TO HEAR?
VERY WELL.
WAIT--!

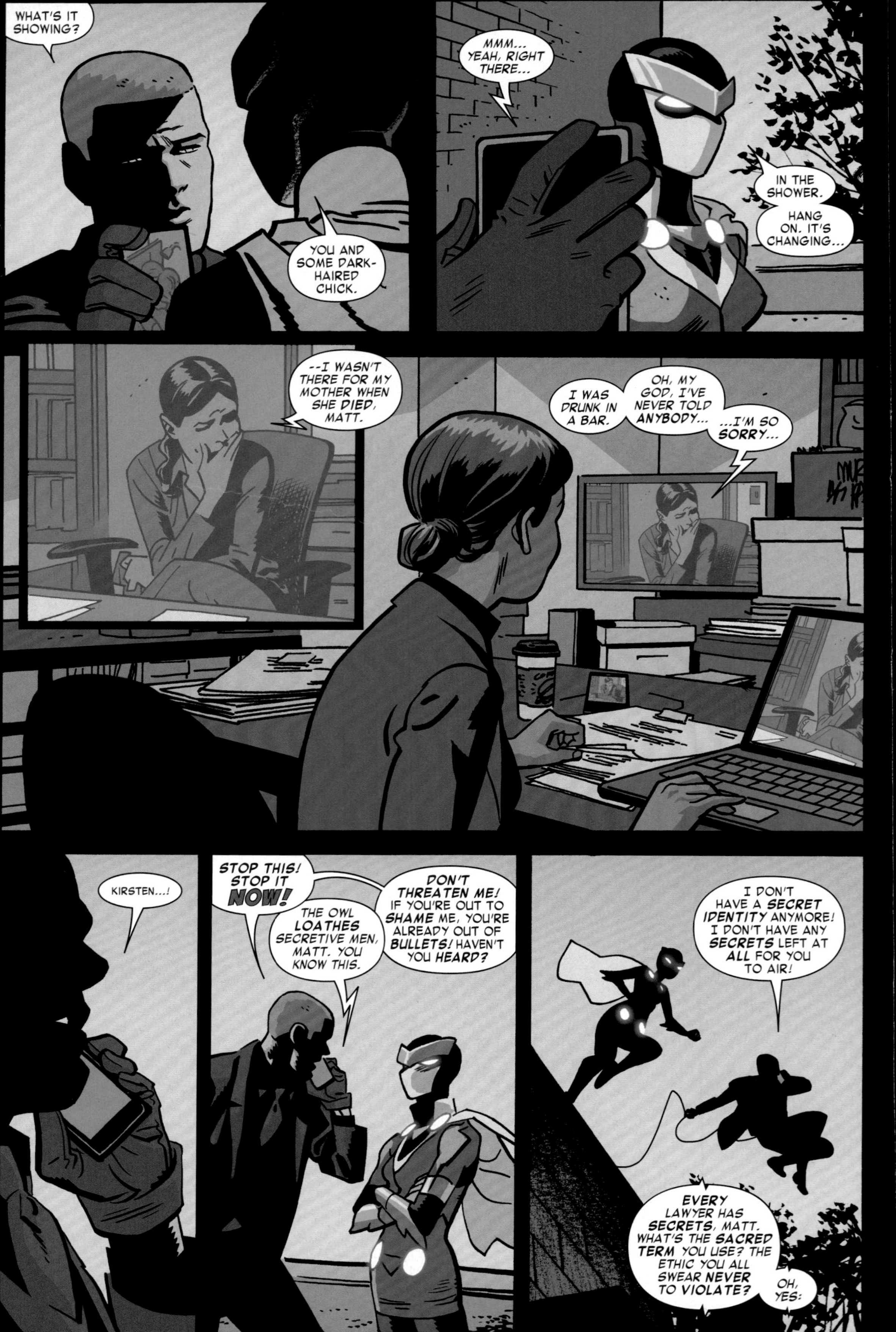
WHAT'S IT SHOWING?
YOU AND SOME DARK-HAIRED CHICK.
MMM... YEAH, RIGHT THERE...
IN THE SHOWER.
HANG ON. IT'S CHANGING...
--I WASN'T THERE FOR MY MOTHER WHEN SHE DIED, MATT.
I WAS DRUNK IN A BAR.
OH, MY GOD, I'VE NEVER TOLD ANYBODY...
...I'M SO SORRY...
KIRSTEN...!
STOP THIS! STOP IT NOW!
THE OWL LOATHES SECRETIVE MEN, MATT. YOU KNOW THIS.
DON'T THREATEN ME! IF YOU'RE OUT TO SHAME ME, YOU'RE ALREADY OUT OF BULLETS! HAVEN'T YOU HEARD?
I DON'T HAVE A SECRET IDENTITY ANYMORE! I DON'T HAVE ANY SECRETS LEFT AT ALL FOR YOU TO AIR!
EVERY LAWYER HAS SECRETS, MATT. WHAT'S THE SACRED TERM YOU USE? THE ETHIC YOU ALL SWEAR NEVER TO VIOLATE?
OH, YES:

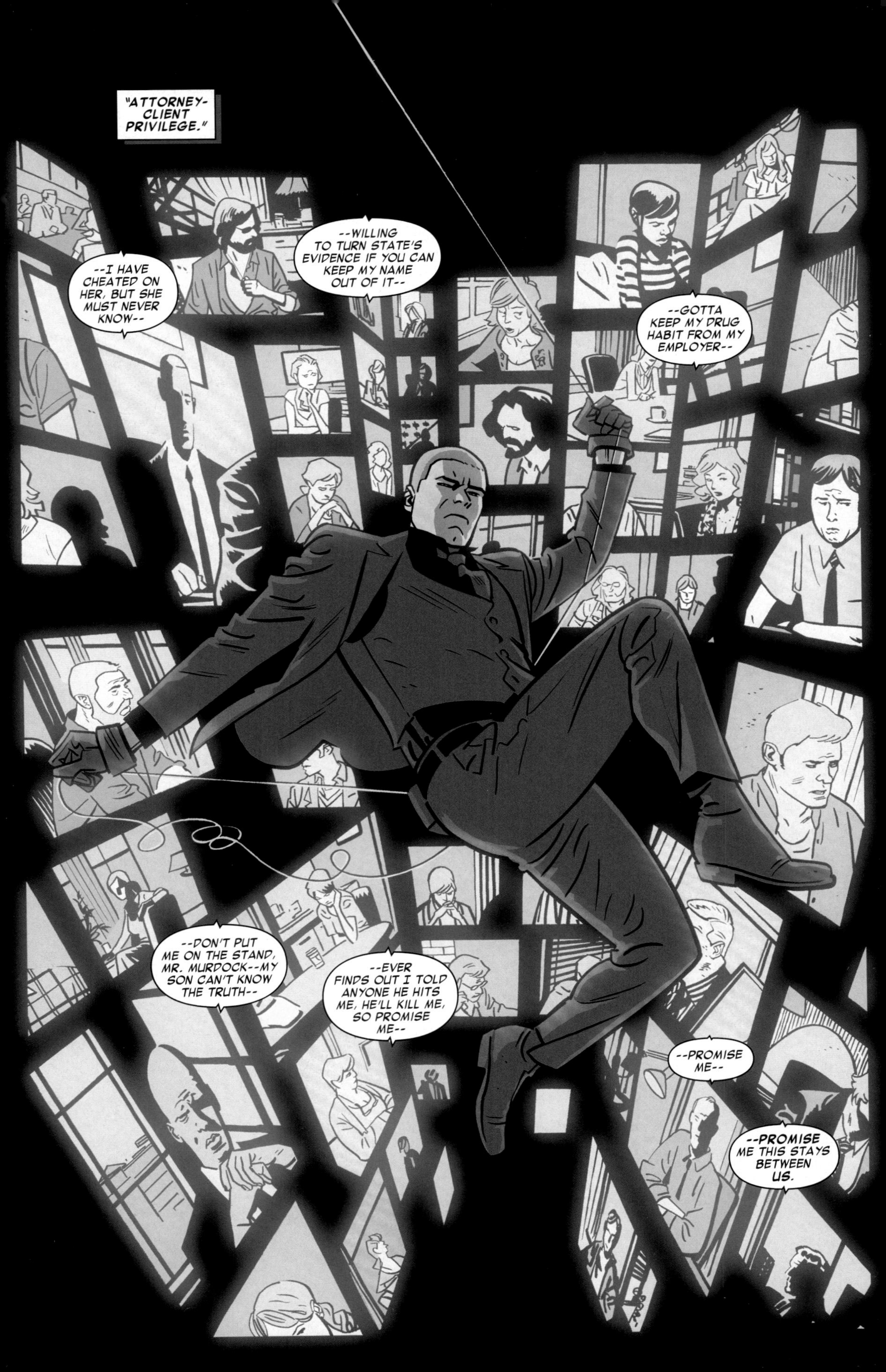
"ATTORNEY-CLIENT PRIVILEGE."
--I HAVE CHEATED ON HER, BUT SHE MUST NEVER KNOW--
--WILLING TO TURN STATE'S EVIDENCE IF YOU CAN KEEP MY NAME OUT OF IT--
--GOTTA KEEP MY DRUG HABIT FROM MY EMPLOYER--
--DON'T PUT ME ON THE STAND, MR. MURDOCK--MY SON CAN'T KNOW THE TRUTH--
--EVER FINDS OUT I TOLD ANYONE HE HITS ME, HE'LL KILL ME, SO PROMISE ME--
--PROMISE ME--
--PROMISE ME THIS STAYS BETWEEN US.

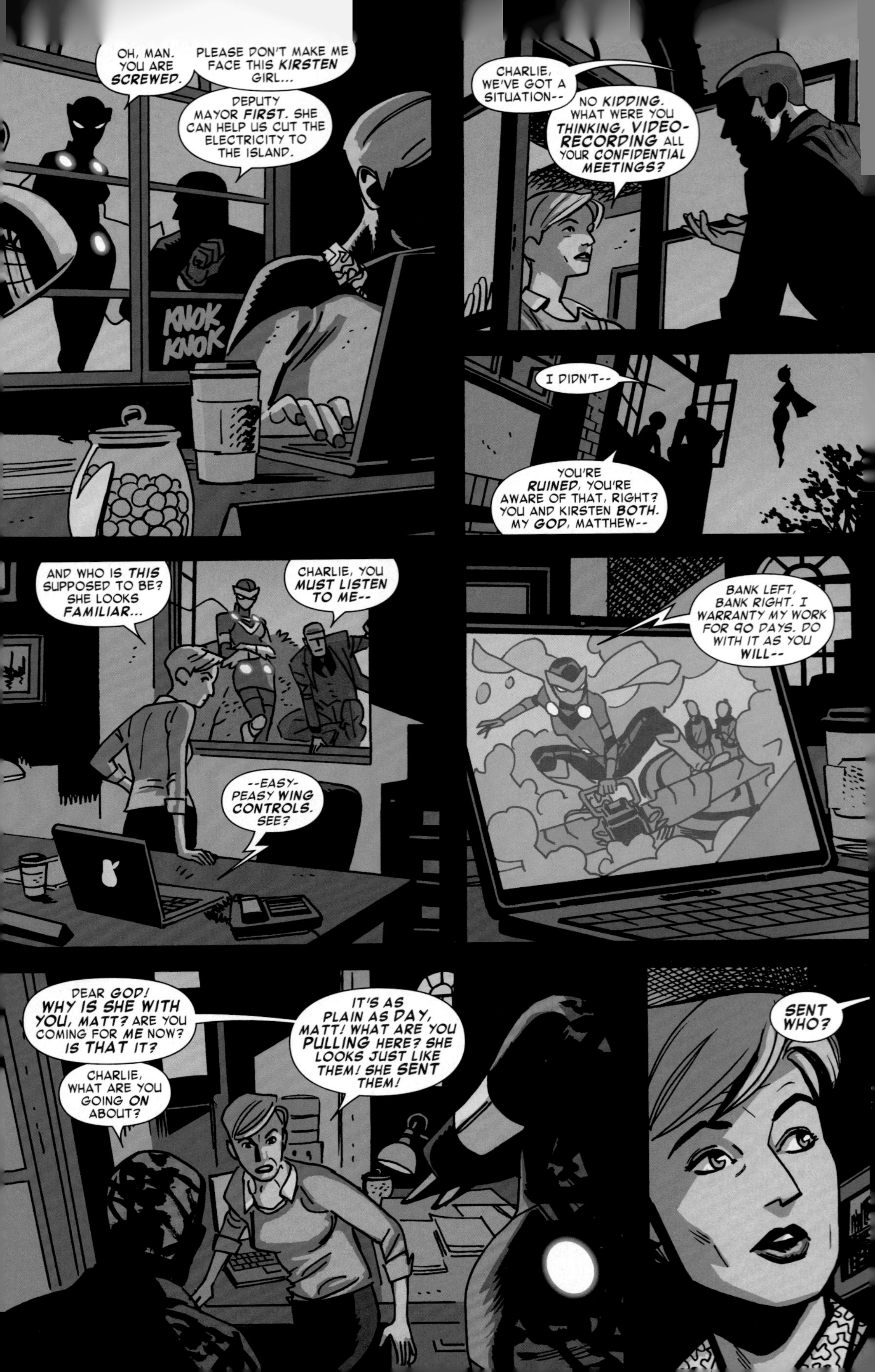
OH, MAN. YOU ARE SCREWED.
PLEASE DON'T MAKE ME FACE THIS KIRSTEN GIRL...
DEPUTY MAYOR FIRST. SHE CAN HELP US CUT THE ELECTRICITY TO THE ISLAND.
KNOK KNOK
CHARLIE, WE'VE GOT A SITUATION--
NO KIDDING. WHAT WERE YOU THINKING, VIDEO-RECORDING ALL YOUR CONFIDENTIAL MEETINGS?
I DIDN'T--
YOU'RE RUINED, YOU'RE AWARE OF THAT, RIGHT? YOU AND KIRSTEN BOTH. MY GOD, MATTHEW--
AND WHO IS THIS SUPPOSED TO BE? SHE LOOKS FAMILIAR...
CHARLIE, YOU MUST LISTEN TO ME--
--EASY-PEASY WING CONTROLS. SEE?
BANK LEFT, BANK RIGHT. I WARRANTY MY WORK FOR 90 DAYS. DO WITH IT AS YOU WILL--
DEAR GOD! WHY IS SHE WITH YOU, MATT? ARE YOU COMING FOR ME NOW? IS THAT IT?
CHARLIE, WHAT ARE YOU GOING ON ABOUT?
IT'S AS PLAIN AS DAY, MATT! WHAT ARE YOU PULLING HERE? SHE LOOKS JUST LIKE THEM! SHE SENT THEM!
SENT WHO?

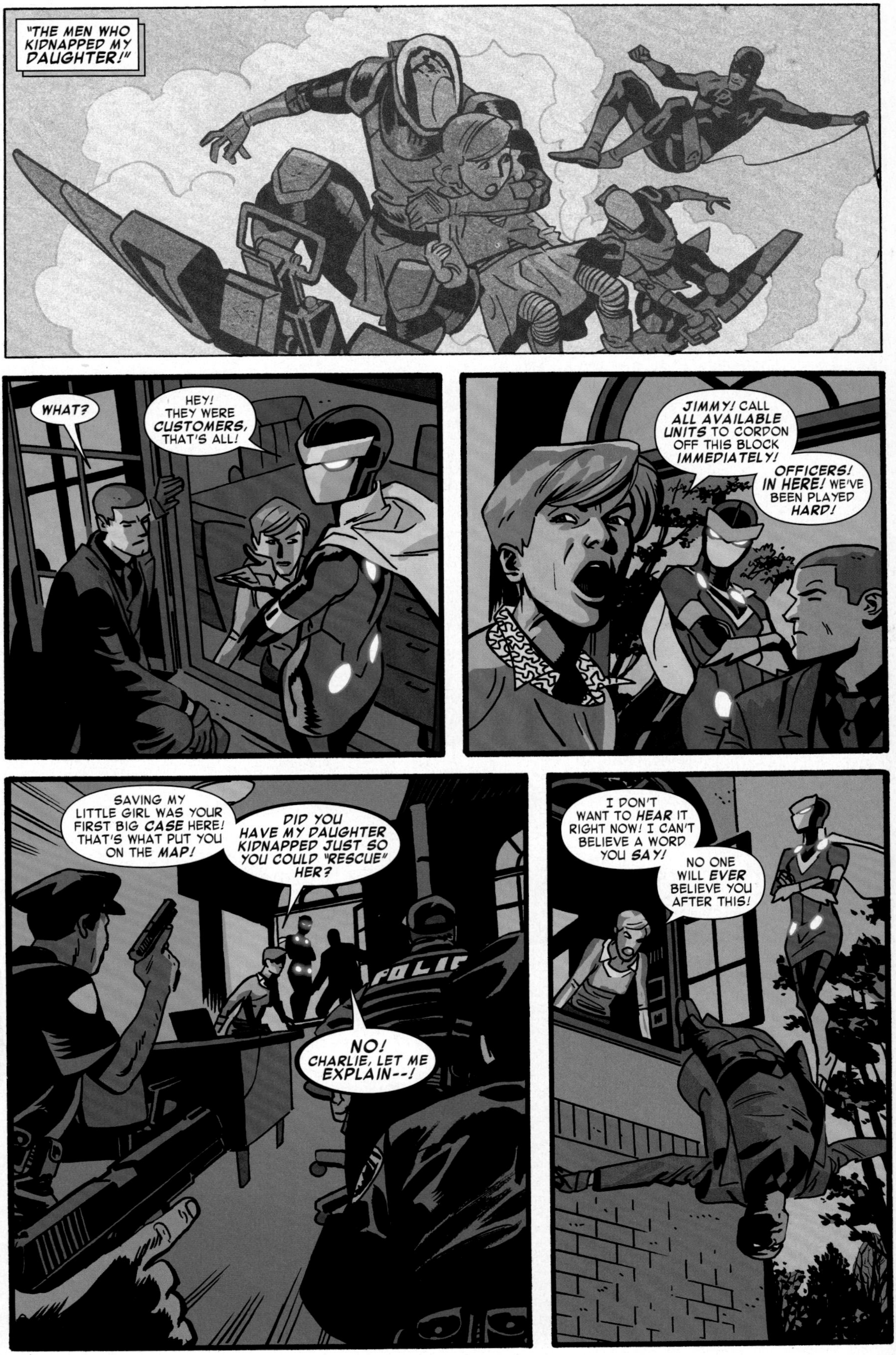
"THE MEN WHO KIDNAPPED MY DAUGHTER!"
WHAT?
HEY! THEY WERE CUSTOMERS, THAT'S ALL!
JIMMY! CALL ALL AVAILABLE UNITS TO CORDON OFF THIS BLOCK IMMEDIATELY!
OFFICERS! IN HERE! WE'VE BEEN PLAYED HARD!
SAVING MY LITTLE GIRL WAS YOUR FIRST BIG CASE HERE! THAT'S WHAT PUT YOU ON THE MAP!
DID YOU HAVE MY DAUGHTER KIDNAPPED JUST SO YOU COULD "RESCUE" HER?
NO! CHARLIE, LET ME EXPLAIN--!
I DON'T WANT TO HEAR IT RIGHT NOW! I CAN'T BELIEVE A WORD YOU SAY!
NO ONE WILL EVER BELIEVE YOU AFTER THIS!

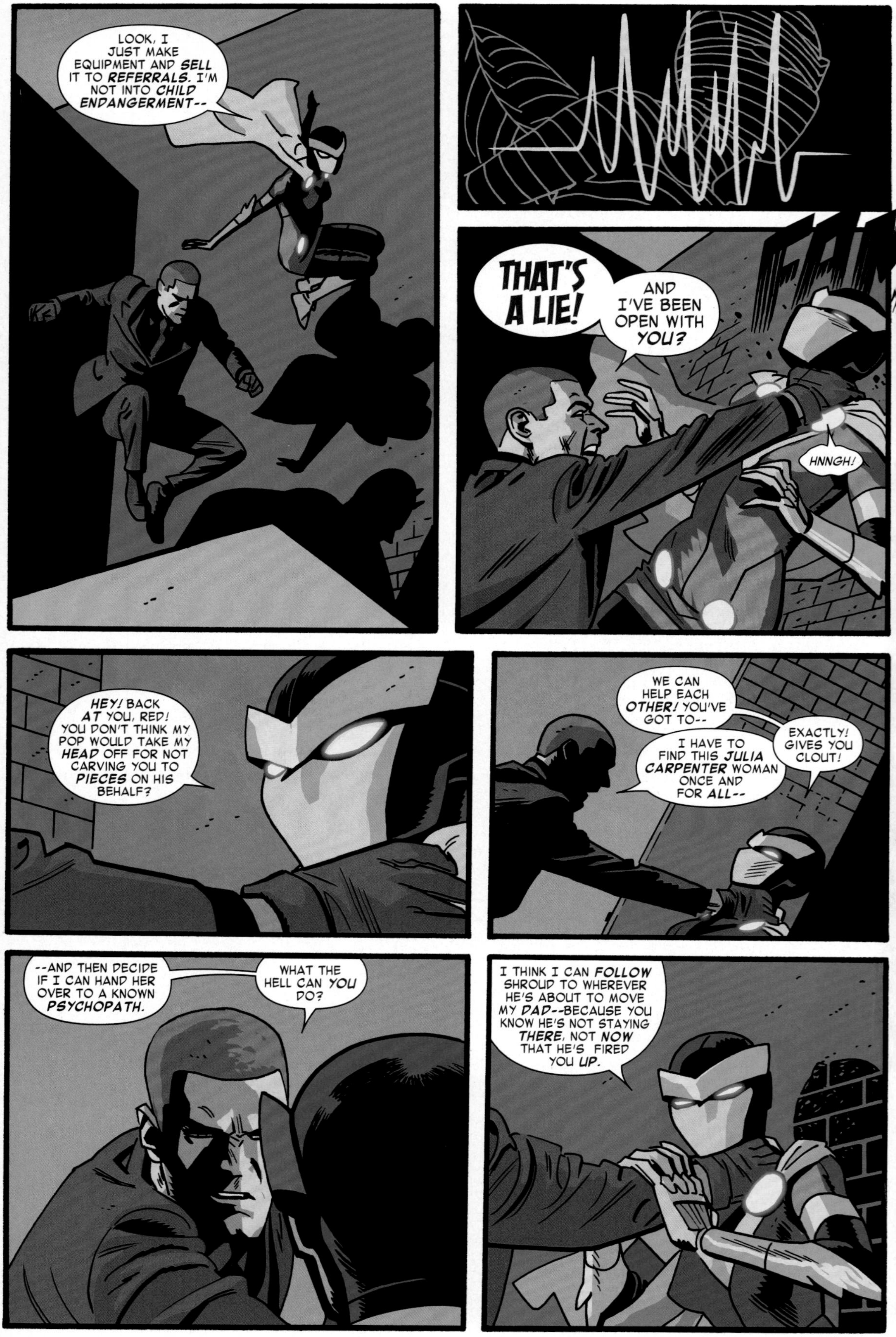
LOOK, I JUST MAKE EQUIPMENT AND SELL IT TO REFERRALS. I'M NOT INTO CHILD ENDANGERMENT--
THAT'S A LIE!
AND I'VE BEEN OPEN WITH YOU?
HNNGH!
HEY! BACK AT YOU, RED! YOU DON'T THINK MY POP WOULD TAKE MY HEAD OFF FOR NOT CARVING YOU TO PIECES ON HIS BEHALF?
WE CAN HELP EACH OTHER! YOU'VE GOT TO--
EXACTLY! GIVES YOU CLOUT!
I HAVE TO FIND THIS JULIA CARPENTER WOMAN ONCE AND FOR ALL--
--AND THEN DECIDE IF I CAN HAND HER OVER TO A KNOWN PSYCHOPATH.
WHAT THE HELL CAN YOU DO?
I THINK I CAN FOLLOW SHROUD TO WHEREVER HE'S ABOUT TO MOVE MY DAD--BECAUSE YOU KNOW HE'S NOT STAYING THERE, NOT NOW THAT HE'S FIRED YOU UP.

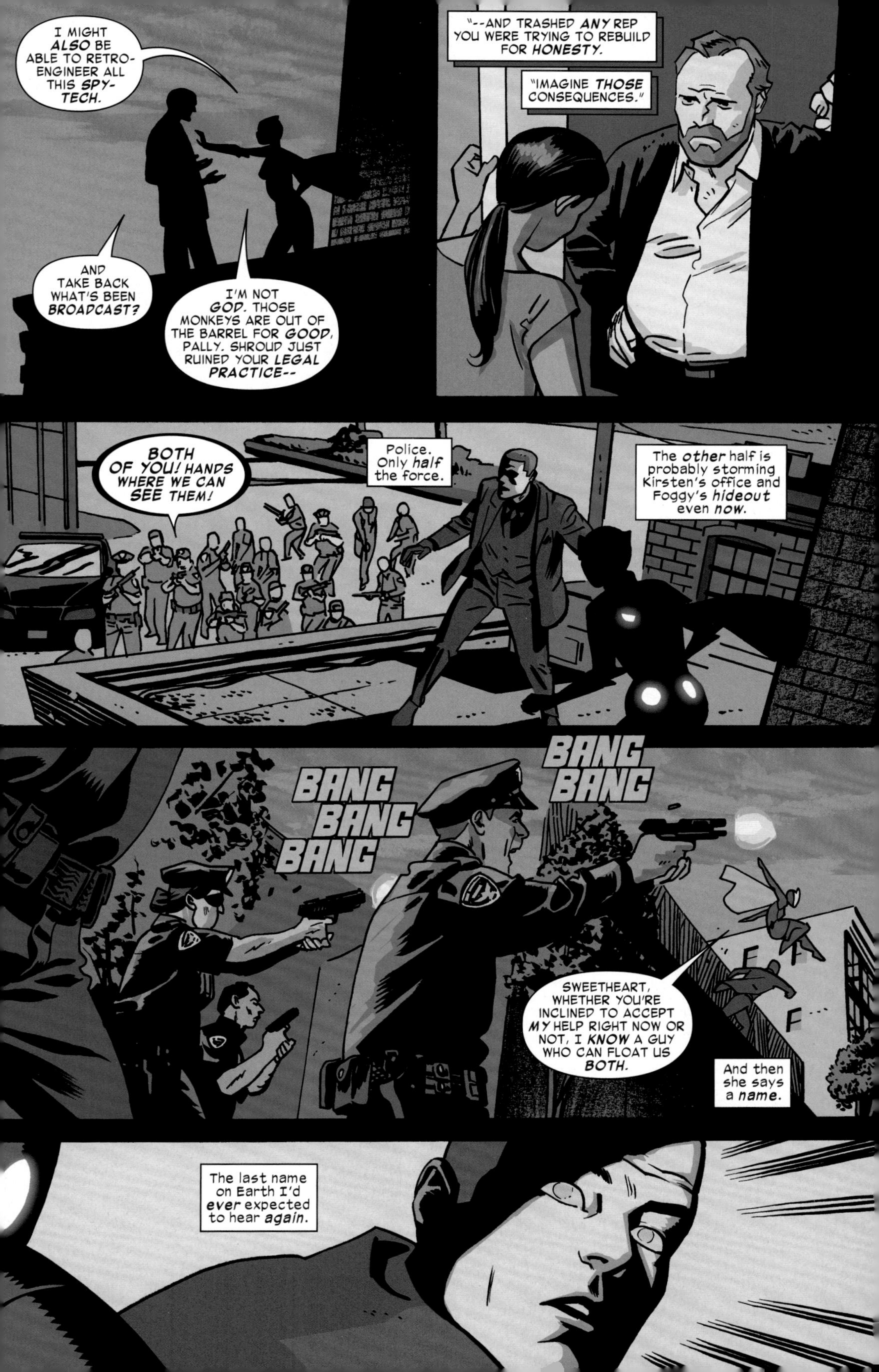
I MIGHT ALSO BE ABLE TO RETRO-ENGINEER ALL THIS SPY-TECH.
AND TAKE BACK WHAT'S BEEN BROADCAST?
I'M NOT GOD. THOSE MONKEYS ARE OUT OF THE BARREL FOR GOOD, PALLY. SHROUD JUST RUINED YOUR LEGAL PRACTICE--
"--AND TRASHED ANY REP YOU WERE TRYING TO REBUILD FOR HONESTY.
"IMAGINE THOSE CONSEQUENCES."
BOTH OF YOU! HANDS WHERE WE CAN SEE THEM!
Police. Only half the force.
The other half is probably storming Kirsten's office and Foggy's hideout even now.
BANG BANG BANG
BANG BANG
SWEETHEART, WHETHER YOU'RE INCLINED TO ACCEPT MY HELP RIGHT NOW OR NOT, I KNOW A GUY WHO CAN FLOAT US BOTH.
And then she says a name.
The last name on Earth I'd ever expected to hear again.

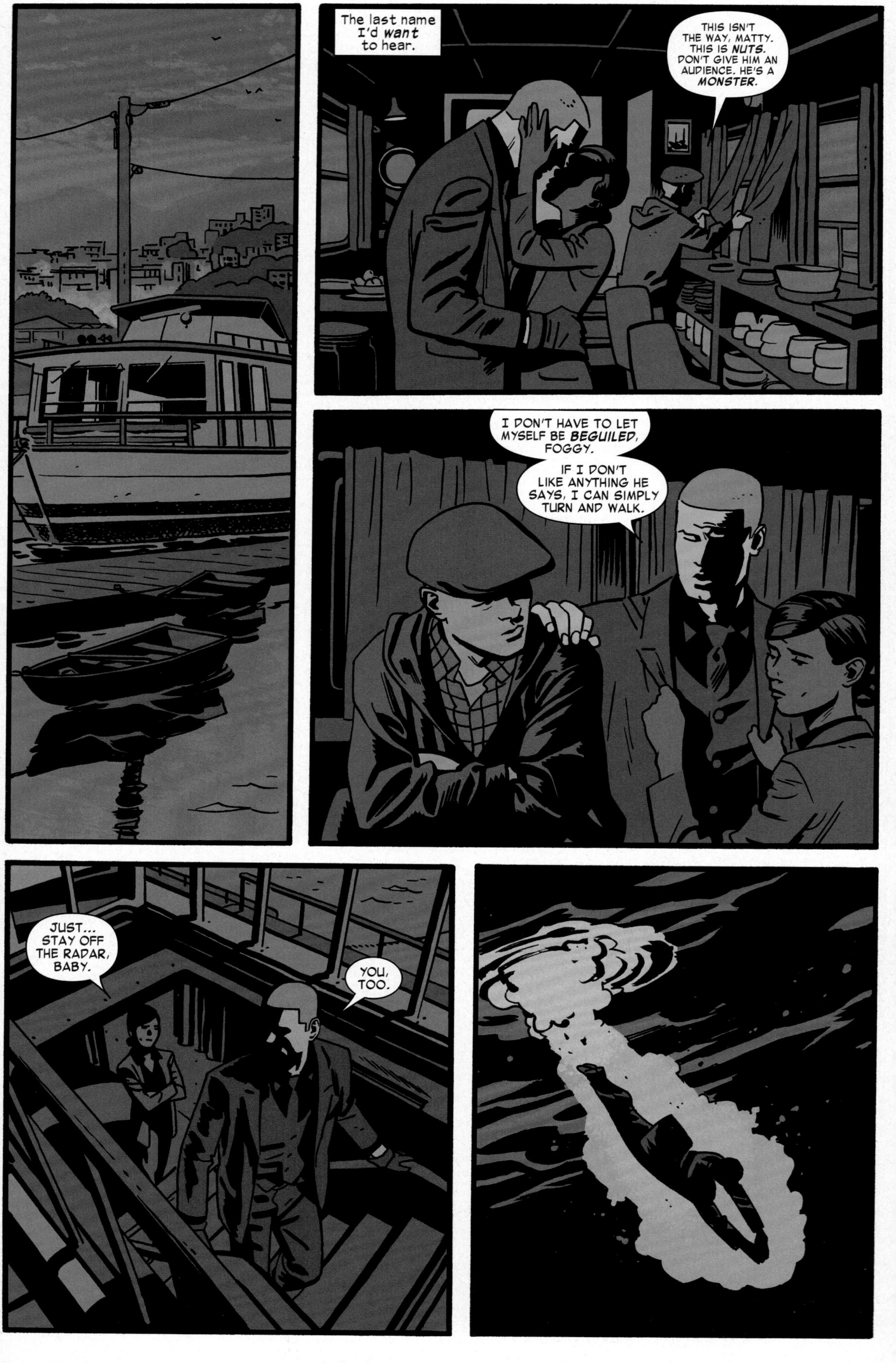
The last name I'd *want* to hear.
THIS ISN'T THE WAY, MATTY. THIS IS *NUTS.* DON'T GIVE HIM AN AUDIENCE. HE'S A *MONSTER.*
I DON'T HAVE TO LET MYSELF BE *BEGUILED,* FOGGY.
IF I DON'T LIKE ANYTHING HE SAYS, I CAN SIMPLY TURN AND WALK.
JUST... STAY OFF THE RADAR, BABY.
YOU, TOO.

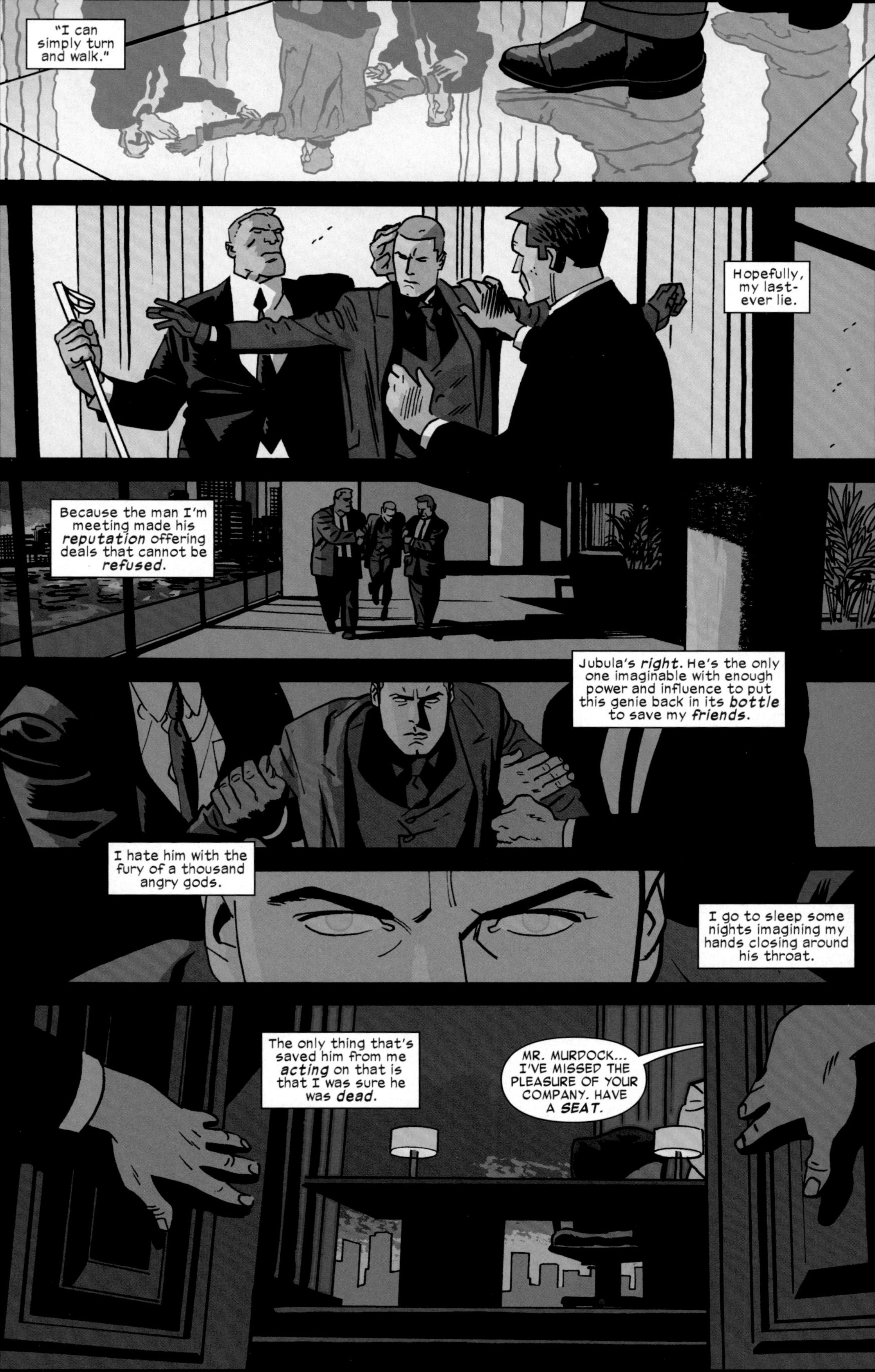
"I can simply turn and walk."
Hopefully, my last-ever lie.
Because the man I'm meeting made his *reputation* offering deals that cannot be *refused*.
Jubula's *right*. He's the only one imaginable with enough power and influence to put this genie back in its *bottle* to save my *friends*.
I hate him with the fury of a thousand angry gods.
I go to sleep some nights imagining my hands closing around his throat.
The only thing that's saved him from me *acting* on that is that I was sure he was *dead*.
MR. MURDOCK... I'VE MISSED THE PLEASURE OF YOUR COMPANY. HAVE A *SEAT*.

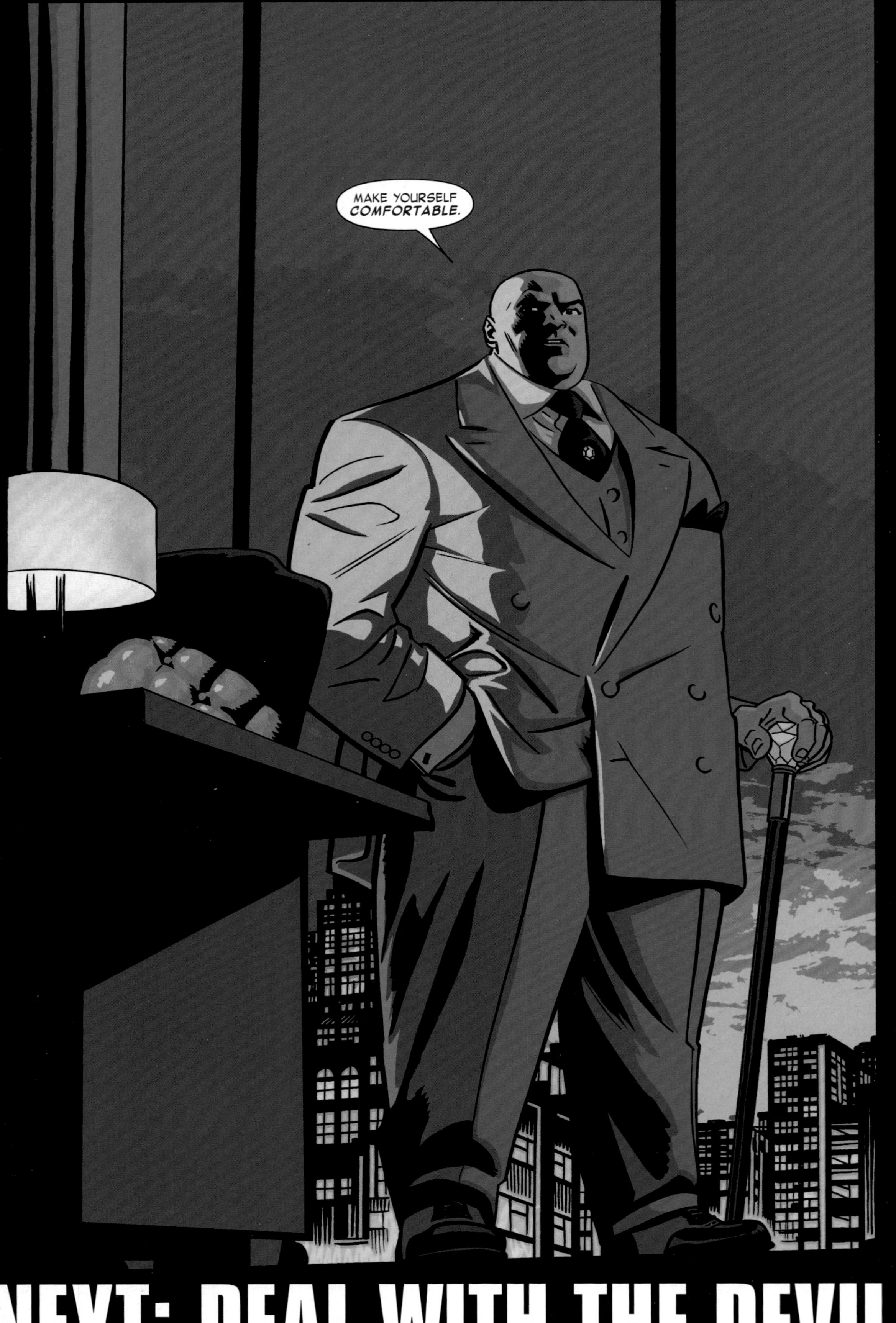
MAKE YOURSELF COMFORTABLE.

NEXT: DEAL WITH THE DEVIL

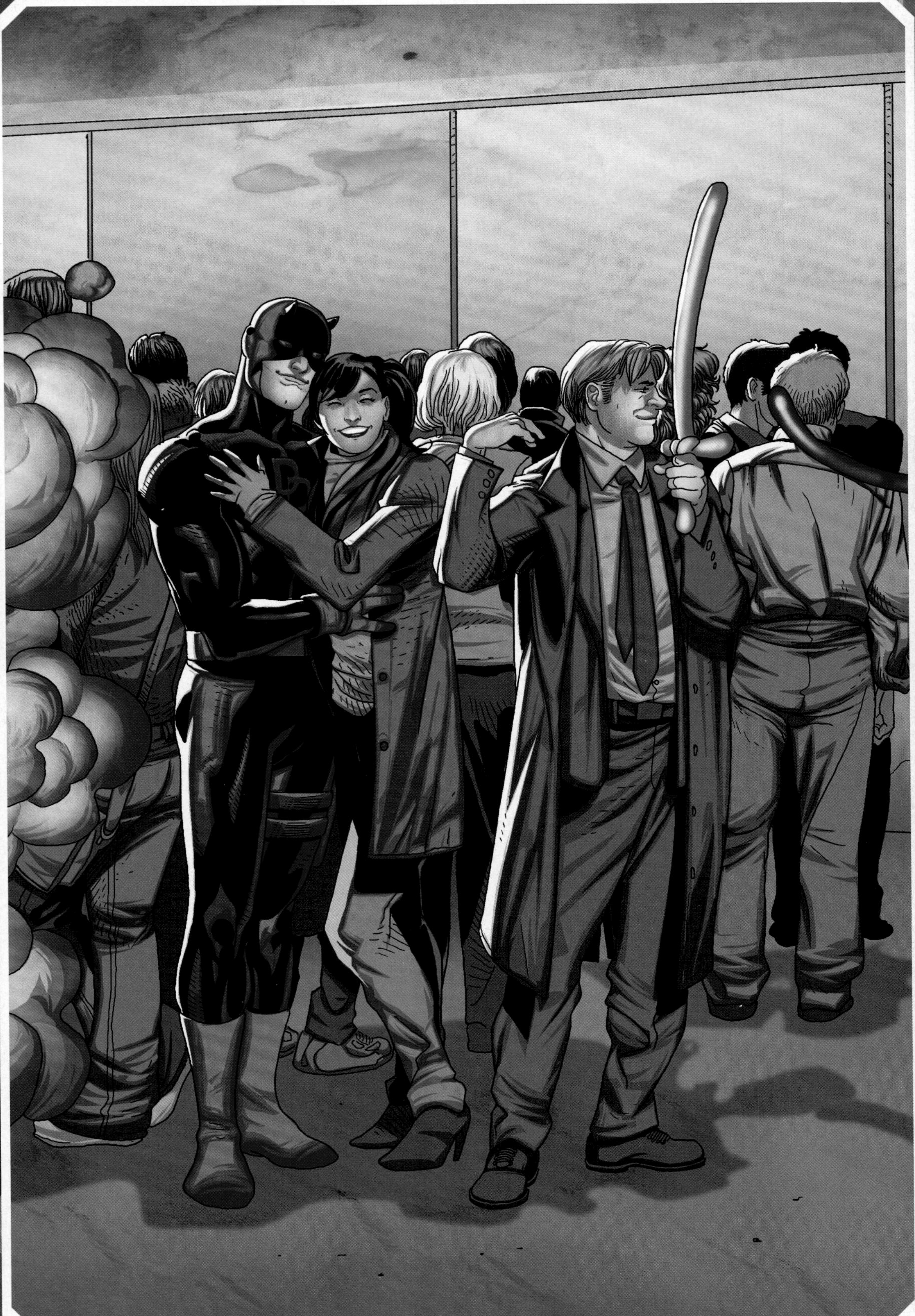

DAREDEVIL #12 WELCOME HOME VARIANT
BY SALVADOR LARROCA & ISRAEL SILVA

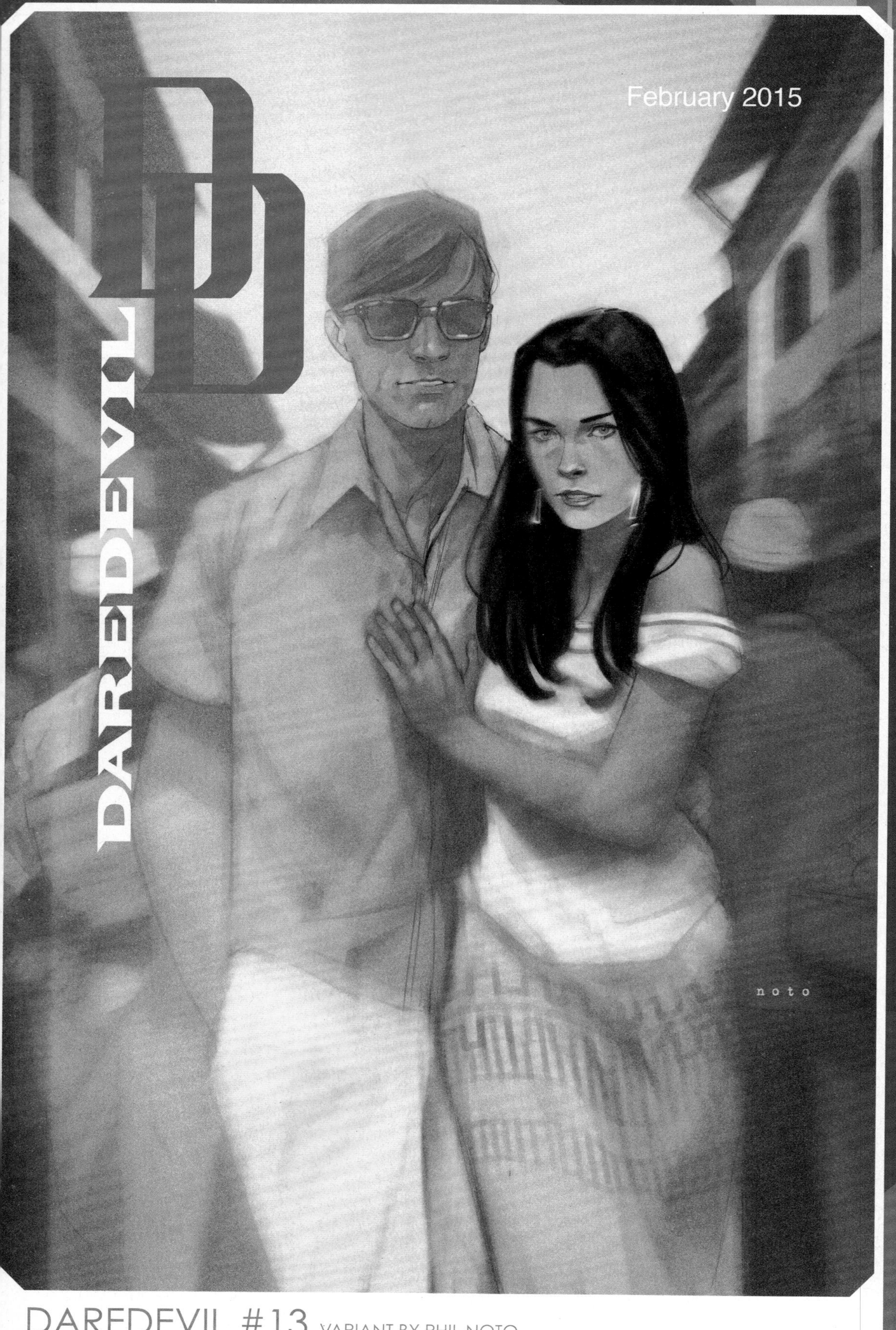
February 2015
DD
DAREDEVIL
noto
DAREDEVIL #13 VARIANT BY PHIL NOTO